BRIGHT LIGHTS, BAKED ZITI

The Unofficial, Unauthorised
Guide to *The Sopranos*

BRIGHT LIGHTS, BAKED ZITI

The Unofficial, Unauthorised Guide to *The Sopranos*

David Bishop

First published in 2001 by
Virgin Books Ltd
Thames Wharf Studios
Rainville Road
London
W6 9HA

ISBN 0 7535 0584 3

Typeset by TW Typesetting, Plymouth, Devon
Printed and bound in Great Britain by
Mackays of Chatham PLC

Dedication

In memory of Aldo Fioravanti, one of the twenty million,
who lost at the big casino. Salut.

Acknowledgements

To Kerri and Rebecca – thanks for the chance
To Shaun and Rob – thanks for the tapes
To David Chase – thanks for the show
To Alison – thanks for the love

Contents

Preface   ix

Season One   1

Season Two   83

Season Three   161

Matriarchy Rules   256

Generation XXX   261

A Hit is a Hit   266

Unseen Sopranos   274

Speculations on Season Four   279

Bright Lights, Baked Ziti On-line!   285

Contents

Preface

If you've picked up this book, chances are you've already seen and enjoyed *The Sopranos*. That alone proves you are a person of considerable taste and intelligence. It also shows that you'd like to know more about this critically acclaimed, award-winning American television series. Well, you've come to the right place. But don't worry if you've never seen *The Sopranos*. It's not too late to catch up – and this book is the perfect introduction.

Praise for *The Sopranos* has been overwhelming. The *New York Times* called the programme 'a groundbreaker' and 'the best television drama ever made'. The *New Yorker* thought it was 'a phenomenon . . . brilliant'. Britain's the *Guardian* called it 'a wickedly funny mixture of mindless savagery', while the *Observer* labelled it 'a modern master-piece'. *Radio Times* said the show was 'slick, shocking and very funny' while the *Daily Telegraph* said '*The Sopranos* is touched with genius' and 'dangerously addictive'. Rarely has a television programme been so universally acclaimed.

The Sopranos has pushed back the boundaries of television drama. It explores issues at the heart of modern culture in the Western World such as violence, the disintegration of the family and generational divides – in the context of compelling drama. It contrasts family values with the values of a Mafia family. It makes the viewer empathise with a central character who steals, extorts and murders for money. It is a show about morality and hypocrisy, yet it makes no moral judgements about the characters it portrays.

Bright Lights, Baked Ziti is an all-encompassing primer to one of the best things on television for many, many years. This programme guide is completely unofficial and has not been prepared, approved or licensed by any entity that created or produced *The Sopranos*. That means it doesn't have to pull any punches or abide by any HBO omerta – if an episode sucks, *Bright Lights, Baked Ziti* will not hesitate to say so.

This guide aims to detail, analyse and illuminate the many aspects of its multi-faceted subject. The book highlights the humour and the humanity of *The Sopranos*. It points out hidden delights you may not have noticed and gives a fresh perspective on one of the 21st century's most acclaimed TV shows. It enables you to relive your favourite moments without exhausting the batteries in your remote control. Each episode is analysed using the following categories:

Episode Number: Episodes of *The Sopranos* do not feature an on-screen production code like most American TV shows. However, the official HBO website and press releases do refer to episodes by their place in broadcast order, numbering from #01 for the pilot onwards. So the final episode of Season One is #13, the opening episode of Season Two is #14 and so on.

Story Title: No episode titles appear on screen in *The Sopranos*. However, all official press releases, websites and releases on video and DVD use episode titles and these have been adopted for use in this guide. There is some confusion over the proper name for the very first episode, with contradictory indications. So this book calls it by both names suggested: 'Pilot/*The Sopranos*'.

Writer: Anywhere between one and three writers are given on-screen credit for writing individual episodes of *The Sopranos*. In interviews creator David Chase says as executive producer he does some rewriting on most episodes but he likes to give credit where credit is due.

Cast: This section lists all the non-recurring characters who appear in an episode and are named in the credits. This covers everyone with a speaking part, but not the many non-speaking extras. Each season is preceded by a short introduction listing the recurring characters and in which episodes they appear. The main actors are named in the credits of every episode, even if they do not appear in that episode.

Storyline: This gives a useful summary of the crucial plot points from each episode, some of which gain a greater significance in subsequent instalments. *The Sopranos* is especially adept at layering in little moments whose importance only becomes obvious in retrospect.

Deep and Meaningful: This section celebrates the scenes that make *The Sopranos* one of the best shows on television. It highlights the sequences where characters reveal their hidden depths. In a drama full of lies, deception and ultra-subtle subtext, these are the moments of emotional truth that turn a work of television entertainment into something, well, deep and meaningful.

Mobspeak: Don't know your agita from your action? Can't tell the difference between mezzofinook and mezzo morte? Here's an invaluable glossary to the slang used by characters in *The Sopranos*. Each new word or phrase is noted and explained. Read them and you'll know exactly how to react if some calls you a buchiach.

Mama Mia: A collection of the many scathing sayings of monstrous matriarch Livia Soprano. Witness Livia's withering commentary on her friends and family. Brave readers can attempt the Livia drinking game, where a drink must be downed every time she uses one of her catchphrases. Here's a few to get you started: 'I wish the Lord would take me'; 'He was a saint!'; and everyone's favourite, 'I gave my life to my children on a silver platter!'

Bright Lights, Baked Ziti: Rarely has a television series featured so many scenes of so many characters eating. Food is almost a supporting character in *The Sopranos*. Whet your appetite with these descriptions of the mouthwatering Italian cooking.

Mobbed Up: *The Sopranos* is packed with pop culture references, especially the mobsters' fascination with Mafia movies. Ironically, life imitated art in 1999 when real mobsters were recorded by law enforcement agencies having a conversation about *The Sopranos*. This section details the many sly mentions and homages, especially concentrating on film references.

How Do You Feel?: Tony's therapy sessions with Dr Jennifer Melfi are a central part of the series. Chart Tony's progress with Prozac, panic attacks and penis dreams.

How Do You Feel, Doctor?: In its second season, *The Sopranos* began showing viewers Dr Melfi's therapy sessions with her own shrink, Dr Elliot Kupferberg. Follow Melfi's escalating problems with drink and drugs, which are fuelled by her treatment of Tony Soprano.

Sleeping With the Fishes: *The Sopranos* is reputed to be one of the most violent shows on American television, although its depiction of violence is never gratuitous. Despite its reputation, the series actually has fewer killings than a mystery show like *Diagnosis Murder* – they just tend to be more explicit. Keep up with the body count in this blood-soaked section.

Always With the . . . : During its first season, characters were frequently exclaiming variations of this catchphrase. A favourite example comes from the second episode: 'Always with the rape of the culture!' Sadly, this catchphrase virtually disappeared in subsequent seasons. Relive its heyday here.

I Dream of Jeannie Cusamano: Many TV series indulge themselves in dream sequences – *The Sopranos* has turned them into a signature piece of surrealism. Where other shows use dreams as a lazy way of imparting crucial information, dreams in *The Sopranos* resemble the strange, inexplicable slices of the bizarre you actually have when asleep. Savour the insignificance of bubble cars, Black Forest sausages and sexual fantasies in all their splendour.

Quote/Unquote: A selection of the best zingers and important utterances. Who could forget favourites like 'What, no fucking ziti?' or 'I'm not a cat, I don't shit in a box.' All the side splitters collected in one section.

Soundtrack: *The Sopranos* refuses to use incidental instrumental music to prompt an emotional response from its audience. Instead it spends a hefty sum each episode securing the rights to use hand-picked music, both famous and infuriatingly obscure, to complement or counterpoint crucial moments. Identifying these tracks has turned into an obsession for a number of American fans who run special internet sites devoted solely to that purpose. The list for each episode is being constantly updated – the listings in this section were the latest available at the time of going to press with this edition.

Surveillance Report: In a multi-layered series like *The Sopranos*, there are many hidden facts and moments that escape even the most eagle-eyed viewer at first. This is a selection of little gems to watch out for. Also included are relevant facts about the cast, guest stars and creation of each episode.

The Verdict: Judgement is passed on each instalment of this critically acclaimed programme, praising its high points and acknowledging its flaws. See if your opinion matches that of the author.

Other categories occasionally appear as necessary – most should be fairly self-explanatory. The book ends with a speculative look at what could happen in Season Four, and several essays examining the show's history, themes and impact.

'No man can wear one face to himself and another to the multitude without finally getting bewildered as to which may be true.'

Hawthorn

Season One
(1999)

Company Credits

Created by David Chase
Produced by Ilene S Landress
Producer: Allen Coulter (7–13)
Co-Producer: Martin Bruestle
Executive Producers: Brad Grey, David Chase
Co-Executive Producers: Robin Green and Mitchell Burgess
Supervising Producer: Frank Renzulli (2–13)

Regular Cast:

James Gandolfini (Tony Soprano)
Lorraine Bracco (Dr Jennifer Melfi)
Edie Falco (Carmela Soprano)
Michael Imperioli (Christopher Moltisanti)
Dominic Chianese (Corrado 'Junior' Soprano)
Vincent Pastore (Salvatore 'Big Pussy' Bonpensiero)
Steven Van Zandt (Silvio Dante)
Tony Sirico (Peter 'Paulie Walnuts' Gualtieri)
Robert Iler (Anthony Soprano Jr, also known as AJ)
Jamie-Lynn Sigler (Meadow Soprano)
Nancy Marchand (Livia Soprano)

Recurring Cast:

John Ventimiglia (Arthur 'Artie' Bucco, 1, 3, 9, 13)
Jerry Adler (Herman 'Hesh' Rabkin, 1, 3–4, 6, 10)
Michele de Cesare (Hunter Scangarelo, 1, 3–4)
Drea de Matteo (Hostess in 1, Adriana in 2–4, 8, 10, 13)
Katherine Narducci (Charmaine Bucco, 1, 3, 9, 13)
Elaine Del Valle (Sandrine in 1, Waitress in 9)
Michael Rispoli (Giancomo 'Jackie' Aprile, 2–4)
Bruce Smolanoff (Emil Kolar, 1, 8)
Al Sapienza (Mikey Palmice, 2–4, 6, 8–9, 11–13)
Anthony Desando (Brendan Filone, 2–4)
Frank Santorelli (Georgie, 2, 6, 8)
Johann Carlo (Bonnie DiCaprio, 2, 11)
Sharon Angela (Rosalie Aprile, 3–4, 13)
Oksana Babiy (Irina Peltsin, 3–6, 10)
John Heard (Detective Vin Makasian, 4, 6, 9, 11)
Tony Darrow (Larry Boy Barese, 4, 6, 8–9, 13)
George Loros (Raymond Curto, 4, 6, 8, 11, 13)
Joe Badalucco, Jr (Jimmy Altieri, 4, 6, 8–9, 11–13)
Annika Pergament (Newscaster in 4, 8–9 and 13,
Female Anchor in 11)
Paul Schulze (Father Phil, 5–6, 12–13)
Frank Pando (Agent Grasso, 8, 13)
Matt Servitto (Agent Harris, 8, 12–13)
Michele Santopietro (JoJo Palmice, 11, 13)
Sal Ruffino (Chucky Signore, 11–13)

1

Pilot (a.k.a. The Sopranos)

US Transmission Date: 10 January 1999
UK Transmission Date: 15 July 1999

Writer: David Chase
Director: David Chase
Cast: Michael Gaston (Mahaffey), Joe Lisi (Dick Barone),
Alton Clinton (MRI Technician),
Phil Coccioletti (Nils Borglund),

Giuseppe Delipiano (Restaurant Owner),
Siberia Federico (Irina),
Justine Miceli (Nursing Home Director),
Joe Pucillo (Beppy), Michael Santoro (Father Phil)

Storyline: Tony Soprano attends his first appointment with
a psychiatrist, Dr Jennifer Melfi. He suffered a blackout
but medical tests showed nothing physically wrong with
him. Tony describes himself as a waste-management consultant. In flashback, Tony recalls events from the day he
blacked out.

He begins by saying how he thinks the best is over; how
in his father's day people had pride and standards. The day
of the blackout was his son AJ's thirteenth birthday and
Tony's wife Carmela was planning a big party for family
and friends. Tony had become obsessed with a family of
wild ducks nesting near his swimming pool.

His daughter, Meadow, is agitating for permission to go
skiing at Aspen with her school friends.

Tony goes to work with Christopher Moltisanti. They
run down and beat a gambler heavily in debt and behind
on his payments. Later, Tony meets his crew to discuss the
Kolar Brothers, rivals for the garbage-hauling business
Tony controls. Christopher volunteers to deal with the
Kolars.

Tony hears that his uncle, Corrado 'Junior' Soprano,
plans to have another gangster murdered at Vesuvio
restaurant. Tony thinks that would ruin the business,
which is run by an old school friend of Tony called Artie
Bucco.

Tony visits his mother, Livia, at her home, bringing her
a CD player as a present, but she shows no interest in it.
He tries to persuade his mother to move into a retirement
community. He also asks her to intervene with Uncle
Junior about the planned hit.

At the birthday barbecue, Tony sees the ducks fly away.
He blacks out.

Christopher murders Emil Kolar without permission.
Later, Christopher and Big Pussy Bonpensiero dispose of

the body after unsuccessfully attempting to throw the corpse into a Kolar Brothers dumpster.

Carmela catches Meadow breaking curfew and cancels the Aspen trip.

Tony has brought events up to date. Dr Melfi presses Tony to admit he is depressed, but he refuses and storms out.

Tony and his family take Livia for a tour of a retirement community. During the tour Tony blacks out again. Soon after, he returns to therapy and Dr Melfi prescribes Prozac.

Hesh, a Jewish friend of Tony, tells Tony and his crew that Uncle Junior is driven by insecurities. Hesh suggests Artie should be lured out of town so Vesuvio will be closed when the planned hit is to take place. Tony tries to get Artie out of town with free tickets for a cruise. But Artie's wife Charmaine refuses them because she does not want to be connected with mobsters, and Artie hands the tickets back.

Tony takes his mistress Irina to a popular restaurant. He bumps into Dr Melfi and her date, and gets them a table, even though the restaurant is very busy. In the same week Tony returns with Carmela. The owner welcomes Tony as if it had been months, not days, since his last visit. Over dinner Tony tells Carmela that he is seeing a therapist and on medication. She is overjoyed that he has sought help. Tony fears for his life if anyone else finds out that he is seeing a psychiatrist.

To prevent the hit, Tony has Silvio Dante blow up Vesuvio.

Tony starts to feel better and believes the Prozac is responsible. Dr Melfi points out that it takes several weeks for the drug to build up effective levels. Any progress is due to the therapy, not the Prozac. Tony tells her about a dream and realises he fears losing his family, as he lost the ducks. He starts to cry.

Artie is a guest at the rescheduled barbecue party for AJ. Artie is very upset at the loss of his restaurant. Tony talks to Christopher, who is sulking because he didn't get any thanks for resolving the problem with the Kolars. Christopher says he's considering writing a screenplay about organised crime. Tony shows his displeasure and tells Christopher everything will be all right with him if he puts aside such distractions.

Junior is outraged by Tony's interference. He tells Livia that he may have to move against her son. She says nothing . . .

Deep and Meaningful: Tony takes Meadow inside the chapel at her high school. It's been years since he has been there. He looks around with wonder at the interior. He says it was built by a crew of labourers, including Meadow's great-grandfather and his brother. They were stone and marble workers who came over from Italy looking for work. The interior is stunning and even the brattish Meadow is impressed by what her ancestors did. For Tony, this place is highly symbolic – both of his ancestry and what artisans working together can achieve. He notes sardonically that, a century after the construction of the chapel, few workmen exist who could put decent grout round a bathtub.

Mobspeak: Tony describes himself as a waste-management consultant (a euphemism for being a mobster). Tony and Christopher see Mahaffey with a boo-boo (prostitute). Uncle Junior plans to whack (murder) a gangster at Vesuvio restaurant. Christopher says he just wet (executed) a guy after killing Emil Kolar. Tony complains that nobody keeps the code of silence (a Mafia vow of silence during police interrogation) any more when they get pinched (arrested). Christopher wants to become a made man (be indoctrinated into the mob). Uncle Junior says Tony is all agita (agitation) all the time.

Mama Mia: Livia says she never answers the telephone when it's dark outside. She also never drives when rain is predicted.

Livia undermines Tony at every opportunity. She scoffs at him, sarcastically announcing that he knows everything. She also badmouths her brother-in-law, complaining that Junior comes to visit her.

Twice she fights back tears when remembering her late husband. 'He was a saint,' she sobs. This will become one of Livia's catchphrases.

She is set against moving to Green Grove retirement community, which she describes as a nursing home. She claims to have seen women in wheelchairs there, babbling like idiots. Livia says her son thinks she'll die faster in a nursing home.

Finally, she complains when Tony uses mesquite on the barbecue, because it makes the sausage taste peculiar.

Bright Lights, Baked Ziti: There's a feast of food in the pilot. At breakfast, Carmela tries to feed Meadow and Hunter some of the previous night's leftover sfogliatella (a pastry filled with ricotta cheese), saying they can't just have cranberry juice. AJ dunks a croissant in the milk jug, disgusting his sister.

Tony has a breakfast meeting outside a pork store but no one eats. Silvio comes by to get some capicolli (strongly spiced ham). Tony and Christopher go to Vesuvio for lunch. Uncle Junior is already there, eating with some friends.

Livia offers Tony eggplant (aubergine) when he visits but her son says he's already eaten.

Father Phil brings a box of crème anglais to AJ's birthday barbecue. AJ takes a call from his grandmother – she won't be coming. The chubby boy seems more concerned about missing out on Livia's speciality baked pasta dish. 'So what, no fucking ziti now?'

Carmela and Father Phil are about to enjoy popcorn while watching a movie but are interrupted by Meadow trying to sneak out of the house. Carmela cancels the skiing trip. As revenge, Meadow later refuses to join her mother for their annual trip to have tea and scones at the New York Plaza Hotel.

Christopher eats meatballs while Tony tries to give Artie Bucco tickets for a Caribbean cruise. When he tries to persuade his wife that they should accept the tickets, Artie says he will go 'postal' if he has to stick his hand up the ass of another lobster without taking a break.

Pussy scoffs an ice cream while he and Hesh menace Mahaffey, a gambler heavily in debt to Hesh. Pussy throws the ice cream over a waterfall to show how easily Mahaffey could fall to his own doom.

After Tony and Carmela have dined out, Carmela brings her primavera (vegetable pasta) home for Meadow as a peace offering. The sulking teen turns down her favourite food, finishing a bowl of cereal instead.

Tony is the barbecue chef at the birthday party, but he lets Artie cook to help him feel better.

Mobbed Up: Carmela and Father Phil discuss mob movies. Tony watches *The Godfather Part II* on laserdisc all the time. He likes the part where Vito goes back to Sicily. Carmela doesn't think much of the third film in Coppola's trilogy. 'Three was, like, what happened?' Father Phil wants to know where Tony ranks *Goodfellas* among great mob movies, but the conversation gets interrupted.

Christopher misquotes one of the most famous lines from *The Godfather* – 'Luca Brassi sleeps with the fishes' – as 'Louis Brassi'. Pussy corrects him.

How Do You Feel?: Tony tells Dr Melfi that he feels fine and is back to work after the initial blackout. He admits to feelings of loss but questions the value of therapy. He prefers American men to be strong, silent types like Gary Cooper, who aren't in touch with their feelings, but just do what they have to do.

Tony admits having qualms about his profession. He compares himself to a sad clown, laughing on the surface while crying inside.

By the end of the episode, Tony says he had constant feelings of dread, but doesn't know what he's afraid of.

Sleeping With the Fishes: Emil Kolar, shot repeatedly by Christopher during a secret meeting at the pork store. Christopher tries to dump the body in a garbage dumpster owned by the Kolars, but is dissuaded by Pussy. He offers to help cut up and dispose of the corpse.

Always with the . . .: When Tony is about to have a CAT scan, he tells Carmela he's had some good times. 'Here he goes now with the nostalgia,' she replies.

Tony tells Carmela over dinner that he has a confession to make. Before he can go any further, Carmela gets ready a glass of wine to throw in his face, infuriating Tony. 'Always with the drama, you!'

I Dream of Jeannie Cusamano: Tony tells Dr Melfi about a dream in which he unscrews his belly button and his penis falls off. While Tony is looking for a mechanic to repair him, a bird swoops down and grabs the penis in its beak before flying away. Dr Melfi links this to the family of ducks in Tony's swimming pool that flew away.

Quote/Unquote: Tony remembers how his mother slowly destroyed his father, a tough mobster. 'He was a squeaking little gerbil when he died.'

Tony takes his mother a ghetto blaster but she rejects it, preferring to drag up old grievances. 'I bought CDs for a broken record,' Tony laments.

Tony complains that modern mobsters don't follow the code of silence, even if it leads to prison. 'Guys today have no room for the penal experience.'

Silvio Dante offers a typical non sequitur: 'Sadness accrues.'

Soundtrack: 'Woke Up This Morning' by A3. 'Who Can You Trust?' by Morcheeba. 'Shame, Shame, Shame' by Shirley and Co. 'I'm So Happy I Can't Stop Crying' by Sting. 'I Wonder Why' by Dion and the Belmonts. 'Rumble' by Link Wray. 'Welcome (Back)' by Land of the Loops. 'The Other Side Of This Life' by Jefferson Airplane. 'Can't be Still' by Booker T & The MGs. 'Rockford Files (Theme)' by Mike Post. 'Lumina' by Joan Osborne. 'Minuet' by Beethoven. 'Tardes De Bolonha' by Madredeus. 'Who's Sorry Now' by Connie Francis. 'I'm A Man' by Bo Diddley. 'Fired Up' by Funky Green Dogs. 'Little Star' by the Elegants. 'No More I Love Yous' by Annie Lennox. 'The Beast In Me' by Nick Lowe.

Surveillance Report: In the pilot, the pork store where Tony's crew hang out is called Centanni's. However, in the title sequence for this episode and in all future appearances the pork store is called Satriale's.

Two characters in the pilot are portrayed by different actors from those who play the parts in subsequent episodes. Here Father Phil is played by Michael Santoro and Tony's mistress Irina is played by Siberia Federico. In future episodes they will be played by Paul Schulze and Oksana Babiy.

The Verdict: 'Hope comes in many forms.' New Jersey mobster Tony Soprano goes into therapy but the problems with his family and his (mob) Family will take more than a few sessions to sort out . . .

The pilot is a remarkably assured debut for this groundbreaking show. Written and directed by the show's creator, David Chase, 'Pilot/The Sopranos' adroitly establishes all the key characters, conflicts and themes. Already crucial plot points are being set up to pay off later in the season.

This episode also works perfectly as a satisfying, standalone drama in its own right. The ducks in the pool is an adept framing device, as well as being a metaphor for Tony's sense of loss. By the end of the pilot, he is happier and healthier – but the swimming pool is still empty in the closing shot. There will be no quick fixes for Tony Soprano . . .

2
46 Long

US Transmission Date: 17 January 1999
UK Transmission Date: 22 July 1999

Writer: David Chase
Director: Daniel Attias
Cast: Debrah Ellen Waller (Perrilyn), Mike Epps (Jerome),
Yancey Epps (Arnaz),
Tibor Feldman (US Attorney Braun),

Harvey Levin (Talk Show Host),
Steven Randazzo (Vincent Rizzo),
Kate Anthony (Counter Person),
Anthony Caso (Martin Scorcese), Victor Colicchio (Joe),
Marcia Haufrecht (Fanny), Desiree Kehoe (Nude Dancer),
Michael Parr (Bouncer), Sharif Rashed (Antjuan),
Charles Santy (Truck Driver),
David Schulman (Mr Miller),
Manny Silverio (2nd Truck Driver),
JD Williams (Special K)

Storyline: A pre-credits sequence shows Tony and his crew
relaxing, joking around and counting their cash. On TV a
famous reformed mobster is giving an interview. They all
scorn such behaviour.

Christopher Moltisanti and his drug addict friend Brendan Filone hijack a truck shipping DVD players. All of
Tony's crew get a share of the spoils.

Anthony Jr announces at breakfast that the car of his
science teacher, Mr Miller, was stolen from the school.
Carmela persuades Tony to have someone investigate.

The Bada Bing! strip club has a new phone system but
the barman, Georgie, keeps losing calls. Tony phones his
mother while she is cooking. Livia gets distracted and her
mushrooms catch fire, threatening to burn down the house.
The fire brigade put out the blaze. Carmela invites Livia to
live with the family, but the old woman refuses.

Big Pussy gets a lead on the stolen car. The Saturn was
taken to a garage by someone wearing the uniform of a
coffee house chain. Pussy and Paulie Walnuts go in search
of the thief.

In the aftermath of the fire, Livia agrees to having a
home help. Carmela has an agency send a Trinidadian
woman, Perrilyn. When Tony visits his mother, she says
Perrilyn is stealing.

Tony meets with Uncle Junior and Jackie Aprile. Jackie is
acting boss while the real boss is in prison. The truck hijacked
by Christopher and Brendan was from a firm called Comley,
which pays protection money to Junior. Jackie rules that

whoever hit the truck should make restitution to Junior. The acting boss is suffering side effects of chemotherapy for cancer.

Carmela visits Livia just as Perrilyn quits and storms out of the house.

Christopher is dragging his heels about paying restitution to Junior. Tony makes it clear that he will hurt Christopher and Brendan unless they pay. He offers to mediate between them and Junior for a commission.

Pussy and Paulie find the thieves. But, when all four reach the garage, the car has already been chopped for parts and its number plates put on another vehicle. Pussy and Paulie force the thieves to take back the plates and steal another Saturn to put them on.

Livia accidentally runs down her friend Fanny, breaking her own wrist and smashing Fanny's pelvis. Doctors say Livia should not live alone any more, but she is unwilling to shift into Green Grove retirement community.

Christopher and Brendan discuss their situation. Brendan says there's another Comley truck worth hitting soon, full of Italian suits. Christopher says the mobs are in chaos. Do they still have a future in the new millennium?

Tony tries to persuade Livia to shift into Green Grove. When she refuses, he threatens to get a durable power of attorney and place her there.

Christopher decides against hitting the Comley. He believes there's no point in being a gangster unless they respect the chain of command. Brendan hits the truck anyway and the driver is accidentally killed.

Tony and Carmela move Livia into Green Grove. Christopher calls with news about the hijack. Tony tells him to take the shipment back to Comley.

At school, Mr Miller's Saturn reappears in its parking space. However, the keys are different and the paint is still wet on the chassis.

Tony nearly passes out while clearing possessions from his mother's house. At a therapy session, Dr Melfi asks Tony if he can admit he has feelings of hatred for his mother. He needs to own his anger, instead of displacing it. Tony storms out in disgust.

Back at the Bada Bing!, Georgie still can't cope with the phones. Tony loses patience and beats the barman unconscious with the receiver. It seems Tony has not yet learnt to own his anger . . .

Deep and Meaningful: Christopher shows some maturity for the first time, turning down the chance to hit a Comley Truck loaded with Italian suits. He tells Brendan that there was a time when being part of Tony's crew was all he ever dreamed of. Christopher decides that directly disobeying orders is wrong, and speculates that ignoring middle management is a major reason for the Mafia being in crisis. Unless he follows the rules, what is the point of being in a crew?

Mobspeak: On a TV talk show watched by Tony and his crew, the host asks whether disregard for the rules that served the old dons (heads of the Families) lead to the decline of Mafia power. The host introduces one of his guests, Vincent Rizzo, as a former soldier (a bottom-level member of an organised-crime Family) in the Genovese Family (an organised-crime clan), and a real wiseguy (a made man). Rizzo talks about when mobsters started to rat (to divulge information to the police). The TV host also mentions the Omerta (a Mafia code of silence, punishable by death).

Tony and Uncle Junior meet with Jackie Aprile, their acting boss (the head of the Family, he decides who gets made and who gets whacked – he also gets money from all Family business).

Tony tells Christopher the books are closed (there is no chance for promotion to full membership of the Family). He berates Christopher for not paying tributes (giving higher-ranked mobsters their due slice of proceeds from criminal activity).

Christopher says there was a time when being with the Tony Soprano crew (the group of soldiers under a capo's command) was all he ever dreamed of. He tells Brendan to shut up or else Christopher will get clipped (murdered).

Mama Mia: Livia has a very busy episode, but ends it in the one place she did not want to be. Tony phones his mother, who complains that he never calls – even though he had called her the day before. She dismisses the answering machine at Tony's house as fancy and manages to set fire to her kitchen.

Livia refuses an invitation to move into Tony and Carmela's home, saying she knows when she's not wanted. Livia doesn't want to leave the house that she and her husband shared. He was a saint. Unusually, she does ask about Tony's health.

Livia finally agrees to have a home help but determines to get rid of Perrilyn, the woman sent by the agency. The old woman accuses Perrilyn of stealing and eventually succeeds in driving her out of the house.

Tony is proud of his mother because she drives her friends around. But Livia gets her gears wrong and runs over her best friend. Livia still refuses to shift to Green Grove. When Tony threatens to get power of attorney over her, Livia implores him to kill her instead. 'Go into the ham, and take the carving knife and stab me, here, now please! It would hurt me less than what you just said!'

By the end of the episode, Livia has been moved into Green Grove. She just refuses to talk to anybody, especially Tony.

Bright Lights, Baked Ziti: After the feast of food in the pilot, meals take a back seat in this episode. At breakfast AJ eats scrambled eggs, sausage and toast when Meadow picks at fruit. Tony drinks orange juice and steals a sausage from AJ's plate.

After the kitchen fire, Carmela offers to make Livia a little dish of cooked pasta but the old woman refuses. Later, Carmela brings her mother-in-law some fresh bread and a box of other food.

Paulie says Americans ate pootsie before the Italian people gave them the gift of cuisine, such as pizza, calzone, buffalo mozzarella and olive oil.

Just before Livia runs down her best friend, Carmela is preparing a meal for the extended Soprano family. Carmela's parents and Livia are both bringing some antipasto. Carmela has chopped the ingredients for a salad.

Tony eats a lunch of cold meat and peppers at Livia's house. He praises the quality of her Virginia ham, but turns down another helping.

After Livia is moved into Green Grove, Tony offers to make his wife some lunch. Carmela says there's some fantastic prosciutto (cured ham) in the fridge.

Mobbed Up: Silvio Dante tries to cheer up Tony by imitating Al Pacino in *The Godfather Part III*: 'Just when I thought I was out, they pulled me back in!'

Tony's crew discuss the lesser range of movies available on DVD, compared with laserdiscs. Brendan says the sound is way improved. Tony sarcastically says nothing beats listening to *Men In Black*.

Pussy refers to a TV series *The Sopranos*' creator David Chase previously worked on when he gets frustrated when a mechanic at his garage gives him insufficient information to track down the stolen car. 'Watchung Avenue and what? I'm fuckin' Rockford over here!'

When Tony and Junior argue about the hijack, Tony offers Junior his DVD player from the robbery. He suggests his uncle watch *Grumpy Old Men*.

Later Tony extols the virtues of WC Fields on DVD, giving a passable imitation of a line from *The Bank Dick*.

Goodfellas' director, Martin Scorcese, sweeps into a nightclub while Christopher and Brendan are waiting behind the velvet rope. Christopher calls out that he liked the Buddhist epic *Kundun*, unintentionally damning Scorcese's film with faint praise.

How Do You Feel?: No matter what he does, Tony feels guilty. He can't let Livia live with him because, he says, Carmela won't allow it. Tony says his sisters cut themselves off from Livia a long time ago. He believes he should take care of his mother and describes her as an old sweetie pie. But, when Dr Melfi challenges him to relate a warm, loving experience with Livia, he struggles to cite an example. Finally he recalls when his father tripped and the whole family laughed, including his mother.

After Livia's car crash, Dr Melfi points out that depression can cause accidents, alluding to Tony's blackouts in the pilot. He takes this as suggesting his mother tried to whack her best friend!

Tony is sad after shifting his mother into Green Grove. Dr Melfi angers Tony by suggesting he has feeling of hatred for his mother. But he cannot acknowledge this and walks out of the session.

Sleeping With the Fishes: Hector Anthony, a driver for Comley Trucking. He is accidentally shot and killed by one of Brendan's accomplices when they hijack a truck full of Italian suits.

Always With the . . .: Paulie is infuriated that others have co-opted Italian cuisine. (This becomes ironic when Paulie gets to sample true Italian cuisine in Season Two.) Most galling for him is the vogue for coffee house culture. Italians invented espresso and now everyone else is getting rich off it, he says. Pussy loses patience with his friend: 'Oh, again with the rape of the culture?' In retaliation, Paulie steals a coffee pot from a trendy coffee house.

I Dream of Jeannie Cusamano: Nobody has a dream this episode, but Christopher does profess to using the technique of positive visualisation.

Quote/Unquote: Tony's crew contemplate a letter to the local newspaper asking what if scientists had cloned Princess Di. Silvio wonders about her death. 'You think the royal family had her whacked?'

There's a wicked spoof of Starbucks and similar upmarket coffee houses, which are misnamed as Buttfucks by a mechanic at Pussy's garage. When Paulie tries to order just coffee, the woman at the till points to a sign behind her. 'Our café du jour is New Zealand Peaberry.'

Brendan and Christopher complain about their treatment by Uncle Junior. 'It's like, not only does he shit on our heads, we're supposed to say thanks for the hat.'

Dr Melfi describes Green Grove as a beautiful facility which is more like a hotel at Cap D'Antibes. When Tony

tries to use this line on his mother, it comes out as being
more like a hotel at Captain Teebs. Livia is understandably
baffled and asks who he is. 'The captain who owns luxury
hotels or something. That's not the point!'

Tony is outraged when he learns that his mother has
given her jewellery away to his cousin Josephine, but she is
trying to gift him an armchair. 'You gave a fuckin' cousin
Cartier dinner rings and you give me a vibrating chair?'

Soundtrack: Tony serenades Carmela with an inaccurate,
rambling version of Procol Harum's 'A Whiter Shade of
Pale' at breakfast. 'This Time' by Richard Blandon & The
Dubs. 'Bop Hop' by Brooklyn Funk Essentials. 'Chico
Bonita (Levante Las Manos)' by Artie The One Man
Party. 'Party Girl' by Ultra Nate. 'Symphony #3, Op 36'
by Dio. 'Battleflag' by Pigeonhead featuring the Lo-
Fidelity All Stars.

Surveillance Report: This episode has a rare pre-credits
sequence when Tony and his crew watch TV. The acting
boss, Jackie Aprile, is played by Michael Rispoli, who
co-starred as Joe Fusco Jr in *While You Were Sleeping* with
Sandra Bullock. Drea de Matteo caught David Chase's eye
while playing a restaurant hostess in the pilot. When *The
Sopranos* was commissioned for a full series by HBO, she
was picked to play Christopher's girlfriend, Adriana.

The Verdict: 'Time and patience change the mulberry leaf
to silk.' This episode is full of bleak comedy and despair.
Crisis in the mobs is the larger theme of this episode, with
the Mafia under attack from without and within. For Tony,
the pressure just keeps building. The agita between him and
Junior is worsened by the hits on Comley Trucking.

But the real problem revolves around his relationship
with his mother. He spends the whole episode trying to get
Livia into Green Grove. When he finally succeeds, it just
makes him feel worse. The light at the end of the tunnel
Tony saw last episode now seems more like an oncoming
train . . .

3
Denial, Anger, Acceptance

US Transmission Date: 24 January 1999
UK Transmission Date: 29 July 1999

Writer: Mike Saraceni
Director: Nick Gomez
Cast: Ned Eisenberg (Shlomo Teittleman),
Chuck Low (Ariel), Sig Libowitz (Hillel),
Sasha Nesterov (Russian Man),
Bernadette Penotti (Nurse), Slava Schoot (Russian Man),
Angelica Torn (Woman at Party),
Joseph Tudisco (Trucker), Jennifer Wiltsie (Miss Marris)

Storyline: Christopher and Brendan return the truck Brendan hijacked in the previous episode. Uncle Junior is still fuming about the hijack. Comley Trucking gives the credit for this to Tony Soprano, which only infuriates Junior further.

Tony is intrigued by a painting in Dr Melfi's waiting room, which shows a farm with a barn and a tree on it. He believes it's a trick picture, designed to mess with his mind.

Tony and his crew visit Jackie in hospital, where he's undergoing chemotherapy for recurring cancer of the intestine. Silvio says a Hassidic Jew, Shlomo Teittleman, is having problems with a son-in-law, Ariel, who won't agree to a divorce. The son-in-law wants 50 per cent of a family-run motel. Hesh counsels against getting involved.

Meadow and her friend Hunter are feeling the pressure at school, trying to cram for SAT exams and rehearse for their choir.

Carmela and Tony visit Artie and Charmaine Bucco in their new, smaller home. The pair had to move house after losing their restaurant, Vesuvio, which Tony had fire-bombed to prevent a hit happening there.

Tony meets with Teittleman and agrees to intercede, in return for 25 per cent of the motel. Paulie and Silvio visit the son-in-law, Ariel, but he will not change his mind.

Paulie beats Ariel with the reception desk bell at the motel to try to persuade him – without success.

Carmela hires Artie and Charmaine to cater a fundraiser for a paediatric hospital. While Charmaine is visiting the house, she sees Carmela beckon for a maid with a wave of her fingers.

Meadow and Hunter ask Christopher to get some amphetamines, to help them stay awake for studying, but he refuses. When they go, Christopher's girlfriend Adriana asks him to think again. If the two girls try to get the drugs from street dealers they could get raped, poisoned or killed.

Tony arranges for Jackie to get a very special sponge bath in hospital by one of the exotic dancers from the Bada Bing! strip club.

At a therapy session Dr Melfi says Jackie's chances of survival don't sound good. Later she and Tony argue about the significance of the painting in the waiting room. He storms out of the office.

Christopher gives Meadow the drugs she wanted, but warns her never to tell Tony. If she does, Christopher is a dead man.

Artie and Charmaine argue about whether to take money from Tony Soprano to help them through their economic crisis.

The fundraiser is a big success, thanks to the catering. During the evening Carmela beckons to Charmaine with her fingers, just as she did to her maid earlier. The former school friend is insulted, but hides it.

Tony sneaks away from the party to visit his mistress, Irina. But he is summoned away by Silvio and Paulie, who need help dealing with Ariel. All three of them threaten to kill Ariel, but he is not scared of death. After consulting with Hesh, Tony opts for threatened castration as a fresh approach.

The morning after the fundraiser, Charmaine gets her revenge for being treated like a glorified waitress by Carmela. Charmaine says she dated and slept with Tony before he and Carmela were married.

Teittleman tries to renegotiate the deal with Tony after Ariel agrees to a divorce. Tony responds with violence and Teittleman calls him a living golem.

Junior visits Livia at Green Grove retirement community. He seeks her advice about how to deal with Christopher and Brendan.

Jackie's condition is getting rapidly worse. Tony is down after seeing his friend. He tells Dr Melfi about being called a Frankenstein monster, but doesn't respond when she asks if he lacks human feelings.

After the session Tony goes to his daughter's concert and is cheered by seeing Meadow sing and sharing the experience with Carmela.

Meanwhile, Junior makes his move. Christopher is handcuffed, beaten and subjected to a mock execution. He thinks Tony has found out about his getting drugs for Meadow. Mikey Palmice murders Brendan, shooting him through the eyeball.

Deep and Meaningful: Carmela treats her old school friend like a waitress at the fundraiser when she gets Charmaine's attention with a supercilious hand gesture, just as she had done to her maid earlier. Charmaine gets revenge by spilling the beans about sleeping with Tony before he and Carmela were married. Charmaine says she and Carmela both made their choices – a clear reference to Carmela's being married to a mobster. Carmela gets the jibe, but doesn't understand the cause.

Mobspeak: Silvio says Teittleman is offering 25 large ($25,000) to get his son-in-law to sign divorce papers. Tony asks if the insurance company think Artie Bucco is mobbed up (connected to the Mafia) when Artie says there is to be a second arson investigation. Meadow asks Christopher to cop (obtain) some crystal (amphetamine) for her and Hunter while they study for their SATs. Tony describes Ariel to Hesh as his non-shellfish-eating friend (Jew). Christopher identifies his two attackers as friends of Tony's goomah (Mafia mistress).

Mama Mia: Livia makes only one appearance this episode but it is a telling one. Junior visits her at Green Grove to help put up some pictures, and tells her about the rapid

decline in Jackie Aprile's health. Livia asks what is really
on his mind. Junior seeks her advice about dealing with
Christopher and Brendan. He says they're hiding behind
Tony.

Livia doesn't want Christopher killed, saying she loves
him like a son. She suggests he could use a little talking to.
Livia sentences Brendan Filone to death with just a shake
of her hand. Junior says she has a lot of sense for an old
gal. Livia absolves herself of any guilt by saying that she
is just a babbling idiot. 'That's why my son put me in a
nursing home.'

Bright Lights, Baked Ziti: Uncle Junior and Mikey eat a
soup-based dish at a restaurant. Later, Mikey is at Jackie's
bedside when Tony and his crew arrive to visit, bringing
gift-wrapped boxes of food. Jackie jokingly asks his wife to
bring him back a plate of brasciole (small rolls of beef
stuffed with savoury ingredients and cooked in a tomato
sauce) from the cafeteria. As Mikey leaves, Tony asks for
a quart of vinegar peppers Junior owes him.

As Artie prepares food for the fundraiser, Charmaine
berates him for squeezing the quail too hard. The food is
a big hit at the event, especially the veal, and the arancin
(little rice balls). In the kitchen Tony argues with Artie, so
the chef throws a slice of prosciutto ham, which sticks to
Tony's forehead. The pair have a food fight.

Silvio is eating a massive ham sandwich when Tony
arrives to help sort out Ariel. Tony declines Silvio's offer
of something to munch on.

Mobbed Up: Junior and Mikey discuss the situation with
Christopher and Brendan. Mikey gets very agitated but
Junior calms him down by saying they're not making a
Western here.

When Tony puts the squeeze on Teittleman, the Jew
calls Tony a Frankenstein monster.

How Do You Feel?: Tony gets paranoid about the painting
in Dr Melfi's waiting room. To him it says that psychiatrists are smart and its asks what he thinks of the spooky

depressing barn and rotted-out tree in the picture. Despite this, Tony says he's having a really good week. Then he reveals that a friend of his is in hospital with cancer.

Later he questions Dr Melfi about Jackie's prospects and gets angry when she suggests it doesn't sound very good. Dr Melfi says Tony is getting closer to confronting his true feelings. There's nothing in the picture to indicate the tree is rotted out, she adds. Tony takes this as proof of trickery and storms out of the office.

When Jackie deteriorates, Tony returns for another session. He admires the Hassidic people for having their beliefs and not being afraid of death. He denies being afraid of death, but is troubled by the accusation that he is a Frankenstein monster, lacking humanity.

Sleeping With the Fishes: Brendan Filone, who dies in the bath. He is shot through the eyeball by Mikey, while Uncle Junior looks on happily. Christopher thinks he is going to be executed by the Russians but they just scare the shit out of him – quite literally. Tony, Paulie and Silvio almost kill Ariel, but instead use the threat of castration by bolt-cutter to get their way.

Quote/Unquote: Artie Bucco contemplates becoming a plumber. Tony says there's only one concept to master: 'Shit runs downhill.'

When Tony visits his mistress, he asks Irina what a painting on the wall means to her. It shows water splashing in a swimming pool, as if someone had just dived in. Irina shrugs and reveals a passing knowledge of British twentieth-century painters. 'It just reminds me of David Hockey [sic].'

Facing death from Tony, Paulie and Silvio, Ariel tells them about the Masada – 900 Jews who held their own against 15,000 Roman soldiers. Ariel asks whatever happened to the Romans? 'You're looking at them, asshole,' Tony replies.

Tony ponders the big philosophical issues of life, death and self-awareness in his own, inimitable style. 'If all this shit's for nothing, why do I got to think about it?'

Soundtrack: 'Tenderly' by Chet Baker. 'Happy Feet' by Paolo Conte. 'Gawk' by Ethyline. 'Melodia del Rio' by Ruben Gonzalez. 'Turn Of The Century' by Damon & Naomi. Meadow and her school choir sing 'All Through the Night'. 'Complicated Shadows' by Elvis Costello and the Attractions.

Surveillance Report: The closing scenes juxtapose Meadow and her choir singing with the execution of Brendan and the mock execution of Christopher. This is a homage to *The Godfather* films, which often juxtapose a series of brutal killings with a family or religious event.

The Verdict: 'When a Jew gets a divorce, even the altar sheds tears.' Tony makes an ill-advised foray into the world of Hassidic divorce brokering, while Carmela alienates a childhood friend with her high-handed patronage.

Death permeates events like a black cloud. The acting boss, Jackie Aprile, is dying from cancer, Brendan Filone gets executed by order of Uncle Junior and Tony confronts his own mortality. For the second episode running he storms out of a session with Dr Melfi.

Much of the episode is dealing with the fallout from previous events, or setting up plotlines for later development. But the Hassidic divorce subplot provides welcome comic relief, as well as giving food for thought to Tony.

4
Meadowlands

US Transmission Date: 31 January 1999
UK Transmission Date: 5 August 1999

Writer: Jason Cahill
Director: John Patterson
Cast: Mark Blum (Randall Curtin), John Arocho (Kid #2),
Michael Buscemi (Lewis Pantowski),
TJ Coluca (Jeremy Piocosta),
Guillermo Dias (Salesperson), Daniel Hilt (Kid #3),

Ray Michael Karl (Teacher), Theresa Lynn (Stripper),
Shawn McLean (Yo Yo Mendez),
Sal Patraccione (George Piocosta),
James Spector (Kid #1), Corrine Stella (Woman),
Anthony Tavaglione (Lance)

Storyline: Adriana picks up Christopher from hospital,
where he has been recovering from the mock execution. He
is deeply paranoid, believing it was ordered by Tony
because Christopher gave amphetamine to Meadow.
Adriana asks if it's true he did 'number two' in his pants
while being threatened. Adriana and Christopher go to
Brendan Filone's apartment, where they discover his dead
body in the bath.

Anthony Jr gets into a fight with his former friend,
Jeremy Piacosta, at school. AJ's shirt is badly ripped in the
confrontation.

Tony arrives for a session with Dr Melfi and almost
bumps into Silvio Dante, who sees a dentist in the opposite
office. Tony gets worried about how safe it is for him to be
treated by a psychiatrist.

Christopher accuses Meadow of telling Tony about the
amphetamine, which she emphatically denies. Meadow
says she hates being a Soprano.

Carmela discovers AJ's ripped shirt. He promises to get
$40 to replace the shirt, which was a gift from his
grandmother.

Tony visits Livia at Green Grove. He tries to persuade
her to take part in activities at the retirement community
but she would rather be a martyr. Outside Tony meets with
Detective Vin Makasian, a corrupt policeman. Tony wants
information about Dr Melfi's background and daily routine.

Tony and his crew are visiting Jackie Aprile on his
deathbed. Christopher arrives and says that Uncle Junior
has had Brendan executed. The crew speculate that Mikey
Palmice carried out the hit on Junior's orders. Tony leaves
Jackie's deathbed to sort the problem out, stealing a staple
gun from a maintenance worker at the hospital.

Tony goes to the Sit-Tite Loungette to confront his uncle. Outside Tony pauses to attack Mikey Palmice for the attack on Christopher, stapling through Mikey's suit into his chest. Inside Tony and Junior argue. Junior says Christopher should work for him from now on, but Tony rejects the idea. Junior warns his nephew that, if he comes back, Tony should come armed.

Detective Makasian and a colleague follow Dr Melfi, who is on a date with a friend called Randall Curtin. Makasian pulls Curtin over and beats him up. The detective thinks Tony and Dr Melfi are having an affair. He cryptically tells her not to sleep around.

Next day Makasian reports his findings to Tony. Dr Melfi is dating Randall Curtin. She's divorced with one child, aged nineteen. She sees a psychiatrist herself.

Tony discusses the leadership crisis over lunch with three other captains from the Family – Larry Boy Barese, Raymond Curto and Jimmy Altieri. Tony tries to get Curto to take over as acting boss when Jackie dies, but Curto declines. The other captains say the job will have to go to either Tony or Junior.

AJ tries to get the $40 from Jeremy Piocosta and they start fighting again. The pair are pulled apart but resolve to settle the matter the next day by fighting at the school sandpit.

Tony collapses in the kitchen at home after forgetting to take his medication. Carmela asks whether he discusses their marriage with the psychiatrist. Tony is considering quitting therapy because of the security risk. Carmela says their marriage is at stake if he abandons therapy. Tony pretends to his wife that Dr Melfi is a man.

At his next session Tony discusses his problems with Junior. Dr Melfi suggests a book about coping with elder family members. She says sometimes they need to have the illusion of being in control, just as children do.

Christopher tries to collect his regular payment from a street-corner dealer called Yo Yo Mendez. Yo Yo says Junior's boys have already collected from him – they have taken over control of the corner. Christopher attacks Yo Yo, saying he still controls the corner.

Jeremy Piocosta surrenders before he and AJ can begin fighting. He gives forty dollars to a bemused AJ.

A TV news bulletin announces that Jackie has died of cancer. At the Bada Bing!, Tony and his crew toast their dead leader. Christopher bursts in, demanding Tony go to war with Junior after the latest skirmish. Tony nearly throttles Christopher and then leaves to confront Junior. The crew contemplate the bleak prospect of a gang war.

Tony visits Junior at the Sit-Tite and offers him the position of acting boss, in exchange for two of Junior's territories. Junior agrees and they embrace.

AJ seeks Meadow's advice about Jeremy Piocosta backing out of their fight. She shows him websites about gangsters on her computer.

Dr Melfi goes to Randall Curtin's for a date but he is scared to go out after being attacked by Detective Makasian. She recommends a therapist who specialises in post-traumatic stress disorder.

At Jackie's burial, Tony and his crew discuss making Junior boss. Tony says this will keep Junior happy. All the key decisions will still be made by Tony, but Junior is a lightning rod for any attacks from outside. Government agents are photographing the event for their files.

Deep and Meaningful: The episode ends with AJ watching his father at the funeral, seeing him from a new perspective. Over the course of the instalment AJ loses his innocence, learning that his beloved father is actually a member of the Mafia. Tony smiles and winks at his son – he still loves AJ, but the boy now knows his father is involved in all manner of illegal activity and could well be a murderer. It's a touching moment that will be referred to later . . .

Mobspeak: Christopher describes Brendan's execution as a message job (shooting a bullet into a body to send a specific message to that person's crew or Family) through the eye (meaning we're watching you). Tony's crew discuss message jobs. Silvio says that through the eye means the guy was a rat.

Junior warns his nephew that, the next time he visits, Tony should come heavy (carrying a weapon).

Tony, Jimmy Altieri, Raymond Curto and Larry Boy Barese discuss who should succeed Jackie as acting boss. Jimmy asks if Junior is stubborn enough to go to war. Raymond says no one's going to the mattresses (going to war with a rival clan or Family) in this day and age. Tony says one of the captains (a Family member who leads a crew) needs to step up and restore order to the whole Family.

Yo Yo Mendez tells Christopher there's no one to whom he'd rather give his ten points (percentage of income from criminal activity).

Mama Mia: Livia's mask slips for a moment when Tony brings her macaroons. She looks joyful, then swiftly rejects them as too sweet, rather than give her son any pleasure. She doesn't like the people at Green Grove and she doesn't want to go on a trip to New York for dinner and a show. Livia says that city is full of grown men soiling themselves and mothers throwing their babies out of skyscraper windows.

Tony says she isn't making the most of her opportunities but Livia asks what does he care? As long as she's out of sight, she's out of mind. Tony asks whether she wants the macaroons, because he's leaving. Livia says she doesn't care but tells him to leave some out for the lunatics.

Bright Lights, Baked Ziti: Christopher offers to buy Meadow a Happy Meal from McDonald's, as he did when she was little.

Tony takes his mother some of her favourite biscuits, macaroons, but she rejects them. Livia suggests he leave some out for the other residents of Green Grove. Outside the retirement community, Detective Makasian mooches some of the macaroons off Tony.

Junior and his cronies are eating pasta at the Sit-Tite Loungette when Tony confronts his uncle about what happened to Christopher and Brendan.

Tony shares a massive lobster dinner upstairs at the Bada Bing! strip club with three other captains from the Family.

Junior is having a coffee and a sandwich when Tony returns to the Sit-Tite to offer him the position of acting boss.

Mobbed Up: Big Pussy calls the killing of Brendan a Moe Green special. He says that in *The Godfather*, Moe Green's eyes got too big for his stomach so they put a small-calibre slug through one of them. Paulie quibbles whether getting shot through the eye is actually a message job. He believes the film's director, Francis Ford Coppola, just framed the shot that way for the shock value.

As the conflict between Tony and Junior escalates, Christopher says this isn't the time for negotiation. He suggests Tony re-create the finale in *Scarface*, where Al Pacino has a bazooka under each arm.

How Do You Feel?: Tony is nervous, after nearly bumping into Silvio outside Dr Melfi's office. He is concerned about security. If somebody sees him going into a therapy session, it could have dire consequences.

After Tony has another panic attack, she prescribes Xanax to get him over short-term stresses. Dr Melfi suggests Tony let his mother and uncle believe they are in charge.

As the episode draws to a close, Tony tells Dr Melfi he feels fine, the Xanax is helping. He no longer has doubts about therapy. Tony says he gets a lot of good ideas at the sessions.

How Do You Feel, Doctor?: Dr Melfi tells Tony that she's out of touch with the climate of rage and casual violence in American society, mentioning how her date got beaten up by a policeman. These sentiments will come back to haunt her in Season Three . . .

Sleeping With the Fishes: Giancomo 'Jackie' Aprile, from cancer. His death leaves a power vacuum. With the boss, Ercoli 'Ekley' Demeo, serving a life sentence in prison, the Family needs a new acting boss.

Always With the . . .: Tony despairs of his mother's attitude to New York City. 'You're always with the babies out the windows.'

Silvio says Christopher is always with scenarios when the latter suggests the bazooka climax of *Scarface* as a way of resolving problems with Junior.

I Dream of Jeannie Cusamano: Tony has a cryptic dream at the beginning of this episode. He sees himself in Dr Melfi's office when Hesh walks by the window outside. Melfi says Hesh has a three o'clock appointment. Tony goes out into the corridor. AJ is watching him through a partially open doorway. In a waiting room, Silvio is having sex while Pussy and Paulie read newspapers – Paulie's paper is in Japanese.

Tony returns to Melfi's office and asks what's going on? Melfi is in her chair but facing away from Tony. Jackie Aprile sits up on a hospital bed in the corner of the office, smoking a cigarette. He says there are thunderstorms and he can smell rain. Melfi turns around, but she is actually Livia dressed as Dr Melfi, complete with a wig and glasses. Tony wakes up with a start!

Quote/Unquote: Tony worries that his notoriety could lead to unwanted celebrity, but Dr Melfi is unimpressed by his concerns. 'I thought we made some progress on your narcissism.'

Livia opts for high drama when Tony says she has not been forgotten by him or his family. 'I wish the Lord would take me now.'

Tony dismisses a suggestion that the Family be run by a council, because it was established as a paramilitary organisation. 'We need a supreme commander at the top, not the fucking Dave Clark Five.'

Tony complains about his mother's attitude to Green Grove retirement community. 'I pay four grand a month for this place and she acts like I'm an Eskimo pushing her out to sea.'

Soundtrack: Randall Curtin says he has a song by the Doors, 'People Are Strange', stuck on a loop in his head. 'Prisoner Of Love' by Perry Como. 'Ugly Stadium' by Tipsy. 'Floor Essence' by Man With No Name. 'Looking

Down From the Bridge' by Mazzy Star. 'Fired Up' by Funky Green Dogs.

Surveillance Report: Adriana's sunglasses keep appearing and disappearing from her face during the scene where Christopher interrogates Meadow. This episode introduces Detective Vin Makasian, played by the American character actor John Heard. He has previously appeared in films such as *Home Alone*, *In the Line of Fire* and *The Pelican Brief*. Makasian mentions Melfi's psychiatrist, Dr Elliot Kupferburg, who will be a recurring character in Season Two.

The Verdict: 'I'll never forget where I was this day.' AJ makes a shocking discovery about what his father does for a living, while the death of the acting boss, Jackie Aprile, brings the Family to the verge of a civil war.

This episode is the concluding chapter of a trilogy charting a significant power shift in the Family. The scenes between Tony and Junior are very tense, while the moment when Tony offers his uncle the job of acting boss is a genuine twist. Tony may not be able to sort out his family problems in therapy, but it is helping him resolve some of his Family problems. We also get our first meaningful glimpse behind the professional mask of Dr Melfi.

'Meadowlands' is a gripping episode, peppered with humour and pathos. It's the best the show has been since the pilot, at least in part, because it pays off plot lines built up over the two preceding episodes.

5
College

US Transmission Date: 7 February 1999
UK Transmission Date: 12 August 1999

Writer: James Manos Jr and David Chase
Director: Allen Coulter
Cast: Tony Ray Rossi (Fred Peters),
Lisa Arning (Peters's Wife), Ross Gibby (Bartender),

Mark Kamine (Admissions Dean),
Michael Manetta (Gas Station Attendant),
Keith Nobbs (Bowdoin Student),
Luke Reilly (Lon Le Doyenne),
Sarah Thompson (Lucinda),
Olivia Brynn Zaro (Peters's Daughter)

Storyline: Tony is driving Meadow around Maine so she can visit prospective colleges. Carmela is home sick, recovering from the flu.

Meadow asks her father if he is in the Mafia. He initially denies it, but eventually admits that some of his money comes from illegal activities. While they are stopped at a gas station, Tony thinks he sees a former mobster turned informant, Fabian Petrulio, who tours the college circuit giving lectures about his criminal past. He notes down the man's licence plate number and calls Christopher to get it traced.

Carmela's fever breaks and she starts to feel a little better. She sends Anthony Jr to a friend's house to play video games. Carmela's parish priest, Father Phil Intintola, turns up unexpectedly during a rainstorm. He confesses to a craving for her pasta.

Over dinner Meadow and Tony discuss his Mafia membership. Meadow says she thinks AJ also knows. Tony admits he only just scraped into college. He wonders if he joined the mob because his father and uncle were already members and he was too lazy to think for himself. Meadow confesses to having taken amphetamine in the past, but will not reveal her supplier. Father and daughter agree it's good they can tell each other such difficult truths.

Meadow meets girls from one of the colleges she could be attending. Tony suggests she spend time with them. Meanwhile, he calls Christopher, who says the licence plate belongs to Frederic Peters, a Maine resident. Tony thinks that Peters is Petrulio, but wants a positive identification.

Carmela discovers Tony's therapist is a woman when Dr Melfi phones to reschedule an appointment.

Tony goes to Peters's house and gets a better look at his quarry. But Peters realises he is being observed. Peters contacts a few friends to find out if anyone has been asking about him lately. Tony locates Peters's workplace, a travel business run out of a Portakabin in a secluded piece of countryside.

Carmela and Father Phil share a meal, with the priest doing most of the eating. They start watching a film but Carmela becomes upset. Father Phil hears her confession. Carmela says she hasn't truly confessed in twenty years. She has forsaken what is right for what is easy, allowing evil into her house. She thinks Tony has committed terrible acts. Carmela feels that it's only a matter of time before God compensates with outrage for her sins. Father Phil gives Carmela Holy Communion after her confession.

Tony takes a drunken Meadow back to their motel. Peters has tracked them and nearly shoots Tony, but is interrupted by other motel guests. Tony tells Christopher not to come to Maine – Tony will deal with Peters himself.

AJ phones Carmela to say he wants to sleep over at his friend's house, and she agrees. Carmela and Father Phil almost kiss but he has to bolt for the toilet, where he throws up copiously. Next morning he frets about sleeping over on a sofa but Carmela says they have done nothing wrong.

Peters tries to blackmail two drug addicts into killing Tony but they refuse.

Tony drops Meadow off at Bowdoin College for her interview. He drives to Peters's office and strangles the informer, cutting his hand. When Tony returns to pick up Meadow, she notices mud on his shoes and the cut. He lies about what caused them.

Tony and Meadow finally get home. Carmela tells her husband about Father Phil staying the night. Tony isn't impressed, but looks sheepish himself when Carmela asks why he lied about having a female therapist.

Deep and Meaningful: This episode is packed with magic moments which reveal the essence of several central characters, such as Tony's reaction to Meadow asking if he's in the Mafia and Carmela almost kissing Father Phil. But the most insightful has to be Carmela's confession.

Initially, she talks normally but she quickly breaks down under the strain of her own hypocrisy. For the first time in decades, she truly confesses, admitting that she is fully aware of both Tony's illegal and immoral activities, and of her unspoken complicity in those acts. It's this moment that probably won Edie Falco her Emmy for Best Actress in a Drama Series.

Mobspeak: Tony says Peters flipped (changed allegiance from the mob to federal law enforcers) about ten years ago. Christopher worries that Peters could lam (go into hiding) at any time.

Carmela talks about fanook (homosexual) priests.

Bright Lights, Baked Ziti: There's a lot of food in this episode but most of it ends up being ignored or regurgitated. AJ brings Carmela a poached egg and orange juice but she can't face eating it. In Maine Tony takes Meadow to dinner but they leave plenty of food behind on their plates.

Father Phil visits Carmela and says he has a craving for her baked ziti. She reheats a trayful of it from the freezer. The priest says it's so much better that way because the mozzarella cheese gets nice and chewy. He also asks for some wine, if it's open. They drink Chianti while the pasta is reheating.

Father Phil asks Carmela if she thinks he is a schnorrer – a Yiddish word for somebody who always shows up in time for free food. He tosses a salad and finds a jar of Cajun stuffed olives in the fridge.

The priest gorges himself on the baked ziti, adding extra cheese. He says the red pepper flakes make all the difference.

Fred Peters asks a gas-station attendant called Tanky if anyone has been looking for him. Tanky wants to know if Peters will be giving away any homemade cheese this year.

Father Phil and Carmela share holy communion. The priest and Carmela are about to kiss when Father Phil runs to the toilet to vomit.

Next morning Carmela says they have done nothing wrong. 'Is there a commandment against eating ziti?' When

Tony gets home he wants some cold pasta. He's amazed that a whole tray of ziti from the previous Sunday has been eaten. Tony surmises that Monsignor Jughead must have been visiting again.

Mobbed Up: Tony assumes Meadows and her friends got their ideas about the Mafia from watching *The Godfather*. She says they prefer Martin Scorcese's *Casino*, because of Sharon Stone, the 70s clothes and the pills.

Carmela and Father Phil discuss another Scorcese film, *The Last Temptation of Christ*. Carmela cannot picture that Jesus looked like Willem Defoe, even though she rates his performance in the film. She also finds the ending confusing and is unsure whether Jesus really gets down off the cross.

Father Phil says Robert De Niro was supposed to play Jesus. Carmela speculates that this would have made it into a different picture. Father Phil attempts a De Niro accent, blending the actor's famous dialogue from *Taxi Driver* into a Biblical setting. 'You talking to me, Pilate? Well you must be talking to me 'cause I don't see nobody else here. Except Barrabas here.'

The priest is going to leave but Carmela tempts him to stay with *Remains of the Day* on DVD. Father Phil professes a weakness for anything featuring the British actress Emma Thompson.

The next morning, Carmela refers to their having watched *Casablanca* recently. Father Phil says the new print is great. Carmela likens her situation to that of Humphrey Bogart's character. She asks why, of all the priests in the world, she had to get the one who's straight.

How Do You Feel?: Tony does not have a session this episode because he is in Maine with Meadow, but Dr Melfi does phone his house to reschedule an appointment – she is stricken with flu.

Carmela becomes convinced Tony is sleeping with Dr Melfi, because he lied about his therapist being a woman. Carmela is distraught. She thought therapy would help clear up the freak show in Tony's head.

Sleeping With the Fishes: Fred Peters, also known as
Fabian Petrulio. Tony strangles him with a length of
plastic cord because Peters broke the oath of silence and
ratted on members of the Family.

Quote/Unquote: Meadow provides proof for suspecting
that her father is a member of the Mafia. 'Did the
Cusamano kids ever find fifty thousand dollars in kruger-
rands and a forty-five automatic while they were hunting
for Easter eggs?'

Christopher charmingly describes why he should fly to
Maine and execute Peters, instead of Tony doing the job.
'Clipping a famous rat would put me a cunt hair away
from being made.'

Carmela tells Tony that Father Phil stayed the night but
says nothing happened between them. Tony is unconvinced. 'What'd you guys do for twelve hours? Play "name
that pope"?'

Carmela again states that nothing happened, referring to
a top-rating TV miniseries and bestselling novel about a
woman's affair with her priest. 'Do I look like the friggin'
Thorn Bird over here?'

Soundtrack: 'Gold Leaves for GK Chesterton' by Michael
Hoppe. 'Eye On You' by Rocket From The Crypt. 'Maine
Two-Step' by Basin Brothers. 'Cadence To Arms' by
Dropkick Murphys.

Surveillance Report: Only a handful of the regulars appear
in this episode. Tony's mistress Irina tells him a story
about a friend of hers with a prosthetic leg. She will repeat
the same story in Season Two during 'The Knight in White
Satin Armor'.

There's a visual reference back to the ducks in the pilot.
After Tony kills Peters, a flock of birds fly overhead. He
stands and stares up at them.

The Verdict: 'Jimmy says hello from hell, you fuck.' Tony
reveals his dark side through murder while getting closer
to Meadow by being more honest. Carmela has a spiritual
crisis, confessing her sins and then almost kissing a priest.

The character of Carmela gets some real development as she confronts her own complicity in her husband's crimes. She also faces her first test of fidelity and passes only by virtue of Father Phil's fondness for food.

The two sides of Tony are shown in sharp contrast – the loving father bonding with his teenage daughter, and the ruthless mobster who will murder to enforce the Mafia's code of silence. 'College' is one of the strongest episodes from Season One and stands alone as a compelling hour of television. It won the 1999 Emmy for Outstanding Writing in a Drama Series. Three other episodes of *The Sopranos* ('Pilot/The Sopranos', 'Nobody Knows Anything' and 'Isabella') were among the five nominees.

6
Pax Soprano

US Transmission Date: 14 February 1999
UK Transmission Date: 19 August 1999

Writer: Frank Renzulli
Director: Alan Taylor
Cast: Vincent Curatola (Johnny Sack),
Freddy Bastone (Barman), William Conn (Old Man),
Maurizio Corbino (Waiter), Sylvia Kauders (Old Woman),
Salem Ludwig (Mr Capri), Prianga Pieris (Mechanic),
Salvatore Piro (Sammy Grigio),
Christopher Quinn (Rusty Irish),
Dave Salerno (Card Player),
Donn Swaby (Guy on Bridge), Sonny Zito (Eggie)

Storyline: Tony is becoming obsessed with Dr Melfi. He still has Detective Makasian tailing the psychiatrist but gets no new information about her. Tony starts bringing coffee for Dr Melfi and himself to their sessions.

Junior's assistant, Mikey Palmice, breaks up a high-stakes card game on Junior's orders, because the organiser doesn't pay a slice of its earnings to the acting boss.

Junior gets himself measured for a new suit by his tailor. The tailor is unhappy because his grandson committed suicide after buying designer drugs, and the dealer is still walking free. Later Junior visits his sister-in-law at Green Grove retirement community. She suggests he should tax Hesh.

Tony can't get an erection with his Russian mistress Irina. They argue and she throws a burning candle at him.

Hesh seeks Tony's help. Junior wants to tax Hesh's loan-sharking business and Hesh is unhappy at the amount demanded. Tony agrees to see what he can do.

Despite his impotence, Tony is having erotic dreams about Dr Melfi.

During a wedding anniversary dinner with Carmela, Tony has a meeting with Johnny Sack, a representative of the New York Mafia. He agrees to help Tony resolve the situation between Hesh and Junior. Carmela is furious that Tony used their wedding anniversary to discuss business. They are not having sex and she resents his relationship with Dr Melfi.

Dr Melfi tells Tony she cannot accept any gifts from him, not even a cup of coffee. She has to interrupt their session because of a phone call from a garage about problems with her car's starter. The garage wants to charge a high price to fix the problem. Tony admits to suffering from impotence. Dr Melfi suggests the cause may be psychological rather than physical.

Tony gets home to find a load of furniture being delivered. He argues with Carmela, who has been on a spending spree in recent days.

Junior, Tony, Hesh and Johnny Sack have a meeting to discuss the tax. Junior agrees to a smaller percentage and only $250,000 in back taxes.

Tony tries to have Irina dress like Dr Melfi but she misunderstands his suggestion and feels insulted.

Tony retells what happened to Dr Melfi, but substitutes his wife's name for that of his mistress. Tony says he wanted Carmela to dress like Dr Melfi. He kisses the psychiatrist but she pushes him away.

Melfi's car problems mysteriously resolve themselves. A mechanic tells her a new starter has been fitted.

Mikey Palmice and his associate Chucky Signore murder Rusty Irish, the drug dealer blamed for the suicide of the tailor's grandson.

Tony is visited by the other captains, who complain about Junior not sharing the proceeds of his new wealth as acting boss. Rusty Irish was Larry Boy Barese's biggest earner. Tony agrees and tries to intercede. He visits his mother and asks for her help, but Livia says he has to talk directly to Junior.

Carmela seeks Father Phil's counsel about her problems with Tony. Up to now she felt she could deal with his mistresses and viewed them as a form of masturbation for Tony. But Carmela feels challenged by Dr Melfi, as if Tony were cheating on her for the first time. Father Phil says Carmela is not without sin in this matter, and she needs to pray for guidance and forgiveness.

Tony admits to having Dr Melfi's car secretly repaired. He says he is in love with her. The psychiatrist says his feelings are a result of the progress they have made and the role she has played in therapy. She fulfils the things he feels are missing in his wife and mother.

Tony suggests to his uncle that it would be better to share the wealth with the captains. Junior agrees and shares Hesh's $250,000 back taxes among the captains. Tony gives his slice back to Hesh.

Carmela and Tony resolve their differences about Dr Melfi.

Junior is given a celebration dinner by the Family. Everyone present is photographed covertly. Later, in an office, the photographs are arranged on a pinboard to show the new structure of the Family, with Junior replacing the late Jackie Aprile as acting boss. Federal law enforcement is closing in . . .

Deep and Meaningful: This episode's most touching moment comes as Tony and Carmela reconcile with each other by the swimming pool in their back yard. The couple

have been at daggers drawn since Carmela discovered
Tony had lied about Dr Melfi being a woman. Driven by
jealousy, Carmela reacts by having shouted arguments and
having furniture spending sprees to get Tony's attention.
After being counselled by Father Phil, she recognises the
conflict of her own feelings. The husband and wife resolve
this problem together and show that they still love each
other.

Mobspeak: Livia says Junior smells like a French putan'
(short for puttana, whore) because he wears Canoe after-
shave. Junior decides to tax (take a percentage from
someone's illegal earnings) Hesh. Tony wonders if Junior
realises he already gets money from Hesh's shylock business (loan-sharking). The other captains complain that
Junior eats alone (keeps everything for himself). Tony tries
to discuss the situation with his uncle, ending by saying
capice? (do you understand?). Junior says Tony has been
acting mezzo morte (half dead) lately. Junior agrees to take
one and a half per cent of Hesh's shy (the interest charged
on loans by loan sharks).

Mama Mia: Livia is in a surprisingly positive mood this
episode – at least, by her standards. She is almost playful
with Junior when he visits her at Green Grove. Livia
advises him not to let people take advantage now that he
is acting boss. She obliquely prompts Junior into taxing
Hesh. He takes this as proof at how angry she is with
Tony, but Livia denies it.

  When Tony visits his mother she declines an invitation
to bingo from Molly, another resident at the retirement
community. When the woman is out of hearing, Livia
describes her as a degenerate gambler.

  Tony tries to get his mother to intercede with Junior on
behalf of the captains, but she claims not to know that
world and doesn't want to get involved. 'I wish the Lord
would take me,' she announces at random.

Bright Lights, Baked Ziti: Christopher steals some ham
from the slicer as he walks through Satriale's Pork Store.

Tony takes Carmela to a restaurant for their wedding anniversary. She complains that the veal is like rubber, but Tony says it tastes all right. The staff bring a slice of cake with a lit candle on top to the table while singing 'Happy Anniversary' in Italian, to the tune of 'Happy Birthday'.

Tony takes his mother some almond biscuits from Ferrara's, which she accepts for eating with her coffee later.

The captains have a dinner for Junior, to celebrate his promotion to acting boss of the family.

Mobbed Up: Tony feels his life is like an episode of 'provonesomething', likening it to an Italian version of the US TV series *Thirtysomething*.

A fellow captain, Raymond Curto, worries that Tony has turned Junior into a Frankenstein monster by making him acting boss.

How Do You Feel?: Tony tells Dr Melfi that his wife is jealous of her. The psychiatrist asks why Tony chose a female therapist. He says she was the only Italian on the list offered him. He asks why Dr Melfi has him as a patient, when most people avoid him at all costs – but the question goes unanswered.

At their next session Tony says he feels good, very good. He may flush his Prozac because he believes it is making him impotent.

He becomes increasingly obsessed with Dr Melfi. At their next session he says she has a killer body. He admires her for being gentle and sweet-sounding, like a mandolin. Tony kisses her but she pushes him away, just as their session is ending.

At his next appointment, Tony talks about Carmela's extravagant spending. Dr Melfi suggests this is a ploy to get his attention. Tony admits having had the starter in Melfi's car secretly replaced. The therapist says it was a violation of her privacy and she has been scared to death.

Tony says he's in love with her and he can't get excited about another woman. Dr Melfi says this is a by-product of the progress they are making and wants him to return for further sessions. But she still feels someone has been following her on Tony's behalf . . . .

Sleeping With the Fishes: Rusty Irish, a drug dealer. Mikey Palmice and Chucky Signore throw him from a bridge over the Patterson Falls on orders from Junior. The grandson of Junior's tailor committed suicide at the same place after buying designer drugs from Rusty.

Always with the . . .: Tony despairs of Carmela's attitude at their wedding anniversary dinner. 'Why do you always gotta be so dramatic?'

I Dream of Jeannie Cusamano: Tony has two sex dreams in this episode. In the first, he awakens in his own bed but the room is lit with dozens of candles. He is getting a blow job and enjoying himself immensely. The woman giving it to him emerges from under the sheet – it's Dr Melfi, but she speaks with the voice of Irina, Tony's mistress.

In the second dream Tony is interrupted while urinating in his bathroom. A woman is having a shower. She opens the door – it's Dr Melfi again and she's wet and naked. Tony wakes up with a start.

Quote/Unquote: Tony says he might as well be a dildo for all the conversation he gets from his mistress Irina. But she is unhappy with his impotence. 'If you were a dildo, we wouldn't be fighting.'

Big Pussy complains about his luck at cards. 'I've eaten more queens than Lancelot.'

Dr Melfi asks Tony when was the last time he had a prostate exam. 'Hey, I don't even let anyone wag their finger in my face,' he replies.

Junior complains about Hesh's hardline attitude to financial deals. 'Hold on to your cock when you negotiate with these desert people.'

Livia rants about the woman in the next room at Green Grove using too much water. 'She runs the water all day. Water, water, water . . . I'm living next door to Gunga Din.'

Soundtrack: 'When The Boy In Your Arms (Is The Boy In Your Heart)' by Connie Francis. The Green Grove residents sing 'Whistle a Happy Tune' from the musical *The*

King and I. 'What Time Is It?' by Jive Five. 'Willy Nilly' by Rufus Thomas. 'Coconut Boogaloo' by Medeski, Martin & Wood. 'Pampa' by Gustavo Santaolalla. 'Paparazzi' by Xzibit.

Surveillance Report: This episode's title is a reference to Pax Romana, a peace imposed by the Roman Empire. Hesh says he could live off the royalties from six gold records he wrote. Tony points out that two black kids wrote the records – Hesh owned their record company and gave himself a co-writing credit. This will come back to haunt Hesh in a later episode, 'A Hit is a Hit'.

The Verdict: 'My uncle's been boss of the Family for ten fuckin' minutes and already I got agita.' Junior is making waves as acting boss and everybody wants Tony to intercede. But Tony is having problems of his own in bed and can't seem to get Dr Melfi out of his mind.

Uncle Junior proves to be a fair and surprisingly moral leader, but he is also quite easily led. Dr Melfi is beginning to be drawn slowly into the world of Tony Soprano, but still thinks of him as just a patient.

For Tony, the difficulties with Junior are light relief compared with his problems with sex and the women in his life. By the end of the episode he and Carmela resolve some of their problems, but many more remain . . .

7
Down Neck

US Transmission Date: 21 February 1999
UK Transmission Date: 26 August 1999

Writers: Mitchell Burgess and Robin Green
Director: Lorraine Senna
Cast: Joseph Siravo (Johnny Boy Soprano),
Laila Robins (1967 Livia),
Rocco Sisto (1967 Uncle Junior),
David Beach (Dr Galani), Paul Albe (Contractor),

Shirl Bernheim (Pearl), Madeline Blue (Janice),
Bobby Borriello (Young Tony),
Scott Owen Cumberbatch (Rideland Kid #2),
Anthony Fusco (Father Hagy),
Rob Grippay (Byron Barber),
Jason Hauser (Rideland Cop),
Michael Jordan (Rideland Kid), Greg Perrelli (Jared),
Nick Raio (Wiseguy), Steve Santosusso (Guy),
Tim Williams (Mr Meskimmin)

Storyline: Anthony Jr and two friends steal a bottle of
sacramental wine at school. They are drunk in gym class and
AJ's friend, Byron Barber, throws up on the gym teacher.

Tony and Carmela are summoned to the office of Father
Hagy, the school principal. He introduces the school
psychologist, Dr Galani, who believes AJ could suffer from
ADD – attention deficiency disorder. The school wants to test
AJ for psychological, behavioural and medical symptoms.

Livia and Uncle Junior come to dinner with Tony and
his family. Livia says Tony was a car thief by the age of
ten, while Junior describes his nephew as a preteen hellion.
AJ makes a comment that shows he knows about Tony's
real profession. The boy is grounded for three weeks.

Carmela and Tony privately discuss the situation. They
agree it's time to talk with Meadow about the mob, but
will wait for the results of the testing before deciding
whether to tell AJ.

Tony has a flashback to the first time he witnessed his
father beating someone to extort money from them. At a
session with Dr Melfi, she draws a parallel between this
recently recalled memory and Tony's fears about his own
son discovering that he is in the mob.

Carmela and Tony argue about whether they are at fault
for AJ's troubles, either genetically or by the way they have
raised him. Carmela worries that, if AJ is diagnosed as
having ADD, he will be put into special education.

AJ visits his grandmother at Green Grove while suspended from school. He lets slip that Tony is seeing a
psychiatrist. Livia is shocked at this news.

Tony gets a flat tyre while taking AJ to a dental appointment. They talk about Jackie Aprile's funeral and AJ indicates he knows Tony is in the Mafia.

In therapy Tony is struggling to come to terms with AJ's new knowledge. Dr Melfi says those who don't understand history are doomed to repeat it. Tony recalls another incident from 1967 involving his elder sister Janice and his father.

Every Sunday Johnny Boy took Janice out for a drive. Tony stowed away in the boot of his father's car to discover where they went. He saw them go into the Rideland amusement park. Two weeks later he returned to the park by bus and saw his father being arrested by the police. The local mobsters were using their children as an excuse to hold secret meetings at Rideland.

Tony tells Melfi he was proud to be Johnny Soprano's son and he wants AJ to be proud of him. But Tony doesn't want his son to become a mobster.

Tony remembers his parents fighting late one night. Johnny had the opportunity to get in on the early days of Nevada's gambling mecca, Reno, with a neighbour called Rocco Alatore. But Livia refused to move from New Jersey.

Tony goes to Green Grove and confronts his mother about this. The Alatores became billionaires in Nevada. She blames Johnny for not going. She says Tony should visit a psychiatrist if it bothers him, hinting that she knows he is seeing a therapist.

Dr Galani gives Tony and Carmela the test results for AJ. He shows five of the nine symptoms for ADD, which makes him only a borderline case. They are unhappy with the doctor's attitude and believe their son will be fine.

That night Tony and AJ have ice-cream sundaes together at home. They are happy together . . .

Deep and Meaningful: The final scene is the killer in this episode as Tony and AJ prepare their ice-cream sundaes. They eat whipped cream squirted from a spray can straight into their mouths. Tony completely identifies with his son and recognises that he has the same problems as AJ. All through the episode Tony has been recalling the fractured relationship he had with his own father – Janice was always Johnny Boy's favourite child. But Tony and AJ are genuinely comfortable together, able to share simple pleasures.

Mobspeak: At the Bada Bing! strip club Tony asks Pussy if his sons ever asked about this thing of ours (the mob). Christopher comes in with some watches he stole while picking up the Chinaman's vig (the interest paid to a loan shark for a loan). Livia says Junior is full of himself since becoming copa-regime (king of the captains, acting boss).

Mama Mia: Livia says she practically lived in the vice-principal's office while Tony was going to school. She perceptively points out that Tony remembers only what he wants to remember. This triggers a series of flashbacks as Tony remembers what it was really like growing up in the Soprano household.

Livia is shocked when AJ reveals his father is seeing a psychiatrist. Initially she dismisses therapy as a racket for Jews, but becomes upset as she thinks about what her son could be saying. 'I gave my life to my children on a silver platter. And this is how he repays me.'

In 1967 Livia threatens to stick a roasting fork into young Tony's eye. She threatens to smother her children if Johnny tries to move the family to Nevada.

At Green Grove Livia hints to Junior that Tony is seeing a psychiatrist. As soon as he leaves, she badmouths Junior to her son. Tony confronts his mother about how ruthless she was and how she stopped Johnny from escaping New Jersey to have a chance of being a millionaire in Reno. Livia becomes furious and denies all knowledge.

Bright Lights, Baked Ziti: The Sopranos have an extended-family meal of spaghetti and meatballs, with salad and bread.

In 1967 Livia reminds Junior that everyone is going to her sister's for dinner and he promised to bring a pork loin.

Tony says his father loved shellfish such as clams and oysters, especially when sucked from the shell with a little 'Worchester' sauce. His mother never ate anything raw.

AJ eats a pear from a fruit bowl when he visits Livia at Green Grove.

Tony remembers his mother cooking pork bones and veal for gravy, which he called the red lead. When the young Tony stowed away in his father's car, Janice and Johnny were eating sticky waffles.

The next time Tony tracks them to Rideland amusement park, he takes a candy bar but it gets covered in sand or lint from his pockets so he spits it out. Later that night Johnny brings home cherry vanilla ice cream from Nasto's when he is released by the police.

Tony and AJ have ice-cream sundaes with sprinkles, nuts and M&Ms. They eat whipped cream straight from a can.

Mobbed Up: AJ tells Dr Galani that a man missing from a picture could be busy watching *South Park* on television. The boy says the first ever episode is due to be repeated that night, where Cartman gets an alien anal probe and farts fire.

AJ and his father discuss Jackie Aprile's funeral. AJ says there were Feds writing down licence plate numbers and taking pictures, just as in *The Godfather*.

Young Janice and Tony are watching *The Ed Sullivan Show* on television when their father gets home from the police station.

How Do You Feel?: Dr Melfi asks Tony how he feels about what happened in the previous episode between them. He says he can't turn off his feelings for her just because she says it's a by-product of therapy. He proudly says he has a 24-year-old mistress, trying to make Melfi jealous. She doesn't rise to the bait.

Tony works through the flashbacks with Dr Melfi. Tony says he wonders how his life would have been different if Johnny hadn't been a mobster.

Melfi says AJ's fate is not written in stone, that people have choices. Tony points out that the therapist has finally offered an opinion of her own. She insists there are a range of choices for everyone in America – Tony isn't convinced.

Always With the . . .: In 1967 Livia frustrates Johnny by saying she would rather smother her children with a pillow than shift to Reno. 'Always with the drama!'

I Dream of Jeannie Cusamano: Dr Melfi reminds Tony of his dream about the ducks flying away with his penis, and how he saw this as a bad omen that something was going to happen to his family. She asks whether AJ's discovery that his father is a mobster could be what Tony feared? He doesn't know.

Quote/Unquote: Tony describes his father's habits to Dr Melfi. 'Yeah, the belt was his favourite child-development tool.'

Tony says his mother was always high-strung and dramatic. 'Every night to her was a night at the opera.'

Tony describes what happened when his father was in prison. 'They told me he was in Montana, being a cowboy.'

Tony tells his mother that she was more ruthless than his father ever was. 'You're a real stone player, aren't you, Ma?'

Soundtrack: 'Don't Bring Me Down' by Eric Burdon and the Animals. 'White Rabbit' by Jefferson Airplane. 'Carrie Anne' by the Hollies. 'Mystic Eyes' by THEM with Van Morrison. 'Lonely Too Long' by the Young Rascals.

Surveillance Report: In 1967 Livia threatens to smother her children with a pillow rather than move to Nevada. Tony reminds her of this threat. It nearly comes back to haunt her before the end of this season. In the flashback sequences we see Junior playing catch with young Tony, just as he recalled in the pilot.

In 1967 Johnny told his son Tony to pay attention to what teachers say. One generation on, Tony's son AJ is diagnosed as having borderline attention deficiency disorder.

Janice makes her first appearance, seen as a girl in the flashback sequences. Tony tells Dr Melfi his sister calls herself Vishnamatha or something – the name Soprano isn't good enough for her. He describes his sister as a 'fucking wannabe dot-head'.

The Verdict: 'Like father like son, right?' AJ gets into trouble at school and his parents worry whether they are responsible. For Tony this triggers memories of his own childhood and discovering his father was a mobster.

Nature versus nurture is the issue in this episode, along with a debate about fate versus free will. The flashbacks to 1967 offer an intriguing insight into how Tony grew up and show his mother as a lifelong harridan. But for her, the Sopranos could have been a family of legitimate millionaires in Nevada.

The conflict between Tony and Livia continues to escalate, with Livia beginning to use her newly acquired knowledge about Tony's therapy. The seeds are already being sown for the season finale . . .

8
The Legend of Tennessee Moltisanti

US Transmission Date: 28 February 1999
UK Transmission Date: 2 September 1999

Writers: Frank Renzulli and David Chase
Director: Tim Van Patten
Cast: Richard Romanus (Richard La Penna),
Sam Coppola (Dr Reis), Brian Geraghty (Counter Boy),
Will McCormack (Jason La Penna),
Ed Crasnick (Comedian),
Joseph Gannascoli (Bakery Customer),
Barbara Haas (Aida Melfi),
Timothy Nolen (Jeffrey Wernick),
Barbara Lavalle (Band Leader),
Robert Anthony Lavalle (Band Leader #2),
Brooke Marie Procia (Bride),
Bill Richardone (Joseph Melfi)

Storyline: Christopher is haunted by a man he murdered, Emil Kolar.

At a wedding reception for Larry Boy Barese's daughter, word spreads that federal indictments are coming soon. Junior orders the captains to sit tight and, at Tony's prompting, suggests everyone hide the evidence of their illegal activities in case of surprise searches by the FBI.

Christopher is struggling to write his film script, provisionally entitled *Made Man*. A TV news show confirms that the indictments are imminent. A pundit speculates that part of the investigation will focus on the murder of Brendan Filone, who is described as a Soprano family associate and soldier. Christopher is outraged by this inaccuracy, as he is still waiting to be promoted to soldier.

Dr Melfi has dinner with her parents, son and estranged husband, Richard. She lets slip that she is treating a mobster. They debate whether Italian Americans are denigrated by their frequent portrayal as mobsters in films. Richard is involved with the Italian American anti-defamation lobby. He says a recent study showed that the Mafia had fewer than 5,000 members at its peak, out of 20 million Italian Americans.

Christopher is sent by Tony to get pastries for the crew while they sweep the Bada Bing! strip club for surveillance devices. Christopher is forced to wait in a long queue and finally threatens the counter boy with a gun to get served. He shoots the counter boy in the foot.

Carmela takes Livia away from Green Grove for a surprise brunch. In fact, this is a ruse so Tony can secrete illegal guns and cash in Livia's room while she is away from the retirement community.

Tony warns Dr Melfi he may miss an appointment because of a 'vacation' which could happen at short notice. She connects this with TV news reports about the forthcoming federal indictments.

Christopher complains to Paulie and Pussy that he has no character arc or identity. Brendan is now famous in death but Christopher is still unknown. He is also worried that the nightmares are a warning about some problem with Emil Kolar's corpse. Christopher and Georgie from the Bada Bing! dig up the corpse and move it to a new location.

Dr Melfi and Richard decide to sell a block of land they still own to support their son, Jason. Melfi chides Richard for obsessing about her patient's profession.

Tony confronts Christopher about his recent actions, warning him to get his act together. Christopher denies being depressed or suicidal, but does say he worries about getting cancer like Jackie Aprile.

The FBI search Tony's house for evidence of illegal activity. As a result Tony misses his therapy appointment. After the FBI has gone, Tony and his family discuss all the good done by Italians and Italian Americans.

Tony and Dr Melfi argue about whether he should pay for the missed session. Tony throws cash at the psychiatrist before stomping out.

Junior tells Livia he is worried that there is a bad apple in the organisation. She says Tony is seeing a psychiatrist.

Christopher gets a message that his name is mentioned with other gangsters in New Jersey's *Star-Ledger* newspaper. He rushes out and buys a whole stack, overjoyed at public recognition.

Deep and Meaningful: There's a delightful scene in this episode where Christopher is agonising to Paulie about his lack of identity. He draws a parallel to movie scripts, where characters have to have an 'arc' to show progression. Christopher feels he has no arc, whereas the late Brendan Filone now has an identity as a murdered mobster. Paulie is sanguine by comparison, describing himself as half a wise guy who's surviving. He seems more comfortable with his identity than the immature Christopher.

Mobspeak: Christopher believes the FBI will be looking for him because he's OC (FBI shorthand for organised crime). Tony suggests all the captains should do some spring cleaning (hiding evidence of illegal activities). Christopher is angered when Brendan is described on TV as an associate (someone who works with the Family but is not a made man). Tony berates Christopher for shooting a civilian (a member of the public). Meadow asks her father who invented La Cosa Nostra (the original name for the Mafia, which roughly translates as our business or our thing – hence the phrase 'this thing of ours'), before attributing its creation to Charlie 'Lucky' Luciano. Tony talks about Francis Albert (Frank Sinatra).

Mama Mia: At the wedding reception, Livia embarrasses Larry Boy Barese by asking whether he is still an adulterer.

Carmela pays a surprise visit to Livia at Green Grove to take her out for brunch. Livia assumes something must be wrong. She asks if Meadow is suffering from an eating disorder or whether Tony is being unfaithful to Carmela. Despite previous protestations of ignorance about the mob, Livia says she is worried about the effects of the coming indictments on her son.

Junior visits Livia at Green Grove. He is worried there's a rat in the Family. Livia says that Tony is seeing a psychiatrist and could be telling them anything, but she forbids Junior to cause any repercussions.

Bright Lights, Baked Ziti: In Christopher's dream Adriana and Carmela eat sausage. Emil Kolar asks for a salami sub without mayo, then changes his meat order to Black Forest. He says repeatedly that Christopher will have Czech sausages.

At the wedding reception the captains and their families have to leave before they can enjoy the starter course.

The extended Melfi family have a meal of pasta and meatballs, with green salad and bread. Jason praises his grandmother's 'ginzo gravy' – pasta sauce. Richard complains that pizza and mob movies are all that most Americans associate with Italian Americans.

Christopher goes to Russo's Bakery to get a box of sfogliatella, cannolis (pastry shells filled with special cream) and other pastries for the guys at the Bada Bing!. Another customer tries to order two Neapolitan loaves. Christopher forces the counter boy to load a box with free pastries for him.

After the FBI have searched the house, Tony and the family have Chinese takeaway food for dinner, including crispy duck and ribs.

Mobbed Up: Christopher explains to Adriana how much he loves movies. 'That smell in Blockbuster, that candy-and-carpet smell, I get high off of it.' He mentions that his cousin Gregory's girlfriend works for Quentin Tarantino and she says mob stories are always hot.

Dr Melfi's ex-husband complains that most Americans associate Italian Americans with *The Godfather* and *Goodfellas*. Their son Jason says they are good films and good movies to eat pizza by. He suggests that mob movies are classic American cinema, like Westerns.

Christopher complains to Paulie that he has no arc, as characters in movie scripts are supposed to have. He cites Richard Kimble in *The Fugitive*, but quickly dismisses it as a bad example. 'His arc is just run, run, jump off a dam, run.' Christopher prefers *The Devil's Advocate* with Keanu Reeves and Al Pacino as a better example of a character arc.

A comedian at Green Grove makes a joke about a Polish version of Kurasawa's *Rashomon*, where everybody remembers the rape exactly the same. The comedian suggests that the retirement community should make a Zapruder film of its salad bar, referring to the famous home movie of President John F Kennedy's assassination.

How Do You Feel?: When Tony throws the money for his missed session at Dr Melfi, she says she doesn't appreciate being made to feel afraid. Tony replies that he doesn't appreciate feeling that he pours his heart out to a call girl, which is how he sees her now.

How Do You Feel, Doctor?: Dr Melfi goes to family therapy with her estranged husband and their son. She admits to being frightened and revolted by Tony. The therapist says his own family had connections with Louis Lepke, a Jewish gangster from the 1930s.

Sleeping With the Fishes: When Christopher and Georgie dig up Emil Kolar's body, they are surprised that the corpse has grown a beard and long fingernails.

I Dream of Jeannie Cusamano: Christopher has a night-mare about being haunted by Emil Kolar. It begins with Christopher drinking coffee at Satriale's in the daytime. He hears the voice of Emil Kolar. Christopher floats through the store. He sees Adriana kneeling to eat a large sausage held by a disembodied hand in the meat display fridge. Christopher looks away and, when he looks back, Carmela has replaced Adriana eating the sausage. Kolar appears, dead and wrapped in plastic. Suddenly it's a windy night and Christopher is wearing a bloody butcher's smock. He makes Emil a meat sandwich. Emil says Christopher fucked up and gives him four bullets. Christopher tries to give them to the hand in the fridge to hide but the hand grabs him instead. Christopher is jolted from sleep, covered in sweat.

Later Christopher tells Paulie and Pussy about being haunted in dreams by his victim. Pussy says the more people Christopher kills, the better he will sleep. Pussy had one victim chasing him for months in his dreams.

Quote/Unquote: Christopher complains that he doesn't have a character arc, but Pussy is unimpressed. 'You know who had an arc? Noah.'

Dr Melfi's estranged husband cuts to the core of her dilemma about treating Tony. 'After a while, you're gonna get beyond psychotherapy with its cheesy moral relativism. Finally, you're gonna get to good and evil. And he's evil.'

Tony confronts Christopher about shooting the bakery counter boy because the police have a description of Christopher and his car. 'Why don't you just leave a urine sample next time?'

Christopher denies he is depressed and would never contemplate taking Prozac. 'Not this skinny guinea.'

Tony asks if he can help Agent Harris find anything when the FBI search the Soprano household. 'Any incriminating evidence would be nice.'

Soundtrack: A band performs 'Wind Beneath My Wings' and 'Turn the Beat Around' at Melissa Barese's wedding reception. 'Summertime' by Booker T & The MGs. 'You' by The Aquatones. 'Welcome Back' by Land of the Loops. 'Frank Sinatra' by Cake.

Surveillance Report: Several characters watch a news programme on television featuring the fictional character Jeffrey Wernick, a syndicated columnist and author of many books about the mob. Wernick is quoted extensively in *The Sopranos: A Family History*, an official tie-in book to the series first published in 2000, and at the website, www.jeffreywernick.com.

During the spring-cleaning sequence after the wedding reception, Pussy is shown burning papers in his back yard. He is helped by a nonspeaking extra dressed as if she also attended the wedding reception and seems to be his wife. However, the actress is not Toni Kalem, who first appears as Angie Bonpensiero in Season Two.

The scene where Christopher shoots the bakery counter boy in the foot is a sly reversal of a similar scene from Martin Scorcese's *Goodfellas*. In the film Joe Pesci shoots the character Spider (played by Michael Imperioli) in the foot. In this episode Christopher (played by Michael Imperioli) shoots the counter boy in the foot.

Several significant characters have their first appearance in this episode. Agent Harris of the FBI makes his debut, as does Dr Melfi's extended family.

When news of the imminent indictments leaks out, Junior suspects there is a bad apple in the Family – the first person to do so. This storyline will have increasing importance in succeeding episodes.

The Verdict: 'It's like just the fuckin' regular-ness of life is too fucking hard for me or something.' News of imminent federal indictments sends the Family into a panic while Christopher is troubled by the lack of recognition for his work.

The role of Italian Americans in society, and how they are depicted by the entertainment industry, is debated by several different groups in this episode. These discussions cleverly undercut the very debate that the success of *The Sopranos* would subsequently spark.

The FBI emerge from the shadows to become a real threat to the Soprano Family in this episode, while more intriguing insights into the life of Dr Melfi outside her office are revealed. The various plot strands of this debut series are slowly being brought to the boil . . .

9
Boca

US Transmission Date: 7 March 1999
UK Transmission Date: 9 September 1999

Writers: Jason Cahill, Robin Green and Mitchell Burgess
Director: Andy Wolk
Cast: Robyn Peterson (Bobbi Sanfillipo),
Kevin O'Rourke (Coach Don Hauser),
Richard Portnow (Attorney Melvoin),
Cara Jedell (Ally Vandermeed),
Candace Bailey (Deena Hauser),
Jaclyn Tohn (Heather Dante), Danna Marie Recco (Bebe),
Nell Balaban (Receptionist), Moises Belizario (FBI Man),
Mary Ellen Cravens (Taylor),
Steve 'Inky' Ferguson (Moldonado),
Brian Guzman (Delivery Boy), Mark Hartmann
(Capman), Patrick Husten (Waiter), Marissa Jedell
(Becky), Joyce Lynn O'Connor (Shelly Hauser), John
Nacco (Contractor), Bill Winkler (Soccer Ref)

Storyline: Everyone is getting excited about the success of the Falcons, the girls' soccer team at Meadow's school. The coach, Don Hauser, gets the plaudits for the team reaching the sectional playoffs.

Detective Vin Makasian tells Tony that Uncle Junior's sidekick, Mikey Palmice, has hired a private investigator to follow Tony.

Junior is getting stressed about the forthcoming federal indictments. Mikey believes that any leak to the government is coming from Tony's crew.

Meadow finds her friend Ally trying to cut her wrists with a penknife. It is not the first time she has attempted suicide.

Junior skims $20,000 from the Jointfitters' Union development fund to take his girlfriend Bobbi Sanfillipo on holiday to Boca Raton in Florida.

Tony meets with Larry Boy Barese and Jimmy Altieri at Green Grove. All the captains are moving their mothers into the retirement community, to use it as a front for secret meetings and hiding contraband.

A newspaper reveals that Coach Hauser is shifting to the University of Rhode Island. Silvio Dante and Artie Bucco confront him but Hauser says Rhode Island has doubled his salary. The Falcons are surly with their coach.

Junior and Bobbi enjoy their break at the Waldorf Towers Hotel. Bobbi praises Junior's prowess at oral sex but he warns her not to talk about this. Cunnilingus is considered a sign of weakness among mobsters.

Later they go dancing and the FBI have them under surveillance, taking photographs.

Bobbi visits her beauty salon and tells her consultant (also Carmela's) they shouldn't talk about sex any more, although she's previously told the woman all about Junior's preferences.

Paulie delivers a fifty-inch television to Coach Hauser as an inducement for him to stay with the Falcons, but he refuses to accept it.

At a Soprano family dinner Meadow says she has quit the soccer team. Carmela makes jokes about Junior's liking for giving oral sex. Later Tony tickles his wife into revealing the truth about Junior and cunnilingus.

Tony steps up the pressure on Coach Hauser, having Christopher steal and then return the Hauser family dog.

Next day Meadow tells her parents that the coach had sex with Ally. Ally is in love with Coach Hauser but he won't leave his wife.

Tony decides the coach must die and Silvio agrees to make the hit. Artie hears what has happened and agrees that Hauser deserves to die.

Tony and Silvio have a round of golf with Junior and Mikey. Tony infuriates Junior by teasing him about oral sex. Junior hints about knowing that Tony is seeing a psychiatrist.

Artie and his wife argue about Tony dispensing justice on Coach Hauser. Charmaine says any vigilante action would make only the men feel better, not the people actually involved.

Junior tells Mikey that Tony is seeing a psychiatrist. Junior is worried what Tony tells the therapist and whether it could be raised in court. Junior is seriously contemplating having Tony murdered.

Tony and Dr Melfi argue about his plans to punish the coach. Later, Artie asks Tony not to go ahead with the hit because it would not be just.

Junior confronts Bobbi about letting slip his liking for cunnilingus. He rubs a lemon meringue pie in her face and sacks her from the union job. She's distraught.

Tony calls off the hit. On the late news Coach Hauser is arrested after an anonymous tip-off to the police. Tony arrives home, drunk and dazed thanks to a combination of drink and prescription drugs. He is celebrating because he resisted his natural urge to resort to violence against the coach. Carmela beds him down on the floor of the lounge, watched by Meadow . . .

Deep and Meaningful: Junior proves himself to be a man torn between his old school mobster beliefs and the feelings of his heart. Outraged that Bobbi has told others about his prowess at oral sex, Junior feels he has no option but to humiliate and dump her. He wants to beat her but instead rubs a lemon meringue pie in Bobbi's face. Junior storms out of the room and stands outside beneath a street light. His face is a picture of hurt and despair. The angle changes to an overhead bird's-eye view, showing Junior from above – small and borne down by his responsibilities. Finally, he stomps away . . .

Mobspeak: Tony says Coach Hauser doesn't have the coglione (balls) to finish what he started with the soccer team.

Mama Mia: Livia warns her grandson against playing with dogs at the cemetery. She says they could take his hand off or start foaming at the mouth. She complains to Junior about Tony seeing a psychiatrist. 'My son, the mental patient.'

At a family dinner Livia complains that nobody tells her anything. Tony tells his mother to butt out of family problems, so Livia stomps out, saying she will not eat in the house and demanding that Junior take her home.

Bright Lights, Baked Ziti: There's a feast of food scenes in this episode. Junior and his crew have sandwiches delivered to them at the offices of Junior's law firm. Mikey has peppers and eggs, which Junior wishes he had ordered.

Livia is eating lunch with another resident at Green Grove when Tony arrives for a meeting with Larry Boy Barese and Jimmy Altieri. Jimmy is carrying a sandwich.

Junior and Bobbi sip champagne in Boca Raton. Bobbi feeds Junior red peppers from a plate of cold meats, cheeses and other antipasto.

Artie and Tony are eating dessert in a restaurant when Tony pauses to intimidate another diner into removing their baseball cap.

Meadow and Ally are having diet drinks and popcorn while they watch music videos at the Sopranos' house.

Livia and Junior join the Sopranos for a family meal of pasta, cold meats, salad and bread. Next morning at breakfast AJ and Meadow have cereal and orange juice while Tony drinks coffee. Later Tony has scrambled eggs, bacon and toast at the Bada Bing!, but he hardly touches his food. Tony also ignores a sandwich of meat and cheese at the strip club while he contemplates whether to go ahead with the hit on Coach Hauser.

Bobbi has bought a dinner of barbecued chicken, some salad and lemon meringue pie for her and Junior, but he shoves the pie in her face.

Mobbed Up: Coach Hauser invokes a catchphrase from *The Godfather*, saying the University of Rhode Island made him an offer he couldn't refuse.

Junior's rubbing the lemon meringue pie in Bobbi's face is a homage to the 1931 gangster film *The Public Enemy*, where James Cagney's character rubbed a grapefruit in his girlfriend's face.

How Do You Feel?: Tony tells Dr Melfi that his life is putting Prozac to the test. He would rather talk about the problems with his daughter's soccer coach than the stress caused by the impending indictments. Tony vaguely apologises for calling Dr Melfi a whore in the previous episode. He says he might have been overstating the case a bit.

At a later session Dr Melfi wants to know why Tony feels he should always be dispensing justice. Her question goes unanswered.

Always With the . . . : Artie and Charmaine Bucco argue about Tony's attempts to intimidate Coach Hauser. Charmaine demands to know what the next step in a campaign of harassment will be. 'Always with the extreme scenarios,' Artie protests.

Quote/Unquote: Dr Melfi tells Tony that small cutting is the clinical term for a suicidal gesture. 'What's "large cutting", OJ and the missing tracksuit?' he asks.

Tony has a string of euphemisms for cunnilingus. 'The old man's whistling through the wheat field? He's a bushman of the Kalahari?'

Junior loses patience when everyone is talking on the golf course. 'You yap worse than six barbers.'

Dr Melfi says the judicial system has become much better at dealing with sexual predators, but Tony is unimpressed. 'Oh, yeah, let's impeach him.'

Soundtrack: Tony sings 'Camel Walk' to Carmela at the end of the episode. 'Can't You Feel The Fire' by Little Steven. 'Ahoy' by B-Tribe. 'Frente a Frenta' by Rocio Durcal. 'Little Joe' by The Spaniels. 'Buena' by Morphine.

Surveillance Report: Silvio Dante offers his daughter $100 if she scores a goal. Junior's law firm is Melvoin, Frolov,

Schneider and Arkadie. Junior and Bobbi have been going to Boca Raton on holiday for sixteen years.

The Verdict: 'They think if you suck pussy you'll suck anything.' Uncle Junior's bedroom secrets are revealed while Tony contemplates bloody vengeance against Meadow's soccer coach.

Sexual taboos dominate this episode. Don Hauser is lucky to escape with his life when Tony's crew learn about the coach's liking for teenage girls. But the real shocker is all the talk about oral sex in an American television show. Cunnilingus would never be mentioned on a major network drama, but HBO's subscription status enables *The Sopranos* to push the boundaries.

Tony and his uncle have been at peace since Junior became acting captain. But all the teasing about eating sushi leaves him contemplating the murder of his own nephew. The storm clouds are gathering . . .

10
A Hit Is a Hit

US Transmission Date: 14 March 1999
UK Transmission Date: 16 September 1999

Writers: Joe Bosso and Frank Renzulli
Director: Matthew Penn
Cast: Bokeem Woodbine (Massive Genius),
Bryan Hicks (Orange J), Nick Fowler (Richie Santini),
Gregg Wattenberg (Vito), Chris Gibson (Bass Player),
Ned Stroh (Drummer), Bray Poor (Squid),
Robert Lupone (Dr Bruce Cusamano),
Jim Demarse (Jack Krim),
James Weston (Randy Wagner), Phil Cocciletti (Eric),
Terumi Matthews (Rita), Dan Morse (Mullethead),
Alexandra Neil (Wendy Krim), Ken Prymus (Manager),
Saundra Santiago (Jean Cusamano),
Jessy Terrero (Gallegos),

Elizabeth Ann Townsend (Barb Wagner),
Cedric Turner (Police Officer)

Storyline: Paulie, Christopher and Pussy surprise a drug dealer who has been trespassing on Soprano territory. They net thousands of dollars in cash from the hit, which they share with Tony.

Tony gives a box of illegal Cuban cigars to his neighbour, Dr Cusamano, as a thank-you for the referral to Dr Melfi. In return Cusamano invites Tony to play with some friends at their private golf club.

Christopher takes Adriana to a Broadway show. On the way home they stop for burgers and meet the gangsta rapper and media mogul Massive Genius. He invites them to a party at his house. There he asks Christopher to arrange a meeting for him with Hesh about some outstanding royalties owed to a relative of Massive.

Tony and Carmela are invited to a barbecue by a neighbour, Barbara Wagner. Carmela worries about how she could pay for Meadow's college education if something should happen to Tony.

Adriana wants to get into music management. She is friends with the lead singer of a band formerly known as Defiler. Adriana wonders if Massive Genius would help. Christopher agrees to bankroll Adriana's new career.

Massive Genius and his crew meet with Hesh, Tony and his crew at Hesh's stud farm. Massive wants Hesh to pay $400,000 in reparations to the surviving relatives of a dead singer called Little Jimmy Willis, who had hits on Hesh's F-Note Records in the 1950s and 1960s.

Dr Melfi goes to a dinner party held by the Cusamanos, where the Sopranos are a major topic of conversation.

Adriana and Christopher take Massive to see Defiler – now renamed Visiting Day – in concert. The gangsta rapper says he's interested, but his interest seems to be mainly in Adriana.

Tony and Carmela go to the barbecue at the Wagners' house. Tony is frozen out of conversations by the men but Carmela picks up a stock market tip.

Christopher pays for Visiting Day to make a demo CD but the sessions are troubled. Christopher tries to get the lead singer, Richie, back on drugs to enhance his performance, then smashes a guitar over Richie's back.

Carmela buys 5,000 shares of the company recommended to her.

Tony plays golf with Dr Cusamano and his friends at the private course. Everyone keeps pestering Tony with questions about famous mobsters, making him feel very uncomfortable.

Adriana plays the Visiting Day demo CD to Massive and he is enthusiastic. Christopher plays it to Hesh, who hates it.

Hesh calls Massive Genius and refuses to pay reparation. The gangsta rapper says he will sue, so Hesh threatens to countersue over a sample lifted from an F-Note Records disc. Massive says he'll see Hesh in court.

Christopher tells Adriana that Visiting Day sucks and Massive only wants to get in her pants. They argue and she storms out.

Carmela's new stocks split three ways, tripling her investment overnight.

Tony gets his revenge on Dr Cusamano. He asks him to look after a mysterious package for a while, which is actually filled with sand. The Cusamanos stare suspiciously at the box, wondering whether it contains drugs, guns or something worse . . .

Deep and Meaningful: This episode shows both Tony and Dr Melfi squirming in the company of people they thought were friends. Dr Melfi attends a dinner party at the Cusamanos', where the other guests discuss Tony and Carmela disparagingly. They discuss the film portrayal of gangsters, whereas Dr Melfi is privy to another side of mobster life.

Tony tries to integrate himself with Dr Cusamano and friends during a golf match. Instead he finds himself being treated like a dancing bear, there only to entertain them with tales of mob life. Tony may have the power of life and death over many people, but to these people he is an amusement.

Mobspeak: Tony tells Christopher he should invest in stocks and live off the juice (interest, usually referring to money from loan-sharking).

Tony describes the Wagners as mayonnaises (Italian Americans who have been assimilated into suburban culture).

Christopher tells Adriana he is arranging a sit-down (a meeting to settle disputes) between Hesh and Massive Genius.

Tony tells Dr Melfi that Dr Cusamano is what his father called a Wonder Bread Wop (same meaning as mayonnaise).

Tony approaches Dr Cusamano, saying he needs a little solid (favour).

Bright Lights, Baked Ziti: Christopher takes Adriana to dinner at Le Cirque but she's embarrassed to be hungry again afterwards. They order a couple of burger baskets from a fast-food outlet.

Tony eats ham from the fridge and drinks bottled mineral water while discussing the cost of college education with Carmela.

The Cusamanos host a dinner party, where the food served includes chicken and asparagus.

Visiting Day's lead singer, Richie, once got third-degree burns when he tried to grill a trout with a downed power line.

At the barbecue Randy Wagner is cooking sausages from a little place in Garfield. All the men drink bottled beer.

Mobbed Up: When Christopher turns down a night of debauchery with Tony and his crew for a date with Adriana, Paulie misquotes Edward G Robinson's final line from the classic 1930 gangster film *Little Caesar*: 'Mother of Mercy! Is this the end of Rico?'

Massive Genius's associate, Orange J, calls Christopher Donnie Brasco outside a burger bar to get his attention. At Massive's house, the gangsta rapper says he has seen *The*

Godfather two hundred times. He thinks *The Godfather Part II* was definitely the shit, but a lot of people didn't like the third film in the series. He thinks it was just misunderstood.

On the golf course Tony does his WC Fields imitation. His playing partners ask him how real was *The Godfather*.

How Do You Feel?: Tony tells Dr Melfi he wants to branch out and make new friends, but he's afraid of the reaction from his crew.

At a subsequent session with Dr Melfi, Tony recalls when he was a kid how he and his friends pretended to like a guy called Jimmy Smash, who had a cleft palette. They used to get him to speak so they could make fun of him. Tony likens this to his golf game with Cusamano and friends, who treated him like 'a dancing bear'. He thought his neighbour was becoming his friend – now he knows better.

Sleeping With the Fishes: An unidentified drug dealer, executed by Paulie in a Newark apartment for trespassing on Soprano territory.

Always With the . . .: Adriana despairs when Christopher mouths off in a crowded burger bar. 'Always with the attitude, Christopher.'

Quote/Unquote: When Massive Genius says he wants Hesh to pay reparations for stealing royalties, Christopher thinks it's unlikely Hesh will agree: 'I've heard his opinions about giving back pieces of Israel. I can only imagine what he's gonna say about this shit.'

Carmela wonders what she should do if something ever happened to Tony, but he is unconcerned. 'You dig out my blue suit. You call up old man Coletti. You tell him not to put too much make-up on my face.'

Carmela despairs of Tony's attitude, likening him to a multiple-choice question. 'I can't tell if you're old-fashioned, paranoid or just a fucking asshole.'

Who could forget the soulful lyrics of Defiler? 'Stay out of our way, don't be so gay. We're coming to defile, defile you.'

After Tony has been made to feel uncomfortable by his neighbour, Cusamano, he starts calling him 'Cooz' – slang for female genitals or an easy woman.

Soundtrack: 'You Give Love a Bad Name' by Bon Jovi. 'De Cara A La Pared' by Lhasa De Sela. 'Defile You' by Defiler. 'Erase Myself' by Visiting Day. 'Why?' by Annie Lennox. 'A Dreamer's Holiday' by Ray Anthony & His Orchestra. 'DJ Keep Playin' (Get Your Music On)' by Yvette Michelle. 'Nobody Loves Me But You' by Dori Hartley.

Surveillance Report: The songs by Defiler and Visiting Day were written especially for this episode by Nick Fowler and Gregg Wattenberg, who play Visiting Day's lead singer and guitarist respectively. The band and its songs were designed to be astoundingly average.

Christopher talks about Silvio having owned rock clubs in New Jersey. Silvio Dante is played by Steven Van Zandt, who is also a guitarist with Bruce Springsteen's E Street Band – New Jersey's most famous rock group.

Tony's revenge on Dr Cusamano with the mysterious box is a homage to a scene in *The Godfather Part II*, where Bruno Kirby gives Robert De Niro a gun to hide, which leads the young Vito Corleone to become a gangster.

The Verdict: 'I think you should mentally prepare for the fucking possibility that Visiting Day sucks.' Christopher tries to establish Adriana as a music manager, as Hesh is haunted by his actions as a corrupt record producer forty years before. Meanwhile, Tony finds making new friends difficult.

This episode about the shadier side of the music industry has its funny moments but seems to slacken the pace after recent developments. Junior and Livia are conspicuous by their absence. Even Tony is reduced to the role of comic relief in the Wonder Bread Wop subplot.

The scenes with Visiting Day are cringe-inducing because they are so well done. Adriana truly believes in the band and truly has no clue just how mediocre it is. This episode would have fitted better earlier in the season but, just three weeks from the grand finale, 'A Hit Is a Hit' feels like a regression.

11
Nobody Knows Anything

US Transmission Date: 21 March 1999
UK Transmission Date: 23 September 1999

Writer: Frank Renzulli
Director: Henry J Bronchtein
Cast: Karen Sillas (Debbie),
Giancarlo 'John' Giunta (Kevin Bonpensiero),
Doug Barron (Dr Mop-N-Glo), Veronica Bero (Girl),
Britt Burr (Traffic Cop), Ramsey Faragallah (Fed #1),
Bobby Rivers (Male Anchor),
Matthew Lawler (Fed #2),
Chance Kelly (Fed #3), Tim Kirkpatrick (Detective #1),
Peter Bretz (Detective #2)

Storyline: Tony, Paulie and Pussy are enjoying a visit to a high-class brothel when Pussy injures his back. Their departure is watched by Detective Vin Makasian.

Four days later the FBI raid a property rented by Jimmy Altieri. They catch Jimmy, Pussy and two others gambling at cards. A search reveals a pool table full of guns. Pussy tries to escape but is easily caught and arrested. He is soon bailed out by his wife.

Detective Makasian tells Tony that Pussy is wearing a wire for law-enforcement agencies. Bonpensiero was facing a mandatory life sentence for dealing heroin and cut a deal. Tony is stunned and demands to see the relevant 302 report as proof of Pussy's complicity.

The Sopranos hold an open-house party. Pussy refuses to help shift a piano because of his back. Tony asks Paulie and Christopher to keep a watch on Pussy. Paulie says an eminent back doctor thought Pussy's back problems were psychological rather than physical.

Tony asks Dr Melfi whether psychological problems could cause such symptoms. She says a heavy burden of responsibility could be responsible, but secrets also bring a heavy load of guilt.

Tony meets with Makasian at the brothel but the detective has no further proof about Pussy. Makasian uses the brothel as a refuge from the world.

Tony goes to see Pussy at home. Pussy hints that things are happening. Tony offers him a chance to come clean, but Pussy says nothing. Afterwards, Tony shares his suspicions with a shocked Paulie, who offers to whack Pussy. Tony makes him vow not to make the hit unless Paulie sees the wire.

Tony drops off some CDs for his mother with Bonnie DiCaprio at Green Grove. He also leaves a message that Livia's house sale is going through.

Paulie takes Pussy for a steam and sauna but Pussy refuses to get undressed. He says the doctors warned him away from heat.

Silvio tells Tony that Makasian owes Pussy $30,000 from gambling and loans, sufficient motivation to lie about Pussy being a government informant. Tony is still not sure – he wants absolute proof.

A police raid on the brothel snares Detective Makasian and the mob captain, Raymond Curto. Makasian is released and put on administrative leave. He drives to the Route One bridge and jumps off.

Tony hears of the detective's suicide, which stymies efforts to discover the truth about Pussy. Tony visits Debbie, the madam at the brothel. She says Makasian didn't have much to say about Tony and his crew, except that he wasn't worried about the money he owed. Makasian trusted Tony, Debbie says.

Junior visits Livia, who is upset that Tony has sold her house. She mentions that the captains are holding secret meetings at Green Grove. She says Larry Boy Barese and Jimmy Altieri have both shifted their mothers into the retirement community. She also lets slip that Johnny Sack from New York has been at the meetings and ventures that perhaps the captains are talking about Junior behind his back. Junior is outraged and believes Tony is organising a move against him.

Jimmy gets out on bail and visits Tony. He asks a lot of pointed questions about the hit on the Colombian drug dealer and its proceeds. Tony realises that something is wrong and becomes evasive in his answers. Once Jimmy has gone, Tony rushes to the office at Satriale's Pork Store.

Tony tells Silvio that Jimmy is the rat, not Pussy. Paulie arrives and Tony demands to know if the hit on Pussy has happened. Paulie says it hasn't. Nobody knows where Pussy has gone.

Chucky Signore delivers a stolen microwave oven to Mikey and JoJo Palmice. He says Junior is going ahead with the hit on Tony and they are to look out of town for the killers . . .

Deep and Meaningful: The crunch comes in this episode when Tony visits Pussy to find out if he is working with the FBI. Pussy admits he is under pressure and hints that things are going on. Tony gives his friend a chance to confess but Pussy doesn't take it. There is a long pause but Pussy is afraid and says nothing. The significance of this becomes apparent during Season Two . . .

Mobspeak: Pussy complains that the FBI robbed him of four dimes ($4,000).

Detective Makasian says Pussy is wired for sound (wearing a surveillance device to record conversations).

Mikey Palmice tells his wife that Junior is old school (a gangster who respects and follows the rules and oaths of being a mobster).

Mama Mia: Livia refuses to attend the open-house party, as she does every year. Tony calls this negative attention getting.

Next day Carmela visits Livia at Green Grove and asks her mother-in-law to stop manipulating Tony with emotional blackmail. Livia pleads ignorance. She has no friends, she's been abandoned and this would never have happened when her husband was alive. 'Johnny was a

saint,' Livia says, sobbing into her ever-present handkerchief. Carmela says it's good that Junior comes to visit but
Livia takes umbrage at any suggestion of a relationship
between herself and her brother-in-law. However, she says
having someone who will listen gives her some purpose in
life.

Livia puts that someone to good use when Junior comes
to visit. She weeps about Tony selling her home but Junior
isn't very sympathetic. Livia tries another tactic, casually
revealing Tony's secret meetings at Green Grove with the
other captains and Johnny Sack from New York. She even
hints that they are discussing Junior. He is outraged, seeing
this as a move against him. He has to act against Tony,
even though they are blood relations. Livia has got her
revenge against her son . . .

Bright Lights, Baked Ziti: Carmela serves a finger buffet
when the Sopranos have their open-house party. Next day
Carmela takes a ricotta pie made with low-fat cheese to
Livia, but the old woman turns her nose up at it. Carmela
leaves it so Junior can have some when he next visits Livia.

Tony goes to Pussy at his home, bringing a box of
cannoli from Spirelli's.

Carmela cooks the family a breakfast of pancakes,
bacon and syrup.

When Jimmy visits after getting out on bail, Tony,
Carmela and AJ are eating lasagne, salad and bread.
Jimmy declines an invitation to join them for dinner.

Chucky brings Mikey and JoJo a microwave oven. JoJo
has prepared bowls of salad and brews some coffee.

Mobbed Up: Paulie's car horn plays the theme music from
The Godfather.

How Do You Feel?: Tony says he feels like someone
walking down the street and looking up, worried that a
safe is going to land on their head. Dr Melfi suggests this
is a feeling of pending doom.

Sleeping With the Fishes: Detective Vin Makasian, who
commits suicide by jumping off the Route One bridge. He

clips his detective's badge on to the breast pocket of his suit before jumping.

Quote/Unquote: Paulie describes the different tests Pussy has had on his back. 'MRIs, CAT scans, dog scans, you name it.'

Paulie says he must be dreaming when Tony tells him Pussy is wearing a wire. 'Get used to it. I've been walking into walls all week.'

Tony reveals his attitude to sexual discussions with his children at breakfast. 'Out there it's the 1990s, but in this house it's 1954.'

When Mikey Palmice tells his dim wife JoJo that Tony Soprano is on his way out and for ever, she asks if Tony is going to jail. 'No, the other forever.'

Soundtrack: 'Micky's Monkey' by Smokey Robinson and the Miracles. 'Lick It Up' by Kiss. 'Walking On A Tightrope' by Johnny Adams. 'The Highs Are Too High' by Johnette Napolitano. 'Slide Slide' by The Hotheads. 'My Heart Is Hanging Heavy' by Johnny Adams. 'Manifold de Amour' by Latin Playboys.

Surveillance Report: There is a caption after the opening scene, to indicate that four days have passed. The manager at Green Grove, Bonnie DiCaprio, sits in a comedically low chair, which means her head and shoulders only just get above the level of her desk. Tony brings his mother's CDs of half-ass tenors.

The Verdict: 'Things are happening, Tony.' Someone in the Family is wearing a wire for the feds and suspicion falls on Pussy. Meanwhile, Livia goads Junior into ordering a hit on her own son.

After the detour of 'A Hit Is a Hit', the season hits the accelerator and surges towards its bloody climax. Livia reveals just how far she is willing to go to punish her own children, forcing Junior into action he doesn't want to take. Detective Makasian takes his leave, but not before dropping a bombshell about Pussy. The impact of that news will resonate all through Season Two.

This is a cracker as the heat gets turned up on Tony and his crew. Just as the second, third and fourth episodes formed a trilogy, so this instalment begins the three-part endgame to Season One.

12
Isabella

US Transmission Date: 28 March 1999
UK Transmission Date: 30 September 1999

Writers: Robin Green and Mitchell Burgess
Director: Allen Coulter
Cast: Maria Grazia Cucinotta (Isabella),
John Eddins (John Clayborn), Touche (Rasheen Ray),
Kareen Germain (Nurse), Johnathan Mondel (Boy),
Jack O'Connell (Vendor), Katalin Pota (Lillian),
Denise Richardson (Newscaster), Bittu Walia (Doctor),
David Wike (Donnie Paduana)

Storyline: Christopher is worried about Tony, who sleeps during the day and seems depressed. Silvio dismisses this, saying all leaders have dark moods.

Carmela tries to get Tony out of bed but he refuses to move. He's taking both lithium and Prozac. Carmela throws open the curtains when she leaves. Tony goes to close them and sees a beautiful woman in the back yard of the Cusamano house next door.

Junior has a meeting with Mikey Palmice and Chucky Signore at a funeral home. Mikey says the hit on Tony will be made tomorrow by two black guys hired through an intermediary.

Next day Christopher visits Tony at home but his concerns are only made worse. Tony wanders out into the yard and discovers a silky camisole on the grass. He goes next door to the Cusamanos' and gives it to the beautiful woman there. She is a dental exchange student called

Isabella, who is looking after the house while the Cusamanos are in Bermuda playing golf.

Christopher follows Tony to Montclair and inadvertently prevents the hit by parking in front of the two black guys, John Clayborn and Rasheen Ray.

Afterwards, Mikey and Chucky meet with the intermediary, Donnie Paduana, to find out what went wrong. Donnie assures them the hit will happen the next day. He jokes about hearing that Tony Soprano's own mother wants him murdered. Mikey kills Paduana on orders from Junior, who has been watching the meeting from the back of a nearby car and thinks Paduana's too mouthy.

At a session Dr Melfi tells Tony that the combined prescription of lithium and Prozac is to give his system a jolt, but he feels nothing. She suggests he check into a residential treatment centre but Tony refuses. Dr Melfi increases the dosage of Prozac.

Outside the chemist Tony meets Isabella and takes her to lunch. While they talk about Italy Tony has a fantasy about Isabella nursing a baby.

That night Livia comes to dinner at the Sopranos', but Junior declines because he feels ill. Livia berates Tony for coming to the dinner table in his bathrobe and complains about her house being sold. Tony goes back upstairs.

Carmela catches Tony looking out of the bedroom window at Isabella, and threatens to cut his penis off.

Junior takes Livia to a film while the hit is happening. She talks about Tony displaying signs of mental illness.

Tony goes to a newsstand to get orange juice and a racing form guide. He sees a black man approaching him with a handgun. The first bullet smashes Tony's bottle of juice, the second takes out his window as Tony gets into his four-wheel drive. Tony grabs the gun arm of the shooter and keeps the barrel pointed away from himself. The second black man runs over and shoots through the passenger-side window, accidentally killing his partner. Tony grabs the second shooter's gun arm and starts driving away. The shooter falls to the road. Before Tony can enjoy his escape, he crashes into a parked vehicle.

At the hospital Tony gets stitches in his left ear but otherwise has only cuts and bruises. Carmela, Meadow and AJ rush to see him but Tony says he is fine. He claims it was only an attempted car-jack. Carmela takes the children outside as Agent Harris of the FBI comes in. He offers Tony and the family immunity and relocation in return for any testimony. Agent Harris says nowhere will be safe for Tony now, and that the assassination problem will not go away. When Agent Harris has gone, Tony and Carmela argue about whether to accept the offer.

Junior and Livia watch a TV news report of the failed hit. Junior panics but Livia decides they should go and visit Tony.

The family and Tony's crew gather at the Soprano house. Christopher realises he prevented the hit the day before and believes Junior is responsible for ordering the attack. Junior and Livia arrive to see how Tony is.

Father Phil shows up and Tony sarcastically asks if he will be staying over. Livia starts acting senile.

Carmela drives Tony to a roadside meeting at night with Dr Melfi. He relates the fantasy about Isabella and the baby. Dr Melfi believes Tony is fantasising about being nursed by Isabella.

Junior confronts Livia about her faked senility.

Tony sees that Dr Cusamano is home and asks him about Isabella, but his neighbour doesn't know what Tony is talking about. Carmela also has no memory of seeing Isabella or threatening to cut off Tony's penis.

Tony phones Dr Melfi to say that Isabella was just a fantasy, never real. His therapist tells him to discontinue the lithium. She says the fantasy has meaning. He obviously craves a loving, caring mother figure – but why now?

Deep and Meaningful: The look on Junior's face when Livia starts faking the first symptoms of senility says more than words ever could. The hit on Tony has failed so Livia conveniently starts forgetting who people are. If looks could kill, Junior would be facing life imprisonment or the death penalty at this moment. He realises that his sister-in-

law is shielding herself and leaving him to face Tony's
wrath for the attempted hit.

Mama Mia: At dinner Livia criticises Tony for his breath
and his sensitivity to criticism. She says the whole world's
gone crazy and cites the case of a woman in Pennsylvania
who shot her three children and set her house on fire. Livia
dismisses Tony's depression, complaining that she has been
thrown into the glue factory and had her home sold out
from under her. She succeeds in driving Tony upstairs,
then bursts into tears, pledging never to come back to the
house again.

Waiting in line for the cinema with Junior, Livia
compares Tony to her cousin Cakey after his lobotomy.
She tries to justify the hit on Tony because he is empty, a
shell. Better he be dead than go on living like that.

Junior panics when he hears that Tony survived the hit
but Livia reveals her true colours. 'My son got shot. And
he got away.' She decides they must visit Tony and
switches on the waterworks, because Tony is her only son.

At Tony's house Livia gets confused about Meadow's
identity, as if the first stages of senility were suddenly
setting in. Later Junior confronts her about this and the
terrific timing of her forgetfulness. She pleads ignorance.

Bright Lights, Baked Ziti: Outside the chemist Isabella has a
long filled roll. She asks Tony why it's called a hero
sandwich. He takes her to lunch but there is no food on their
plates, only bread in a basket and white wine in their glasses.

At the Soprano family dinner the food includes chicken
with the usual pasta, salad and bread.

AJ munches on a huge sandwich while he and Meadow
wait for their father to be treated at the hospital. When
Tony gets home Carmela has a finger buffet for everyone,
including slices of capiccola sausage, peppers and bagels.

Mobbed Up: Paulie alludes to the film *Cool Runnings* when
discussing the attempted hit with AJ and Meadow. 'It
would take more than a Jamaican bobsled team with cap
guns to stop your old man.'

How Do You Feel?: Before the hit Tony tells Dr Melfi he feels nothing, dead, empty. He is King Midas in reverse, turning everything he touches to shit. He doesn't want to live, but refuses to be admitted to a psychiatric hospital.

After the hit he feels pretty good. Tony says getting shot at gives you a nice kick-start. When the attack came, he didn't want to die. Every particle of him was fighting to live.

When Tony tells Dr Melfi that Isabella was just a fantasy, she says it still has meaning. Melfi draws a link between Tony's need for a loving, caring mother and Livia's constant talk about infanticide. Tony says he feels pretty good but he'll feel even better when he finds out who ordered the hit.

Sleeping With the Fishes: The corpses start piling up thick and fast in this episode. Donnie Paduana gets it first, executed by Mikey Palmice on Junior's orders after joking that Livia Soprano wanted her own son murdered. John Clayborn is second, accidentally gunned down by his fellow assassin when they try to slay Tony Soprano.

I Dream of Jeannie Cusamano: The entire Isabella plotline is an elaborate fantasy, apparently fuelled by Tony's lithium and Prozac prescriptions. This does not become clear until the final minutes of the episode, when Tony talks to Dr Cusamano. Tony even has a fantasy within a fantasy during his lunch with Isabella, daydreaming of her nursing him as a baby. This episode certainly has the highest level of fantasy and/or dream sequences up until the final episode of Season Two, 'Funhouse'.

Quote/Unquote: Silvio cites Winston Churchill as an example of a temperamental leader. 'Napoleon, he was a moody fuck, too.'

Junior wonders why nobody collects prayer cards the way they collect baseball cards. 'Thousands of bucks for Honus Wagner and jack shit for Jesus.'

Tony tells Carmela that he cannot testify because he took an oath of silence. 'What are you, a kid in a treehouse?' she replies.

Tony ridicules joining the witness relocation programme. 'You want to move to Utah, be Mr and Mrs Mike Smith? We can sell some Indian relics by the road. Maybe start a rattlesnake ranch. Have some Mormons over to dinner. Eat some tomatoes that have no taste.'

Meadow is appalled that her brother is more worried about trying to get out of going to a dance than the recent attempt on their father's life. 'God, self-involved much?'

Soundtrack: 'Tiny Tears' by Tindersticks. 'Cry' by Thornetta Davis. 'Temptation Waits' by Garbage. 'Ugly Stadium' by Tipsy. 'Milonga Del Angel' by Al Di Meola. 'I Feel Free' by Cream.

Surveillance Report: Isabella is played by Maria Grazia Cucinotta, better known for her starring role in the film *Il Postino*.

The Verdict: 'This fantasy of yours has meaning.' Tony reaches his lowest ebb of depression but gets snapped out of it by an attempted assassination.

This episode is a gripping instalment, building up to the hit and then showing its aftermath. Acting as a counterpoint to these mobster machinations is the Isabella fantasy, which is carried off brilliantly. The audience never suspects that she is the product of Tony's drug-addled senses.

By the end of the episode, Tony and his crew have their suspicions about who ordered the hit – but no proof yet. Dr Melfi has her own suspicions. The truth of both theories is coming in the grand finale to the first season . . .

13
I Dream of Jeannie Cusamano

US Transmission Date: 4 April 1999
UK Transmission Date: 7 October 1999

Writer: David Chase
Director: John Patterson

Cast: Frank Pellegrino (Agent Cubitoso),
John Aprea (US Attorney), George Bass (Janitor),
Gene Canfield (Police Officer), Frank Dallarosa (EMT),
Santiago Douglas (Jeremy Herrera),
Militza Ivanova (Russian Woman),
Candy Trabucco (Ms Giaculo)

Storyline: Junior and his captains have a meeting. Afterwards Junior agrees with Tony that Jimmy Altieri is a rat and approves having Jimmy whacked as a message to everyone.

Christopher takes Jimmy to an apartment for some quality time with two Russian prostitutes. Once Jimmy sits down he is executed by Silvio Dante.

Meadow is on the sofa at home necking with her boyfriend while AJ is upstairs masturbating in his bedroom. All three are disturbed by Livia, who wanders past outside, apparently confused and lost. The police arrive after getting complaints about a woman wandering in the neighbourhood.

Dr Melfi confronts Tony about his mother's recent actions. She suggests Livia has borderline personality disorder with no love or compassion. Tony becomes enraged, smashing Melfi's glass coffee table top and storming out after threatening her physically. Melfi is terrified.

Carmela and Rosalie Aprile have lunch at the newly re-opened Vesuvio restaurant. They are joined by Father Phil. He is wearing the late Jackie Aprile's watch, which Rosalie has given to him.

Jimmy's corpse is found behind a building with a rat stuffed in his mouth.

Tony is persuaded by the FBI to listen to surveillance tapes. They document Livia goading Junior into ordering the hit on Tony.

Artie Bucco visits Livia in the Green Grove nursing unit. She tells him about Tony having the original Vesuvio restaurant torched.

Tony tells his crew that it was definitely Junior and Mikey Palmice that took out the hit. Tony begins plans to strike back. Silvio points out that Junior might want to finish the job on Tony, probably using Mikey's associate Chucky Signore. Tony says that Chucky has to disappear without raising any alarms.

Tony is suffering low self-esteem after absorbing the fact that his own mother wanted him dead. Carmela believes Livia is faking the Alzheimer's symptoms to escape retribution for her actions.

Tony surprises Chucky Signore on his boat, executing him and then dumping the body out at sea with the help of Silvio.

Later, Tony goes back to Dr Melfi, who eventually agrees to let him in for a session but sits behind her desk rather than in a chair opposite Tony. He warns Melfi that she is in danger and should get out of town until he can remove the threat. She is appalled that people will be murdered on her behalf. Tony thanks her for being a good doctor.

Artie confronts Tony behind Satriale's Pork Store, threatening to shoot him with a hunting rifle. Tony tries to convince Artie that he did not burn down the old Vesuvio restaurant. Artie smashes the rifle against his own car and drives away.

Junior and Livia come to the Sopranos' house for the regular Sunday dinner. Livia is ranting about families dying because of uncooked pork. Tony asks about Artie visiting her in the nursing unit, but Livia denies all knowledge.

Artie seeks guidance from Father Phil. The priest suggests Artie tell all to his wife Charmaine and risk losing everything in a police investigation.

Tony tells his crew that he has been seeing a psychiatrist for five months. Paulie admits to having seen a therapist and learning some coping skills as a result.

Carmela takes a bowl of home-cooked food to Father Phil but finds him being served pasta by Rosalie Aprile. Carmela leaves, dumping her food into a rubbish bin outside.

Charmaine hires Adriana to work at the new Vesuvio. Artie decides against telling his wife about what really happened to the old restaurant.

Christopher and Paulie execute Mikey Palmice while he's out for an early-morning jog.

The FBI swoop, arresting Junior, Larry Boy Barese and others on federal racketeering charges. Tony and his family watch Junior doing the perp walk on the TV news. Tony gets a call from his lawyer about the charges. They relate to a telephone calling-card scam and a technical stock racket in which he had no involvement. The feds have stuff on Tony from surveillance and informants, but they just don't have a case yet.

US Attorney Gene Conigliaro tries to persuade Junior to testify against the Family, claiming that Tony is the true acting boss. Junior won't co-operate.

Carmela gets home to find Father Phil already inside. He's brought a DVD to watch. Carmela confronts the priest about his actions, accusing him of playing a game of sexual frustration with a spiritually needy woman. Father Phil leaves, taken aback by what she has said.

Tony goes to the Green Grove nursing unit, intent on smothering his mother with a pillow. Livia is being wheeled out to a hospital after suffering an apparent stroke. Tony tells her he knows she influenced having him whacked and threatens to do the same to her. Security guards pull Tony off his mother, who smiles as she is taken away. Tony drives to Melfi's office as a storm closes in but she has disappeared, officially going on vacation.

Tony and his family are driving around in the storm, unable to get home. They stop at Vesuvio and Artie agrees to cook for them by candlelight. Inside Silvio and Paulie are eating while Christopher and Adriana are sitting at the bar. Tony makes a toast to good moments like this . . .

Deep and Meaningful: The Season One finale is packed with wonderful moments. Innocence falls from Artie's face like a landslide when Livia tells him it was Tony who ordered that Vesuvio be torched. The FBI's Agent Harris squirms with shame as his superior plays Tony the surveillance tapes of Livia and Junior talking about having Tony whacked. Dr Melfi removes her glasses and becomes all the more vulnerable when she realises people will be executed on Tony's orders to protect her.

But a favourite moment happens when Tony sits down Paulie, Silvio and Christopher to tell them he is in therapy. The reactions of his crew are quite telling. After an uncomfortable silence, Paulie reveals he too has seen a therapist in the past. Silvio thinks it would be good if they could all talk about their feelings – but it'll never happen. For Christopher therapy is an alien concept – he likens it to marriage-guidance counselling.

Mobspeak: Junior tells the FBI that his nephew is a strunz (piece of shit).

Mama Mia: Livia turns up at the Soprano house at one in the morning, babbling incoherently. She is shifted into the nursing unit at Green Grove and gets tested for Alzheimer's disease.

When Artie Bucco visits her in the nursing unit, Livia turns her nose up at some home-cooked Italian food because it's a Northern recipe. She cold-bloodedly tells him about Tony torching Vesuvio, hoping this will drive Artie to finish the job on Tony where others failed.

At Sunday dinner, Carmela says Livia has to admit it's a nice nursing unit that lets someone be signed out for family occasions. 'I don't have to admit anything,' Livia says – never were truer words spoken.

Bright Lights, Baked Ziti: Carmela and Rosalie Aprile enjoy a meal at the new Vesuvio. Artie brings them a free plate of Buccatine matriciana with imported pancetta (bacon) and apologises for a bug that was found in their salad. Father Phil joins them for lunch and sings the praises of a zabaglione dessert he had at the Soprano household.

When Artie visits Livia in the nursing unit he brings her a plate of gavadel pasta with a nice duck ragu.

At the Sunday family dinner the Sopranos, Livia and Junior have pork with the usual pasta, salad and bread.

Carmela takes a bowl of pasta and sauce to Father Phil, but he is already eating some home-cooked food, served to him by Rosalie Aprile in his office.

Artie takes a lunch break at Vesuvio, eating spaghetti and sauce.

Carmela cooks the family scrambled eggs for breakfast.

AJ eats ice cream from a carton while watching Junior on the TV news.

Artie cooks a simple meal of pasta and sauce by candlelight for the Sopranos. AJ asks if Vesuvio has any peanut butter in its kitchen. Paulie and Silvio are also eating pasta at Vesuvio in the storm.

Mobbed Up: AJ hums the theme to the US gameshow *Jeopardy* during the Sunday family dinner.

Mikey Palmice claims it was Junior who shot Brendan in the bath but Christopher rejects this, likening Junior to the TV cartoon character Mr Magoo, whose exploits were turned into a bad film starring Leslie Neilsen.

Father Phil brings round a copy of *One True Thing* on DVD to watch with Carmela. But she recalls telling him just a week before that she is not a big Renee Zellwegger fan.

How Do You Feel?: Tony feels bad about his mother being transferred into the nursing unit at Green Grove – the fate she dreaded and feared. Dr Melfi suggests that Livia was involved in ordering the hit on Tony, but he rejects this. Melfi diagnoses Livia as having borderline personality disorder. When she reads out the symptoms from the textbook Tony flies into a rage. He smashes the glass top of Melfi's coffee table and threatens to smash her face into fifty thousand pieces before leaving. The terrified therapist locks her office door.

After Tony has heard the FBI tapes, he returns to see Melfi. Tony says he is humbled that the therapist accepts his assurance that she is not in any danger from him. Melfi suggests Tony is suffering feelings of worthlessness because of his mother's plot to have him killed – he doesn't disagree.

Sleeping With the Fishes: Welcome to the end-of-season bloodbath as three cast members meet their maker. Jimmy Altieri is executed by Silvio for turning into a rat. Chucky

Signore is gunned down as a precautionary measure by Tony, who pulls his firearm from inside a large fish. Christopher and Paulie chase Mikey Palmice through a forest before ventilating him with more than a dozen bullets. Junior escapes a similar fate only because the FBI arrest him first.

I Dream of Jeannie Cusamano: Dr Melfi tells Tony that in his worst dreams, a duck flies off with his penis, symbolising castration.

Tony relates sex dreams he has been having about his neighbour, Jean Cusamano. They are doing it doggy style and Tony climaxes. He describes Jean as having a big ass but Dr Melfi says that Jean is quite slender. Tony moves the conversation on to other topics.

Quote/Unquote: Jimmy Altieri asks Christopher whether he is wearing enough cologne. 'You smell like Paco Rabanne crawled up your ass and died.'

Christopher extols the virtues of East European prostitutes. 'Russian boo-boos, you go for some basic foreplay, they'll detail your car.'

Dr Melfi tells Tony it has been a long odyssey with his mother. 'These last five hundred years just seemed to race by,' he replies.

The FBI want Tony to hear some tapes, but he is unimpressed. 'The Springsteen boxed set. I already got it.'

Tony ponders the twin causes of his problems. 'Cunnilingus and psychiatry brought us to this.'

Tony tries to get back on topic while discussing sex dreams with Dr Melfi. 'We got bigger things to talk about than Jean Cusamano's ass.'

The FBI tell Junior they want the New York mobsters Mangano and Teresi. 'I want to fuck Angie Dickinson. See who gets lucky first,' Junior says.

Soundtrack: 'Inside of Me' by Little Steven and the Disciples. 'Woodcabin' by St Etienne. 'I'll Remember April' by Bobby Darin. 'I've Got You Under My Skin' by the Four Seasons. 'It's Bad You Know' by RL Burnside.

'Rave On' by Buddy Holly and the Crickets. 'Groove Me' by Screemin' Cheetah Wheelies. 'The Four Sections (Andrea Parker Remix)' by Steve Reich. 'El Gorrito' by Lucho Argain. 'State Trooper' by Bruce Springsteen.

Surveillance Report: More than thirty years previously, Livia threatened to smother her children with a pillow. Now Tony contemplates doing the same to her, grabbing a pillow as he enters Green Grove. But Livia is being rushed to hospital after apparently having a stroke, denying him the chance.

Adriana is working two jobs to become a music manager. According to TV news reports, Mikey's mob nickname was Grab Bag.

The Verdict: 'I'm gonna live a nice, long, happy life, which is more than I can say for you.' Tony takes revenge for the attempt on his life while the FBI swoop on Junior and several of the captains.

The season finale is the big pay-off, where virtually all the major plotlines culminate in a gripping conclusion. David Chase's script is dripping with great lines, the body count reaches an all-time high and Carmela resolves her issues with the religious predator, Father Phil.

A great episode for regular viewers who get rewarded for their loyalty but probably too dense and self-referential for any casual watchers. The final scene emphasises the twin concerns of the show – the family and the Family. This episode was written as a grand finale in case *The Sopranos* was not renewed for a second series. This would cause some problems for the second season . . .

Season Two
(2000)

Company Credits
Created by David Chase
Produced by Ilene S Landress
Producer: Allen Coulter
Co-Producer: Martin Bruestle
Executive Producers: Brad Grey, David Chase
Co-Executive Producers: Robin Green and
Mitchell Burgess
Supervising Producer: Frank Renzulli

Regular Cast:

James Gandolfini (Tony Soprano)
Lorraine Bracco (Dr Jennifer Melfi)
Edie Falco (Carmela Soprano)
Michael Imperioli (Christopher Moltisanti)
Dominic Chianese (Corrado 'Junior' Soprano)
Vincent Pastore (Salvatore 'Big Pussy' Bonpensiero)
Steven Van Zandt (Silvio Dante)
Tony Sirico (Peter 'Paulie Walnuts' Gualtieri)
Robert Iler (Anthony Soprano Jr, also known as AJ)
Jamie-Lynn Sigler (Meadow Soprano)
Drea De Matteo (Adriana La Cerva)
Aida Turturro (Janice Soprano,
also known as Parvati, 14–25)
David Proval (Richie Aprile, 16–25)
Nancy Marchand (Livia Soprano)

Recurring Cast:

Jerry Adler (Herman 'Hesh' Rabkin, 14, 18, 22, 24, 26)

John Ventimiglia (Arthur 'Artie' Bucco, 18–19, 23, 26)

Lillo Brancato, Jr (Matt Bevilaqua, 14–15, 19, 21–23)

Chris Tardio (Sean Giamonte, 14–15, 19, 21)

Oksana Babiy (Irina Peltsin, 14, 18, 25)

Nicole Burdette (Barbara Giglione, 14, 19, 26)

David Margulies (Neil Mink, 14, 23–24, 26)

Tom Aldredge (Huge DeAngelis, 14, 21, 26)

John Fiore (Gigi Cestone, 14–15, 18, 26)

Suzanne Shepherd (Mary DeAngelis, 14, 21, 26)

Ed Vassallo (Tom Giglione, 14, 19)

Terence Patrick Winter (Tom Amberson, 14, 24)

Louis Lombardi (Skip Lipari, 15, 17–18, 20, 22–23, 25–26)

Richard Portnow (Attorney Melvoin, 15, 25)

Steven R Schirripa (Bobby 'Bacala' Baccalieri, 15, 17–18, 21, 24–25)

Peter Bogdanovich (Dr Elliot Kupferberg, 16, 18, 22, 24)

Matthew Sussman (Dr Schreck, 16, 24)

Paul Herman (Beansie Gaeta, 16, 21, 23)

Vincent Curatola (Johnny Sack, 16, 18–19)

Donna Smythe (Gia Gaeta, 16, 21)

Sofia Milos (Annalisa, 17, 26)

Federico Castelluccio (Furio, 17–19, 21, 23–26)

Toni Kalem (Angie Bonpensiero, 17, 20, 24, 26)

Sharon Angela (Rosalie Aprile, 17, 24–25)

Maureen Van Zandt (Gabriella Dante, 17, 22, 24–26)

Marisa Redanty (Christine Scatino, 19, 23)

Joseph R Gannascoli (Vito Spataford, 19, 21)

Sig Libowitz (Hillel, 19, 26)

Robert Patrick (David Scatino, 19, 23, 26)

Katalin Pota (Lilliana Wosilius, 21, 23, 25)

Joe Penny (Victor Musto, 23, 25)

Adrian Martinez (Ramone, 23, 25)

Matt Servitto (Agent Harris, 23–24, 26)

Joe Lisi (Dick Barone, 24–25)

Frank Pelligrino (Agent Cubitoso, 25–26)

14
Guy Walks Into a Psychiatrist's Office . . .

US Transmission Date: 16 January 2000
UK Transmission Date: 12 October 2000

Writer: Jason Cahill
Director: Allen Coulter
Cast: John Billeci (Manager), Darrell Carey (Proctor),
Dan Chen (Ernest Wu), Robert Cicchini (Dr De'Alessio),
Mark Fish (Caller #2),
Karen Giordano (Samantha Martin),
Bryan Greenberg (Peter McClure),
Ian Grimaldi (Philly Parisi), Philipp Kaner (Caller #3),
Katrina Lantz (Sylvia), George Loros (Raymond Curto),
Wayne W Pretlow (Caller #1), Kevin Sussman (Kevin),
Roberto Thomas (Lee)

Storyline: A stand-in sits a stockbroker's exam on behalf
of Christopher, enabling him to run the Webistics scam for
Tony (see later this episode).

Pussy is waiting for Tony when he goes to collect his
morning newspaper. Pussy says he has been in Puerto
Rico, where he got involved with a 26-year-old acupuncturist. But Pussy says his financial problems remain, so he
has come back to start earning again. Tony is dubious but
eventually welcomes back his friend.

Philly Parisi has taken over running Junior's crew while
Junior is in jail. Philly goes to the airport to pick up Gigi
Cestone. Gigi is supposed to have just returned from
Boston. Gigi shoots Philly twice in the head for gossiping
about the attempted hit on Tony.

Dr Melfi is seeing clients in a room at the Anthony
Wayne Motel. Tony calls his former therapist to say it's
safe for her to go back to her own home.

Christopher is working as a Stock Exchange Commission compliance officer at a call centre, where stockbrokers
are pushing an Internet stock called Webistics. Adriana
persuades Christopher to have the afternoon off. Two

young wannabe mobsters working at the centre, Matt
Bevilaqua and Sean Giamonte, beat up one of the brokers,
who complains about having to push Webistics.

Hesh and Tony's lawyer, Neil Mink, visit Tony at the
Bada Bing! strip club. Mink says Junior is trying to get out
of jail on medical grounds while awaiting trial. Tony has
no objections – with Junior facing twelve federal charges,
Tony has become the new acting boss. Carmela calls to say
that Tony's sister Janice has come to stay after twenty
years away from New Jersey. Tony decides to stage a
family reunion, excluding his mother.

Pussy meets the rest of the crew again. Paulie and the
others have been collecting on Pussy's behalf. Silvio tells
Tony what happened at the brokerage. Paulie has confirmed Pussy's story about going to a clinic in Puerto Rico.

Next morning at breakfast, Tony welcomes home his
sister. She's on disability benefit, courtesy of the state of
Washington. Her last boyfriend, Rolf, has returned to
Andorra. Janice says she wants to take her turn looking
after their mother. Tony doesn't believe the diagnosis that
Livia had a stroke. Janice thinks she might stay at Livia's
house but Tony says he has put it up for sale.

Tony confronts Christopher about what happened at the
brokerage. He also warns Christopher against letting Matt
and Sean steal cars from the brokerage building.

Tony and Carmela are shocked when they visit Livia's
house with an estate agent. The house has been vandalised,
apparently by local teenagers. Carmela wants Tony to go
back into therapy. He is self-medicating and they have not
had sex recently.

Christopher passes Tony's message on to Matt and
Sean. He also requests a part of their proceeds from any
car crimes.

Janice takes Meadow to visit Livia in hospital.

Tony passes out while driving. He has an accident but is
unhurt. He tries a new therapist but the doctor refuses to
treat Tony because he is a mobster.

The family reunion becomes a barbecue party at the
Sopranos' house. Tony's sister Barbara and her family

come along, as do Carmela's parents. Janice complains to her sister about Tony putting Livia's house up for sale. Barbara says Janice should not get involved. Tony finds the FOR SALE sign from his mother's house in the back of Janice's car.

Adriana and Christopher argue while having a drink with Matt and Sean. Adriana complains about Christopher cooking drugs on her stove. She slaps his face, so Christopher slaps her back. Adriana storms out.

Tony approaches Dr Melfi, who is having lunch at a roadside diner. She refuses to take him back as a patient. One of her patients died because she had to leave her office and her home. Melfi tells Tony to get out of her life.

Deep and Meaningful: This episode introduces Tony's two sisters, Janice and Barbara. They share a very revealing scene during the barbecue when Barbara counsels Janice against getting involved with the dispute between Tony and their mother. Janice shows her true colours, complaining about her brother's plans to sell Livia's house. She says he hardly needs the $180,000 asking price. Barbara's reply speaks volumes: 'You'll get your cut.' Her language betrays her personal knowledge of the world in which Tony lives, and her life experience of how Janice operates. Barbara is a woman without illusions.

Mobspeak: Pussy says he has to get back his action (illegal betting business). Tony tells Pussy that Junior is facing twelve RICO predicates (RICO stands for Racketeer-Influenced and Corrupt Organisation Act; predicates are offences under the statutes of this act).

Christopher tells Matt and Sean that if they steal any Porsches, he wants a taste (percentage of the take). Matt asks if Christopher has capped (murdered) anyone with Tony.

Mama Mia: Livia asks Meadow to let her die in hospital. The old woman says she saw a light and voices were calling out to her. Livia says Tony blames her for everything. She claims the hospital staff beat patients at night. Livia gives Meadow jewellery so she won't be forgotten.

Bright Lights, Baked Ziti: Carmela is twice seen cooking food during the opening montage sequence.

Philly Parisi's wife calls out to remind him to get pastries.

At breakfast, Meadow and AJ eat scrambled eggs, cooked by Carmela. Tony complains about a smell, which Janice says is her miso-and-seaweed soup.

When they visit Livia's vandalised house, Carmela says she needs Tony to pick up sausage. He wants precise instructions on how many pounds are required and whether the sausage should be hot or sweet.

In hospital, Meadow tries to feed Livia food that looks like slop. She understandably turns her nose up at it.

At the family reunion, Carmela's mother makes pound cake. She sends her husband out to get the canned pears for the cake. Tony barbecues the meat at the party, with Pussy helping later. For dessert Carmela has some Ben and Jerry's ice cream to go with the cake. She saves some of both for Janice.

Dr Melfi is having lunch at a roadside diner when Tony approaches her. He asks how the bagels are. After Melfi rebuffs him, Tony goes home, where Carmela microwaves some cold pasta for his lunch.

Mobbed Up: Silvio revives his beloved Michael Corleone impersonation after a request from Pussy. He performs a selection of dialogue, including a Diane Keaton imitation.

Dr De'Alessio refuses to treat Tony and cites the film *Analyse This*, which had a psychiatrist, played by Billy Crystal, treating a mobster, played by Robert De Niro. Tony protests that *Analyse This* was just a comedy.

Carmela's mother likens Livia to *Mommie Dearest*, a scathing book written about Joan Crawford by her daughter, which became a cult film starring Faye Dunaway.

How Do You Feel?: Tony rejects a suggestion from Carmela that he go back into therapy. But he tries a new psychiatrist after passing out while driving. He tells Dr De'Alessio that things were good until Janice turned up. Now his feelings are starting to bleed into his business.

Tony goes back to Dr Melfi but she refuses to treat him or refer his case to another psychiatrist. He swears that nobody got killed because of her but she doesn't believe him.

Sleeping With the Fishes: Philly Parisi, shot twice in the head by Gigi Cestone for gossiping about Tony and Livia.

Quote/Unquote: Tony predicts the outcome of Janice's visit. 'I'm gonna be five grand lighter before she rain-dances back to the commune.'

Tony reveals his catchphrase for this season when talking to Janice about his mother: 'She's dead to me.'

Tony questions the value of Christopher's work at the stock brokerage. 'What did you get your licence for, Christopher, your résumé, huh?'

Carmela's mother is bemused by Janice's change of name to that of a Hindu goddess. 'Parvati – she's a cheese now?'

Soundtrack: 'It Was a Very Good Year' by Frank Sinatra. 'Con Te Partiro' by Andrea Bocelli. 'I've Tried Everything' by the Eurythmics. 'Smoke on the Water' by Deep Purple. 'Nod Off' by Skeleton Key. Tony's crew sing the advertising jingle for a perfume called Charlie. 'Time Is On My Side' by Irma Thomas.

Surveillance Report: Tony tells Janice he's just put Livia's house up for sale. This contradicts events in 'Nobody Knows Anything', when he said the sale had gone through. Presumably, the first sale fell through in between seasons.

Both Tony and Carmela's mother say that Carmela's parents were unwilling to visit the Sopranos while Livia was on the scene. This contradicts events in '46 Long', when Livia was to give Carmela's parents a lift to dinner at the Sopranos' house.

Janice Soprano is played by Aida Turturro, a cousin of the actors John Turturro (star of *Barton Fink*) and Nicholas Turturro (from the TV series *NYPD Blue*). She has appeared in dozens of films, including *Deep Blue Sea*, *Mickey Blue Eyes* and *Manhattan Murder Mystery*.

The Verdict: 'How many more people have to die for your personal growth?' Tony Soprano's sister Janice comes to stay and Pussy returns from Puerto Rico. Tony claims that life is good but his blackouts have returned and the psychiatrist Dr Melfi refuses to take him back as a patient.

The opening episode of Season Two seems like a very slow start after the dramatic finale to Season One. There are a lot of loose threads to resolve, but this first helping hardly scratches the surface. Instead, new agita is introduced by the arrival of Janice while Pussy returns with just a brief explanation. By comparison with the pilot, this episode is much less satisfying.

David Chase admitted in interviews to being terrified by the pressure created by the first season's success. By comparison with most other dramas on TV, this episode of *The Sopranos* is top-quality. By comparison with the show's own high standards, this is average at best.

15
Do Not Resuscitate

US Transmission Date: 23 January 2000
UK Transmission Date: 19 October 2000

Writers: Robin Green, Mitchell Burgess and Frank
Renzulli
Director: Martin Bruestle
Cast: Bill Cobbs (Reverend James Sr),
Gregalan Williams (Reverend James Jr),
Robert Desiderio (Jack Massarone),
Michael Broughton (Protester),
James Collins (Truck Driver),
Katherine Dent (Arlene Riley), Elizabeth Flax (Therapist),
Sam Gray (Judge Greenspan), Timothy Huang (Doctor),
Tertia Lynch (Duty Nurse),
John Mariano (Ralph Giorgio), Tony Rigo (Old Guy),
Laurine Towler (Surgical Nurse),
Kellie Turner (Nurse's Aide),
Beatrice Winde (Funeral Guest)

Storyline: Tony visits his uncle in prison. Junior wants Tony to make peace with Livia, to kill off rumours about recent events between them. Tony refuses and demands a meeting with Bobby 'Bacala' Baccalieri, Junior's new representative outside the prison.

Black protestors are staging a demonstration outside a Masserone Brothers' construction site, preventing further work. The protest is led by Reverend James Jr, aided by his father. The picket line is about the lack of black jointfitters working on the project.

Tony argues with Janice about plans to sell Livia's house. Janice wants a friend of hers to act as estate agent for a cut-price commission. Janice visits her mother at a hospital rehabilitation unit. Livia belittles her daughter.

Tony meets with Jack Massarone, who wants him to act against the protest. The jointfitters' union is under Junior's jurisdiction, but Tony agrees to intervene. He has assisted Massarone before getting work contracts.

Bacala meets with Tony and his crew at Satriale's Pork Store. Tony says Junior can continue to earn, but only enough to pay for his defence lawyers. Tony is taking over many of Junior's interests.

Pussy gets a steroid injection to help his back. He is driven home by Skip Lipari, a law-enforcement agent. Pussy has been an informant for two years. He lies about not having met with Tony since returning from Puerto Rico. Skip says Jimmy Altieri's death means nobody still suspects Pussy is a rat, but Pussy is not so sure.

Junior appears before a judge, who grants him bail on medical grounds. However, Junior is placed under house arrest and made to wear an electronic bracelet at all times, to stop him trying to escape.

Tony goes to Reverend James Jr's home, but he's out. Tony shares a soft drink and talks with Reverend James Sr before leaving.

Junior and Tony meet in a doctor's office – federal law prohibits the use of listening devices in such places. Junior says the owner of Green Grove retirement community, Frederick Capuano, is spreading rumours about Soprano business.

At a family dinner AJ says he has to write a report about DNA for school. Tony agrees to give Janice's friend the real-estate listing on Livia's house.

Frederick Capuano goes missing. The police find his car with the door open and the keys inside. Capuano's hairpiece lies on the road behind the car.

Meadow practises her driving by taking Janice to buy marijuana. Janice quizzes her niece about Livia's hobbies. Meadow suggests music by the De Castro sisters or Mario Lanza.

Junior goes to an optometrist, accompanied by Bacala. Jack Massarone passes through the waiting room, leaving behind an envelope of cash that Bacala picks up for Junior.

Janice takes Livia flowers and a recording of the Italian tenor Luciano Pavarotti. Mother and daughter share a happy moment.

Tony and Bacala have a covert meeting. Tony says the picket line will be broken up the next morning.

At dinner Carmela announces that Meadow passed her driving test. After dinner, Tony and Janice discuss their mother outside. Livia will soon be fit enough to leave the rehab unit, but she needs a place to stay. Tony refuses to have Livia move back into her own home. He suggests she go back to Green Grove, but Janice can't afford the fees.

Tony and Pussy go to watch the picket line being smashed. Tony drives off when two wannabe mobsters, Matt and Sean, try to approach him. Christopher leads the team of heavies who attack the protestors.

Janice visits Livia and suggests they move into Livia's house together. But her mother wants to go back to Green Grove and has a coughing fit when Janice contradicts her. Afterwards a nurse approaches Janice, asking if the Sopranos are willing to sign a 'Do Not Resuscitate' form for Livia.

Janice and Tony argue about the DNR form, which Tony eventually agrees to sign. AJ overhears their conversation.

Meadow drives AJ to visit Livia. He asks his grandmother about her DNR form, whether it has anything to do with DNA.

The next day Janice visits Livia while she is having physical therapy. Livia lets her daughter know she knows about the DNR, then hints she has money hidden somewhere but has forgotten its location.

Junior falls in the shower and hurts his pelvis.

Tony visits Reverend James Jr at home, where guests are leaving a wake for the late Reverend James Sr. Tony gives James his cut of the Masserone payoff – the clergyman was part of the scam from the start.

Tony and Bacala take the injured Junior to hospital.

Deep and Meaningful: The crucial moment in this episode is the revelation that Pussy is a government informant. But there is no melodramatic music or ominous thunderclaps to underline this shocking truth. Instead, it becomes apparent during an offhand conversation between Pussy and a man giving him a lift home after Pussy has had a doctor's appointment.

As they talk the viewer slowly realises that Tony's trusted friend is a rat and the man giving him a lift is an FBI agent called Skip Lipari. The two argue about how little Pussy has divulged during two years as an informant. Pussy also lies about his reconciliation with Tony, proving to the viewer he is either playing one side off against the other or just very conflicted about his situation.

Mobspeak: Tony tells Bacala that Junior can keep his stripes (the title of boss). He will let Junior keep on earning (making money for the Family). Skip Lipari tells Pussy that Jimmy Altieri ate the pill (died) for him. Junior's lawyer objects to his client being characterised as a Mafioso (member of the Mafia). Junior claims Livia did not know she was setting up Tony to be popped (murdered).

Mama Mia: In hospital Livia refuses to eat tapioca but tries to give it to Janice. She complains about the bruise on her hand from the intravenous needle. Livia says Janice could never stand herself and that's why she ran away. Livia asks a nurse to open a window and push her out of it. The old woman then says Janice is there only because her daughter wants to take Livia's house. Finally, she breaks down, sobbing, 'I gave my life to my children on a silver platter.'

Several days later Livia and Janice actually bond for a while when Janice brings her mother fresh flowers and Italian classical music.

Janice tries to persuade Livia to move back home but the contrary old crone now wants to go back to Green Grove. She says it's not that bad and they give you fresh towels every day. When Janice raises objections, Livia has a coughing fit.

AJ tells his grandmother about Janice trying to get Tony to sign the DNR form. Livia tells Janice what she knows, then hints about having money but forgetting where it is. The implication is clear: if Janice wants the money, she'll have to keep Livia alive to get it.

Livia phones Carmela to say she will leave all her money to her grandchildren. She tries to seek help about Janice but Carmela hangs up.

Bright Lights, Baked Ziti: Livia picks at lunch in hospital but refuses to eat the tapioca, requesting strawberry ice cream instead.

Tony describes the obese Bacala as a Calzone with legs and later suggests he start eating more salads.

At dinner the Sopranos have salad, meat and macaroni with cheese. At a subsequent dinner they have sausages and rice with salad. Tony jokes about Janice being a vegetarian.

Livia nearly chokes on a cookie.

When Tony and Janice argue about Livia's DNR form, AJ is scooping ice cream into a bowl. Livia gives him an Italian candy when he visits her later. She watches a cooking show featuring cuisine from the state of Louisiana.

Mobbed Up: Tony says Janice and Livia deserve each other. He says their living together would be like the film *Whatever Happened To Baby Jane?*

Sleeping With the Fishes: Frederick Capuano, who disappears after Junior tells Tony that the director of geriatric services at Green Grove has been spreading rumours about Soprano business. No body is found, but the police discover Capuano's car and hairpiece abandoned on a roadside.

I Dream of Jeannie Cusamano: Janice sees a hospital sign warning about the dangers of rushing down stairs in case of a fire. She fantasises about pushing Livia down stairs and Livia's head appears on the body in the warning sign.

Quote/Unquote: Bacala gets philosophical about the victor always getting the spoils, but Tony dismisses him. 'Why don't you get the fuck out of here before I shove your quotations book up your fat fucking ass!'

Reverend James Sr objects to talk about shit and the Bible. 'Only shit in the Bible came out of Pharaoh's ass when Moses parted the Red Sea.'

Janice asks Meadow what Livia is into. 'I don't know. Negativity?'

Soundtrack: 'Non Ti Scordar Di Me' by Luciano Pavarotti. 'Mother and Child Reunion' by Paul Simon. 'Goodnight My Love' by Benny Goodman with Ella Fitzgerald.

Surveillance Report: Janice is pitching a self-help-video concept called *Lady Kerouac*, about packing for the highway to boost a woman's self-esteem. As a child she sold her ballet shoes to get money for amphetamines.

Prior to his recent bust, Junior hadn't been arrested since 1968. He pays his taxes and was a veteran of World War Two.

The Verdict: 'She's still around – she's too miserable to die.' Janice schemes to get herself into Livia's house and ponders matricide. Junior gets out of jail on a medical but Tony is now fully in control of the Family.

The return of Junior from prison helps kick-start this season, as does the sparring between Janice and Livia. However, Tony's problems with passing out have magically gone by this episode and Dr Melfi doesn't even get a mention. The absence of Tony's therapy sessions leaves a hole in the fabric of the series.

This episode is an improvement on the season opener, with Janice revealing herself as a real chip off the block of her mother. The best moment is when Tony and Reverend James Jr discuss the passing of the older generation. Soon they will be the elders . . .

16
Toodle-Fucking-oo

US Transmission Date: 30 January 2000
UK Transmission Date: 26 October 2000

Writer: Frank Renzulli
Director: Lee Tamahori
Cast: Michele De Cesare (Hunter Scangarello),
Diana Agostini (Miriam),
Getchie Argetsinger (Yoga Instructor),
Leslie Beatty (Nancy), Ed Crasnick (Comedian),
Catrina Ganey (Nurse),
Marc Freeman Hamm (Partygoer),
Linda Mann (Joint Copper), Joe Pacheo (Policeman),
Charles Sammarco (Joey),
Antonette Schwartzberg (Beansie's Mother),
Mike 'Scuch' Quicciarini (Big Frank),
Deirdre Sullivan (Hospital Patient),
Craig Wojcik (Pizza Kid)

Storyline: Tony goes to his mother's vacant home late at night, after a tip-off from a cop. The house has been used as the venue for a teenage party and the police were called. One youth is taken away by ambulance after overdosing on drugs while another is under arrest. Tony finds Meadow inside, looking drunk and sorry for herself. He takes his daughter home and she stumbles off to bed.

Adriana gives a lift to her uncle, Richie Aprile, who has just been released after ten years in prison. He is the brother of the acting boss, Jackie Aprile, who died of cancer. Richie wants to visit his old neighbourhood.

In bed Carmela and Tony discuss how they can punish Meadow for what happened. They both feel powerless.

Richie confronts Beansie Gaeta, who owns three pizza parlours. Beansie used to deal heroin for Richie and Jackie, but he refuses to be intimidated. Richie smashes a glass coffee jug in Beansie's face, smashes a chair over his back and savagely beats him.

Next morning Carmela and Tony berate Meadow for the party. Janice says they should ignore her transgression. Meadow denies any blame and volunteers to surrender her credit card for two weeks. Tony insists on three weeks. Meadow walks away, smiling to herself.

Richie and Tony meet outside Satriale's Pork Store. Christopher arrives and gets a warning from Richie about hitting Adriana. Richie tries to talk business with Tony, who just walks away. Silvio explains that Tony has to be very careful about where he talks business, owing to government surveillance.

Dr Melfi has dinner with two friends. As they leave the restaurant, she bumps into Tony and his crew having dinner. They exchange small talk and Melfi says 'Toodle-oo' as she leaves.

Richie and Janice meet each other at a yoga class.

Tony and Richie meet to talk business at a mall. Tony asks Richie to back off Beansie, whose pizza parlours earn good money as cash businesses.

Janice is furious when she sees what Meadow's friends did to Livia's house. She has a blazing row with Tony and Carmela about how they punished Meadow. Tony storms out and Carmela tells Janice to mind her own business. All this is overheard by Meadow.

Richie meets Junior at his doctor's office. Richie pledges his loyalty to Junior.

Tony and his crew have a party for Richie at the Bada Bing!. Afterwards, Richie hunts down Beansie and tries to shoot him, but Beansie escapes.

Carmela and Janice apologise to each other.

Richie smashes his car into Beansie, backs up, runs over him again and then reverses over Beansie's twitching body.

Next day Richie takes some flowers to Livia at the rehabilitation unit. He is really there to see Janice – twenty years ago they were lovers. They have a drink in the hospital cafeteria and Richie asks Janice out to dinner.

Dr Melfi has a dream about Tony passing out and crashing his car.

Tony visits Beansie in hospital. The doctors say he may never walk again, but Beansie pledges not to rat on Richie.

Richie and Tony meet at the mall again. Tony is furious about Richie crippling Beansie and warns him to start listening to orders – or else.

Tony goes to Livia's house so a locksmith can change all the locks. Inside he sees Meadow cleaning up vomit from the party.

Deep and Meaningful: Tony says Richie Aprile has got a right to be a little fucked up after ten years in prison. Just how fucked up is revealed in the two scenes immediately following Tony's comment. Richie is receiving a complimentary blow job at the Bada Bing! but he can't climax, despite the assistance of two well-endowed young women.

He sends them away and sits in the room on his own, angry, impotent and frustrated. Richie sates himself by hunting down Beansie and eventually crippling the pizza parlour manager. Richie smiles as he drives away – for him, acts of violence have supplanted sexual gratification.

Mobspeak: Richie talks about wrapping up a dime (finishing ten years in prison). Beansie says he moved a lot of 'H' (heroin) for Richie.

Mama Mia: Livia complains about being shifted out of a private room at the hospital. She says Janice changed name to Parvati just to shame her mother. Richie tries to jog Livia's memory by saying she used to yell at him for beeping his car horn. Livia's reply is short and sour: 'Pimps beep.' For good measure, Livia announces that she wishes the Lord would take her.

Bright Lights, Baked Ziti: Beansie orders a free veal parmigiana sandwich for Richie, but the newly released felon rejects the gift.

When Meadow comes down to breakfast she pours a bowl of Cheerios but leaves the kitchen before eating them.

Melfi recommends the veal when she meets Tony and his crew at a restaurant. They are eating pasta.

At the mall Richie bitches about a kid spilling fried rice all over him.

Meadow and Hunter Scangarello make themselves French toast and hot chocolate at the Sopranos' house, turning the kitchen into a pigsty.

The Sopranos have sandwiches and cold meat for lunch.

Mobbed Up: Tony compares Meadow to the eponymous heroine in *Bride of Frankenstein*.

Tony asks Beansie if he can pick up the BBC on the elaborate metal harness holding his broken body in traction.

How Do You Feel, Doctor?: At a therapy session with Dr Elliot Kupferberg, Dr Melfi says she feels so embarrassed about saying 'Toodle-oo' to Tony she can't sleep. She never talks to patients that way. She believes it was a way of hiding from a patient she never wanted to see again. She thinks she regressed into the persona of a girl to escape responsibility for abandoning a patient.

I Dream of Jeannie Cusamano: Melfi has a dream in which Tony drives through pouring rain. He becomes groggy and reaches for a bottle of Prozac, but it's empty. In the background, music from *The Wizard of Oz* plays. He passes out and crashes head-on into a large lorry. Dr Melfi dreams of driving by the accident. Tony is lying on the front of his car, having smashed through the windscreen. His face is bloody and the empty bottle of Prozac is lying beside his head. When Melfi wakes up, she makes brief notes about her dream that describe Tony as Patient S.

Quote/Unquote: Tony warns Carmela not to overplay her hand when punishing Meadow. 'If she finds out we're powerless, we're fucked.'

Tony decides to clear the air with his sister. 'You come riding into town like some Vishnu-come-lately and try to play the concerned daughter. Who the fuck are you kidding?!'

Junior complains about house arrest. 'Federal marshals are so far up my ass, I can taste Brylcreem.'

Tony helps Beansie blow his nose, but the badly injured pizza parlour owner worries he may never be able to wipe his own ass again. 'Your nose is as far as I'm willing to go,' Tony replies.

Soundtrack: 'Holla Holla' by Ja Rule. 'You Never Miss the Water' by Chaka Khan. 'No Scrubs' by TLC. 'You're Out of the Woods/Optimistic Voices' from the *Wizard of Oz* soundtrack. A Muzak version of 'I'll Never Fall In Love Again' plays while Richie looks at underwear in the mall. 'Viking' by Los Lobos.

Surveillance Report: Pussy says that Dr Melfi has nice, pipe-fitter lips which could give world-class blow jobs.

Richie tells Christopher he can hit Adriana all he wants when they get married, but not before.

Janice changed her name to Parvati Wasatch in 1978. She has a son called Harpo, but he changed his name to Hal. He lives in Montreal with his father, Eugene. Janice has petitioned the State Department for custody but believes she is on their enemy radicals list.

Richie Aprile is played by David Proval, who has previously appeared in *The Shawshank Redemption* and Martin Scorcese's *Mean Streets*. Melfi's psychiatrist, Dr Elliot Kupferberg, is played by Peter Bogdanovich, a well-known film director whose credits include *The Last Picture Show*.

This episode features the sole Season Two appearance of Hunter Scangarello, played by David Chase's daughter, Michele De Cesare. This episode is directed by the New Zealand helmer Lee Tamahori, best known for the award-winning *Once Were Warriors*.

The Verdict: 'You and I weren't good for each other twenty years ago. What makes you think it's gonna be different now?' The old-school mobster Richie Aprile gets out of jail after a decade and immediately starts causing agita for Tony. He also makes a move on his former lover, Janice Soprano.

This episode puts the last piece in place for Season Two with the arrival of Richie. With Junior sidelined by house arrest, Richie takes over his role as chief irritant for Tony in the Family. Janice has already usurped Livia as Tony's major female irritant within the family. The combination of these two highly volatile individuals will produce most of the conflict in the coming episodes.

Even Dr Melfi makes a comeback. Previously Tony was talking to her in therapy. Now it's Melfi in therapy talking about Tony. After a couple of slow episodes, Season Two is now firing on all cylinders . . .

17
Commendatori

US Transmission Date: 6 February 2000
UK Transmission Date: 2 November 2000

Writer: David Chase
Director: Tim Van Patten
Cast: Vittorio Duse (Zi Vittorio),
Mike Memphis (Jimmy Bones), Jay Lynch (Partner),
Emme Shaw (Nurse), Ciro Maggio (Raffaelle),
Danton Stone (Mr Sontag), Melissa Weil (Mrs Sontag),
Jason Fuchs (Jr Sontag), Jessica Peters (Sis Sontag),
Gano Grills (Antonio), Anthony Alessandro (Waiter),
Frank Caero (Host), Gina Cutolo (Mother),
Raffaele Giulivo (Nino), Guido Palliggiano (Pino),
Alida Tarallo (Prostitute), Alex Toma (Kid),
Giuseppe Zeno (Tanno), Ricardo Zinna (Hotel Manager)

Storyline: Tony is going to Italy to meet business contacts in Naples. He visits Junior at the doctor's office to seek his advice. Junior used to ship stolen cars in containers to Italy but Tony has inherited the business as acting boss. Junior says he used to deal with Don Zi Vittorio, but lately the contact has been Furio Giunta. Junior regrets never visiting Italy.

Carmela is angry with Tony for not taking her on the trip.

Pussy meets with the FBI's Agent Skip Lipari at a party. He feeds him disinformation, protecting Tony. The pair bump into an Elvis Presley imitator called Jimmy Bones, who asks uncomfortable questions. Pussy panics.

Carmela has lunch with Rosalie Aprile and Pussy's wife, Angie Bonpensiero. Angie says she is depressed and suicidal since Pussy returned from his disappearance. When he came home her heart sank. She found a lump under her arm and is awaiting the results of a biopsy to determine whether the lump is malignant or benign. Either way, she wants a divorce from Pussy.

Tony, Paulie and Christopher arrive at the Hotel Excelsior in Naples. They are met by Furio and his associates. Christopher notices that one of Furio's men, Tanno, has needle marks on his arm from taking heroin.

Carmela and her friends gossip about the Bonpensieros' problems.

Tony and Paulie have dinner with Furio and other representatives of the Vittorio Family. Tony is disappointed that Don Vittorio is not attending. He suggests a price of $90,000 for each stolen car – they are top-of-the-range Mercedes ML series vehicles. Don Vittorio arrives at the dinner in a wheelchair, pushed by his daughter Annalisa. Don Vittorio is senile and can talk only about street names in American cities.

Christopher misses the dinner because he's too busy shooting heroin with Furio's assistant, Tanno.

Tony learns that the Family is now run by Mauro Zucca, but he's in prison serving a life sentence. Furio suggests Tony talk to Annalisa – she is Mauro's wife. Annalisa offers to give Tony a guided tour of Avellino, where his ancestors lived before moving to America. Outside the restaurant a teenage boy throws firecrackers. He is beaten by Furio and others. They also punch the boy's mother. The police just drive away. Tony is impressed by Furio's ruthlessness.

Pussy is having nightmares about Jimmy Bones revealing his secret.

Christopher stays in his hotel room, claiming a bad case of food poisoning from the in-flight meal. That leaves Paulie on his own to check out the docks while Tony meets with Annalisa.

Carmela and Janice argue about the role of Mafia wives. Janice says her sister-in-law is content with too little but Carmela says marriage and family are sacred institutions. She also points out that Janice getting back with Richie Aprile is hardly extending the boundaries of feminism.

Tony goes to stay with Annalisa at the Vittorio family home. She runs the family because all the men have been murdered or sent to prison. Annalisa says Italian men are in love with their mothers, so taking orders from a woman boss is not a major problem.

Paulie wanders around Naples but the locals seem unfriendly.

Tony and Annalisa continue to haggle about the price for the stolen cars. Tony wants to recruit mob soldiers from Naples to join him in America, starting with Furio. Annalisa gets angry and refuses.

Angie tells Pussy her biopsy came back negative – she doesn't have cancer. He is preoccupied and walks out. Pussy drives to Jimmy Bones's house, where he beats the Elvis imitator to death.

Carmela visits Angie, trying to persuade her not to divorce Pussy.

Paulie finally gets close to the locals by sleeping with a prostitute from the same town as his ancestors.

Tony and Annalisa visit the site of the Sibylla of Cumae, a famous oracle of the past. Annalisa offers Tony sex but he refuses because it would be bad for business. They agree a price for the cars and the men.

Tony, Paulie and Christopher fly back to New Jersey. Christopher finally gets around to buying a present for Adriana – at Newark Airport.

Tony gets home. Upstairs, Carmela hears him arrive – but how does she feel about his return?

Deep and Meaningful: Pussy collects Tony, Christopher and Paulie from the airport and drives them home. The three travellers sit in silence, watching the run-down streets pass by. The desolation of the landscape especially reflects the emptiness inside Paulie. He goads Pussy about never having been to Italy when the trip was a depressing and lonely experience for Paulie. He could not communicate with the locals, he didn't like the Italian cooking and had to fuck a prostitute to make some connection with the land of his forefathers. Paulie belongs not in Italy, but to the ugly, decaying landscape of America.

Mobspeak: Tony tells Junior that he's going over to the other side (Italy).

Mama Mia: Annalisa looks after her senile father in her own home. Tony says she takes good care of her father. To Annalisa, this seems only natural. She would never send her parent to a home.

Bright Lights, Baked Ziti: Carmela is cooking a roast dinner when she and Tony argue about his business trip. Meadow is setting the table. She salivates at the idea of real Italian cooking.

Carmela, Rosalie and Angie eat pasta for lunch when Angie talks about divorce. The conversation is being eavesdropped by lunching ladies at the next table. Rosalie yells at them to eat their manicotti (large, tubular pasta filled with meat, cheese and tomato sauce).

At the welcome dinner everyone eats an antipasto of cold meats. This is followed by a course of black pasta, at which Paulie turns up his nose. He requests macaroni and gravy, which is interpreted as spaghetti and tomato sauce. The local mobsters are unimpressed by his taste. 'And you thought the Germans were classless pieces of shit,' one says in Italian.

Tony phones home and interrupts Carmela as she prepares dinner. He says the local food is OK, with lots of fish. She is cooking pasta and roasting meat. Tony suggests she get Chinese takeaway, which infuriates Carmela.

Pussy talks in his sleep about shoving a turnip in Jimmy Bones's mouth.

Christopher claims he got food poisoning from the shrimp hors d'oeuvres on the plane.

Tony eats a pear while he watches Annalisa have her nails trimmed. He and Annalisa eat massive prawns at a seaside café. After they argue, Tony wants to go back to the hotel but Annalisa invites him down to a family dinner. He despairs at how much Italians eat.

Paulie tries a plum from his hotel breakfast tray after sex.

Mobbed Up: Tony and crew sit down to watch an advance DVD bootleg of *The Godfather* with alternative takes. Paulie's favourite scene is where Michael Corleone says, 'I know it was you, Fredo.' Tony doesn't want to have another conversation about the Coppola trilogy. But he says his favourite scene is when Vito goes back to Sicily. Christopher can't get the DVD to work. Paulie says Paramount Pictures should get their shit together as the crew will be stealing thousands of copies.

Sleeping With the Fishes: Jimmy Bones, beaten to death with a ball-peen hammer by Pussy for seeing him with an FBI agent.

I Dream of Jeannie Cusamano: Tony has a dream about Annalisa. She is bending over an ancient stone wall, dressed in a toga. Tony is fucking her from behind while wearing the uniform of a Roman soldier.

Pussy has nightmares about Jimmy Bones revealing his secret. Pussy talks so loud in his sleep, he wakes up Angie in her adjoining bedroom.

Quote/Unquote: Tony scoffs when Paulie says the DVD has alternative takes of *The Godfather*. 'What, are you gonna call Coppola with ideas on how to fix it?'

Junior says any blood relations between the Sopranos and the Vittorios is well diluted. 'It's so far removed, by now Tonto's a closer cousin to you.'

Tony planned to give Don Vittorio a special golf club but Paulie has other advice when they see the Don is senile. 'Ton', you give this guy a golf club, he'll probably try to fuck it.'

Janice defends renewing her relationship with the old-school mobster Richie Aprile. 'Carm, Richie, because of his life experiences in prison, he has a sensitivity to the plight of women.'

Soundtrack: 'Perdido' by Sam Butera and the Witnesses. 'Con Te Partiro' by Andrea Bocelli. 'Marco Polo' by Jovanolfi. 'Piove' by Jovanolfi. 'Certamenta' by Madreblu. 'Cuore Ingrato' by Beniamino Gigli. 'Andalucia' by Pink Martini. 'Blood Is Thicker Than Water' by Wyclef Jean.

Surveillance Report: The series' creator, David Chase, makes a cameo appearance when Paulie is sitting at a café in Naples. Paulie calls out to the men sitting at the next table. Chase regards Paulie with contempt before turning away. Paulie is offended and walks off, muttering 'cock-suckers' under his breath.

In '46 Long', Paulie said that Americans ate shit before Italians gave them the gift of their cuisine. But, when Paulie actually gets to sample real Italian food, he doesn't enjoy the experience and asks for macaroni and gravy.

Tony confirms Carmela's statement in 'Pilot/The So-pranos' that his favourite scene from the *Godfather* trilogy is when Vito returns to Sicily.

The Verdict: 'You are your own worst enemy.' Tony goes to the old country on business and has problems adjusting to dealing with a woman boss. Carmela ponders her future when Angie Bonpensiero decides to divorce Pussy.

In Season One, the 'College' episode sent Tony away from home on business while Carmela stayed home and contemplated her situation. 'Commendatori' attempts the same trick but with less success as the stakes involved are much lower for everyone. Carmela's greatest danger seems to come from an Andrea Bocelli overload as 'Con Te Partiro' is played over and over again.

These problems are offset by the comedy cutaways to Paulie's interaction with Naples and its citizens, and the introduction of Furio. He seems destined to become a significant character in future episodes . . .

18
Big Girls Don't Cry

US Transmission Date: 13 February 2000
UK Transmission Date: 9 November 2000

Writer: Terence Winter
Director: Tim Van Patten
Cast: Linda Emond (Dahlia), Stephen Payne (Dominic),
Lydia Gaston (Rosie), Sasha Nesterov (Russian Man),
Elena Antonenko (Russian Woman),
Oni Faida Lampley (Cynthia),
Scott Lucy (Acting Student), Ajay Naidu (Omar),
Robert Prescott (Mitch), Phyllis Somerville (Brenda)

Storyline: Christopher calls at a local whorehouse to collect protection money, but the owner is short for the third week running.

Tony, Paulie and Silvio have a meal at Artie Bucco's Vesuvio restaurant. Tony asks Artie if he'll hire Furio as kitchen staff to prevent any problems with immigration. Tony will pay Furio's salary. Artie reluctantly agrees.

Christopher begins a class called 'Acting For Writers', which Adriana got him as a birthday present. He gives a false name, Chris MacEveety.

Tony asks Paulie to collect Furio from the airport. He also says Paulie is being promoted. From now on Pussy and Furio will report to Paulie and Silvio.

Melfi tells her therapist about the dream where Tony crashes his car. Dr Kupferberg suggests that treating a mobster gave her a vicarious thrill. She swears at her psychiatrist and walks out of the session.

Tony gets a phone message for his sister from the bank. Janice is trying to get a loan secured on Livia's house. Tony becomes enraged, smashing the phone and throwing it into a dishwasher. He rushes round to Livia's house but the door is answered by Richie, who is wearing only underwear. Richie and Janice are sleeping together again. Tony argues with Janice about the loan before disowning his sister.

In acting class, Christopher is given a scene from Tennessee Williams's *The Glass Menagerie* to prepare as homework.

The Sopranos host a welcome party for Furio. Pussy is unhappy about the new arrival. Tony is unhappy with Christopher's lack of focus. Carmela slams the door on Junior when he arrives to welcome Furio.

Christopher isn't happy with his scene and doesn't find Tennessee Williams's characters credible. He decides to get a different scene to act.

Tony visits Hesh on a business pretext. He wants advice about his blackouts. Hesh says Tony's father suffered from the same symptoms.

Tony takes his mistress Irina to his boat. But he gets into an argument with the Russian couple on a boat in the next mooring. Tony nearly crushes the Russian man's testicles before rushing away.

Late at night Tony retells these events to Hesh, who is trying hard to stay awake. They end up talking at cross purposes, ignoring what each other says.

Christopher wows the acting class with his efforts as James Dean's character in *Rebel Without a Cause*. He spontaneously cries while acting the scene. Embarrassed, he rushes out of the room.

Paulie and Pussy are having lunch at Vesuvio. They are joined by Furio from the kitchen. Pussy teases the Italian about his name. The New York mobster Johnny Sack arrives and Paulie asks Pussy to leave the table while they talk. Afterwards, Pussy meets with his FBI contact, Skip Lipari. They commiserate with each other about being passed over for promotion.

Dr Melfi tells her therapist she is thinking about taking Tony back as a patient. She thinks it will be very therapeutic for her. Dr Kupferberg points out that *this* is her therapy – Tony is her *patient*.

Tony sends Furio into the whorehouse to beat a warning into the late-paying owner. Melfi calls Tony on his car phone and invites him back into therapy. He is not sure he needs her help.

At acting class Christopher is paired with Mitch, the student who played his father in the *Rebel Without a Cause* scene. Mitch says one word and Christopher starts punching him before stomping out of the class. Later, Adriana speculates that the class raised uncomfortable feelings in Christopher about his father's early death.

Tony takes up Melfi's offer of a session. He wants to be in total control but she says this is impossible. Tony tries to goad her but the psychiatrist gives as good as she gets.

In the early hours Christopher gets up, unable to sleep. He junks his screenplay, throwing the printouts and floppy disks into a dumpster.

Deep and Meaningful: The final scene is the killer here. During his acting for the writers' class, Christopher bursts into tears in a scene, which leaves him embarrassed and ashamed. Made men don't cry, and what Christopher wants most of all is to be a made man. He rejects the acting class and attacks the fellow student who prompted him into crying. When Adriana says revealing your innermost feelings is the best kind of writing, she gives Christopher a lot to think about. He gets up in the middle of the night and sits down at his laptop. For a moment the viewer thinks Christopher will have been inspired to become a better writer. Instead he junks his screening, throwing it into the garbage. In effect, he runs away from his own, innermost feelings . . .

Mobspeak: Tony tells Paulie that he is getting a bump (promotion).

Bright Lights, Baked Ziti: At Vesuvio, Artie serves Tony, Paulie and Silvio a new dish, quail à la Bucco – baby quail stuffed with fennel sausage. Tony says that Furio makes the best mozzarella and suggests Artie hire him.

Tony eats slices of ham while watching the news on TV. He dips the slices into an open jar of mayonnaise.

AJ is carrying his lunch on a plate when Tony rips the telephone off the wall after hearing about Janice's loan application. Richie is cooking eggs at Livia's house when Tony arrives.

Carmela serves a finger buffet at Furio's welcome party. Junior brings a box of pignoli cookies, but she slams the door in his face.

Irina feeds junk food to the ducks at the dock until Tony stops her.

Paulie and Pussy are eating pasta at Vesuvio when Johnny Sack arrives. Paulie has a waitress keep Pussy's food warm so Pussy can leave the table.

Pussy eats steak and sweetcorn with Skip Lipari at a diner.

Dr Melfi says she is putting on weight. Her therapist warns Melfi to watch her intake of sugar and sugar substitutes.

Mobbed Up: Christopher tells the acting class that he wants to write for the movies, citing *Goodfellas* as an example.

Tony meets Paulie at the Lou Costello Memorial, which is dedicated to half of the famous comedy duo Abbott and Costello, who starred in eleven films between 1945 and 1955.

Melfi recalls her dream, which had a song from *The Wizard of Oz* as its soundtrack. She compares Tony to the character of Oz himself, a powerful and dominating male. She recalls watching the film on TV at her parents' house, hiding under a blanket with her sister.

At the acting class, the teacher gives out scenes from films for students to perform, including *Barefoot in the Park* and *The Glass Menagerie*. Christopher can't cope with being the Gentleman Caller in the latter, and manages to get it swapped for the James Dean role in *Rebel Without a Cause*. He fancies the idea of playing a Joe Pesci role and imitates the actor's performance in *Jimmy Hollywood* for Adriana.

Furio is surprised to have seen the Oscar-winning Italian film *Two Women*, starring Sophia Loren, on American TV, because it features a rape story. It would not be shown in Italy. His favourite TV show is *NYPD Blue*.

How Do You Feel?: Tony tries to turn Hesh into his therapist, without much success. He tells Hesh about a weird dream and his blackouts. Later he says he feels an aversion to his swimming pool. It depresses him so much he finds himself avoiding the back yard.

Tony initially rejects Dr Melfi's offer of a return to therapy. But he does go back. He tells her about Furio beating the owner of the whorehouse and says he wishes he had been there. The therapist asks whether he wanted to be giving the beating or taking it – Tony doesn't answer.

How Do You Feel, Doctor?: Dr Melfi interprets her dream about Tony as meaning she abandoned her patient. Dr Kupferberg suggests she treats Tony to get a vicarious thrill. Melfi swears at him and walks out of their session – exactly as Tony did during several sessions with her.

When she returns to therapy a week later, she recognises that her actions are imitating those of Tony. This brings her close to tears. She is thinking about taking him back as a patient. Melfi says it will be very therapeutic for her, but Dr Kupferberg points out the contradiction of this statement. Melfi says she doesn't have sexual feelings for Tony but she does have personal feelings for him. 'He can be such a little boy sometimes.'

I Dream of Jeannie Cusamano: Melfi retells her dream about Tony passing out while driving and crashing his car into a truck, as seen in 'Toodle-Fucking-oo'.

Tony tries to tell Hesh about a dream. In it Tony was at the beach, but he had a suit and shoes on. Hesh interrupts before Tony can say any more.

Quote/Unquote: Richie says he and Janice have history, but Tony doesn't think that's a good thing and offers a comparison. 'Yeah, Israel and fucking Palestine.'

Janice tells her brother that she is quite capable of getting a job. 'With your carpal tunnel syndrome? How you gonna hold a beggar's cup?' he says.

Christopher shows a lot of sympathy to a character's physical disability in *The Glass Menagerie*: 'She's a fucking gimp, for Christ's sake!'

Pussy complains about the new arrival, Furio. 'If ever there was a guy in desperate need of a fucking nickname!'

Soundtrack: 'Touch It' by Monifah. 'Big Girls Don't Cry' by Frankie Valli and the Four Seasons. 'You're Out of the Woods/Optimistic Voices' from *The Wizard of Oz* soundtrack. 'Rock the Boat' by the Hues Corporation. 'White Mustang II' by Daniel Lanois.

Surveillance Report: Tony berates Irina for giving junk food to some seabirds. He cites the experience of having a family of mallards living in his pool for two months in 'Pilot/The Sopranos' as proof of his expertise.

The Verdict: 'There's no cure for life.' Furio arrives in New Jersey and makes an immediate impact, while Tony promotes Paulie and sidelines Pussy. Meanwhile, Dr Melfi is drawn into taking Tony back as a patient.

This is a gem of an episode, packed with crackling dialogue and character moments. There are further intriguing revelations about Dr Melfi's state of mind and Christopher has to confront some demons of his own. The funniest moments come from Tony's attempts to turn Hesh into a substitute therapist as the two talk at total cross-purposes. Great stuff.

19
The Happy Wanderer

US Transmission Date: 20 February 2000
UK Transmission Date: 16 November 2000

Writer: Frank Renzulli
Director: John Patterson
Cast: John C Hensley (Eric Scatino), Felix Solis (Fishman), Paul Mazursky (Sunshine), Frank Sinatra Jr (himself),

Lewis J Stadlen (Dr Fried),
Adam Alexi-Malle (College Rep), RJ Brown (Cop),
Angela Covington (Gudren),
Barbara Gulan (Mrs Gaetano), La Tanya Hall (Hooker),
David McCann (Priest), Carmine Sirico (Dealer)

Storyline: Tony and Carmela accompany Meadow to her high school for an evening of presentations from college reps. Tony bumps into Artie Bucco and David 'Davie' Scatino, another friend from his high school days. Davie runs Ramsey Sports and Outdoor Equipment. He also likes to gamble. Davie asks about a very special card game Tony will be staging soon. Tony warns him off, saying the game is too serious for Davie and he could get hurt.

Tony tells Dr Melfi that he is full of anger all the time. He wants to beat up happy people he sees in the street, just because they are happy. Tony resents the fact that therapy makes him feel like a victim.

Davie has a run of bad luck at a card game hosted by Richie Aprile. He ends up owing Richie $8,000.

Meadow and Davie's son Eric practise a duet from the musical *Miss Saigon* for their high school cabaret. Performing in the show could improve their chances of getting into a good college.

Tony meets with Junior to discuss taking over the executive game. Junior established the high-stakes poker game with Tony's father thirty years before. He lets slip that Tony had another uncle called Ercoli, who was retarded. Ercoli spent his life in charity homes and died not long before Tony's father. Tony agrees to give Junior 15 per cent of the profits from the executive game.

Richie goes to the sports store to collect a weekly payment from Davie, but the gambler can't make his full payment. Richie bans Davie from any of Richie's card games until he's caught up on the payments.

Christopher buys some fish for the players at the executive game, accompanied by Matt and Sean. He tells them their role will be cleaning and serving the players, but warns them against talking to Silvio during the game.

The executive game gets started at the motel of which Tony owns 25 per cent. Among the players are Frank Sinatra Jr, Paulie, Silvio, Johnny Sack and Dr Fried, who specialises in penile implants. Davie goes to the motel and asks if he can join the game. Tony tries to dissuade him but Davie is adamant. Tony lends him $5,000 as his stake money.

Tony asks Matt to sweep under Silvio, who has spilled food on the floor. Silvio is losing badly and flies into a rage, ranting at Matt. Davie is having a run of good cards and is well ahead.

Next morning, Eric gives Meadow a lift to school in his four-wheel drive.

At the executive game Tony asks if everyone is ready to quit. Davie is down and owes Tony $45,000. Richie arrives at the game and gets angry when he finds Davie playing. He tries to hit Davie and the game quickly breaks up. Outside, a furious Tony sends Richie home. Tony goes back inside and lays down the law to Davie. He has just two days to pay back all the money he owes, or else he has to pay $2,250 in interest every week. Afterwards, early estimates put the profits from the executive game at about $80,000 for one night's work.

Tony tries to catch up on sleep at home but is awoken by Meadow and Eric practising their duet. Meadow tells him Aunt Barbara's father-in-law has died.

At the funeral Tony finds himself in the same room as his mother, who is brought along by Janice and Richie. In a side room Richie apologises for intruding on the executive game. As tax, Tony rules that Davie Scatino has to pay all of his debt back to Tony before Richie can have a penny.

On the way home Janice chides Richie about following Tony's orders.

Tony confronts Davie at the sports store – he missed his first payment. Tony punches his former friend twice in the head and demands money within 24 hours. Davie goes to Artie for help but Artie pleads poverty. Davie takes away his son's four-wheel-drive vehicle, because Eric didn't keep it clean.

Tony gives the car to Meadow, who recognises it as Eric's. She refuses the present but Tony says it was a by-product of his work, just like everything else in the house that Meadow uses every day.

At the cabaret Eric and Meadow argue about the car. Eric storms off, so Meadow gets to sing a solo instead.

Deep and Meaningful: Meadow gets a jolt of harsh reality in this episode. Tony gives her Eric Scatino's four-wheel drive as a present, but she recognises the vehicle and rejects it, running away to her room. Tony storms after his daughter and points out that everything Meadow has comes from the work he does. She has no right to take the moral high ground. Later Meadow finds herself defending Tony to an understandably angry Eric. He storms out of the cabaret, leaving her to sing alone. Meadow is forced to realise that others will judge her by the actions of her father, not just by what she does . . .

Mobspeak: Tony tells Christopher to give Davie five boxes of ziti (gambling chips in piles equivalent to $1,000 each). Tony wants to know whether the players are ready to close the lights (admit you have lost and end the game). Richie asks Tony to whom he should give the boost (an envelope of cash, given to families at christenings, marriages and funerals).

Mama Mia: Livia doesn't speak, but she sobs heartily at the funeral so everyone knows she's present.

When Dr Melfi asks if Livia makes him feel like a loser, Tony says they have wasted enough oxygen discussing his mother.

Bright Lights, Baked Ziti: Artie Bucco provided the food for the family evening at Meadow's high school. Tony says the food is so good it should guarantee Artie's daughter a place in any college.

Christopher buys enough Brazilian snapper for fifteen people and ten pounds of shrimp. The fish is an ingredient for pizziola.

At the executive game there is a side table covered in food, including cold meats, cheeses, fish and bread. Matt tries to sweep cheese out from under Silvio, who retaliates by ranting, raving and throwing his plate of ham, cheese and bread on the floor. He demands Matt get him more food and renames the wannabe gangster 'Cheese-fuck'. When Richie arrives, Tony tries to distract him by offering some nice, fresh lox.

Mobbed Up: Meadow is going to sing the theme song from *Titanic* as a solo after Eric refuses to do a duet.

How Do You Feel?: Tony describes his feelings to Dr Melfi by saying he'd like to smash her face into hamburger with a brick. He doesn't know why he's always angry, he just is. Tony says Dr Melfi makes him feel like a victim. 'I got the world by the balls and I can't stop feeling like a fucking loser.'

Sleeping With the Fishes: Tom Giglione Sr, who was blown off his roof by a gust of wind while adjusting a satellite dish. It happened the day after he retired, following a life of hard work and devotion to his family.

Quote/Unquote: Tony protests about Dr Melfi's methods, comparing them to those of other females in his life. 'Mother of Christ, is this a woman thing? You asked me how I'm feeling. I tell you how I'm feeling. And now you're gonna torture me with it.'

Junior dismisses Livia's protestations of poverty, saying that Johnny Boy Soprano left her a huge legacy when he died. 'She's like a woman with a Virginia ham under her arm, crying the blues 'cause she has no bread.'

Silvio goes into a lengthy rant about loving to have cheese at his feet, after Matt tries to sweep beneath Silvio's chair. 'I stick motherfucking provolone in my socks at night, so they smell like your sister's crotch in the morning!'

Davie Scatino proves himself to be a master of hypocrisy when he takes away his son's four-wheel drive to help offset his own gambling debts. 'Eric, accountability is everything.'

Soundtrack: A Muzak version of 'Spinning Wheel' plays in the mall. 'Tequila Sunrise' by the Eagles. 'Love Is Strange' by Micky and Silvia. Meadow and Eric practise 'Sun and Moon', a song from the musical *Miss Saigon*. 'The Happy Wanderer' by Frankie Yankovick.

Surveillance Report: Frank Sinatra Jr makes a creditable cameo appearance as one of the gamblers at the executive game.

David Scatino is played by Robert Patrick, who is best known as the T-1000 robot from *Terminator 2: Judgment Day*. Since appearing in *The Sopranos* Patrick has joined the cast of *The X Files* as Scully's new partner.

The Verdict: 'I don't do business with outside friends, you understand.' Tony takes over the fabled executive poker game, but it leads to more agita from Richie Aprile and problems for an old school friend, Davie Scatino.

Tony shows both sides of his nature in 'The Happy Wanderer' – the friendly family man who wants his daughter to get a good education, and the cold-blooded Family man who wants his own way. Davie makes the terrible transition from being a friend of Tony to someone who owes Tony money.

This episode works well in isolation but also sets up crucial plot threads for the rest of the season. The two wannabe gangsters Matt and Sean are treated like dirt, while Janice starts urging Richie to act against Tony. But it's the gambling debts incurred by Davie Scatino that could yet lead to Tony's downfall . . .

20
D-Girl

US Transmission Date: 27 February 2000
UK Transmission Date: 23 November 2000

Writer: Todd A Kessler
Director: Allen Coulter

Cast: Jon Favreau (himself), Sandra Bernhard (herself),
Janeane Garofalo (herself), Alicia Witt (Amy Safir),
Arthur Barnes (Security Guard),
Stephen Bienskie (Hotel Clerk),
John Devlin (Assistant Director),
Dominic Fumusa (Gregory Moltisanti),
Anderson Gabrych (UTA Receptionist),
Bryan Matzkow (Hotel manager),
Andrea Maulella (Michele Foreman),
Jason Minter (Bellman), Frank Pando (Agent Grasso),
Steve Porcelli (Matt Bonpensiero),
Elizabeth Reaser (Stace),
Asa Somers (Blaine Richardson)

Storyline: AJ steals his mother's car to give some girls a ride and scrapes it against the side of a parked truck.

Adriana and Christopher have drinks with cousin Gregory and his girlfriend, Amy Safir. She is head of development for the film star Jon Favreau, who is in New York for a film shoot. Amy asks after Christopher's screenplay. The crowd at the next table keep bumping Amy, so Christopher gets them to move on with a quiet word. Amy is impressed by his presence.

Afterwards Adriana suggests Christopher slip Jon his script. Adriana still has a copy even though Christopher junked the rest.

Carmela discovers the damage to the car. She and Tony interrogate AJ about his actions. He shocks them by saying there is no god. Meadow points out that AJ has been studying philosophy at school.

Skip Lipari comes to Pussy's home at eight in the morning, demanding answers about Tony's relationship with the Philadelphia mob. One of the Philly bosses was blown up by a bomb blast.

Tony tells Dr Melfi about AJ's outbursts. She suggests the teenager has discovered existentialism.

Christopher visits the film set with Amy and meets Jon Favreau. He impresses the actor with his use of colourful vernacular.

AJ tells his father that he doesn't want to be confirmed in church. He tells Tony he's been reading the philosopher, 'Nitch' (Nietzche). Tony says AJ is getting confirmed, whether he likes it or not.

Christopher takes Amy and Jon on a tour of New Jersey. Jon says his next project is a biopic of the gangster Crazy Joe Gallo. He wants Christopher to help make the film grittier and more true to life. Christopher recognises a badly disfigured person as a transvestite who was covered in acid by a mobster who didn't realise he'd been getting a blow job from a man.

Tony takes AJ to Pussy, who is his confirmation sponsor. Tony wants Pussy to talk some sense into the teenager.

Adriana is upset when she discovers that Christopher visited the film set and met Jon Favreau without her.

AJ discusses philosophy with Pussy's son, Matt.

Christopher calls on Amy at the Soho Grand hotel after finding Jon Favreau is not to be disturbed. They discuss his screenplay and end up having sex.

At Pussy's suggestion, AJ visits his grandmother in hospital. But she just makes him feel worse by saying life is a big nothing.

Christopher and Jon meet to discuss the mobster's screenplay. Christopher gives Jon his gun and frightens the actor by punching him and putting him in a headlock. Jon gives him some script suggestions while carefully wiping his own fingerprints off Christopher's gun.

Christopher arrives late for dinner with Adriana, Tony and Carmela. The talk is about weddings and food but Christopher gets angry and walks out. Adriana lets slip about Christopher's screenplay.

FBI Agents Lipari and Grasso put pressure on Pussy to wear a wire to AJ's confirmation and the party afterwards at the Soprano's house.

Christopher goes back to the Soho Grand and has sex with Amy again. He glances over Jon's script and notices that the transvestite incident has been written into it. Christopher gets enraged and demands that Jon take it out, but Favreau has already flown back to Hollywood.

Pussy's wife interrupts him when he is attaching the wire to his chest. He attacks her and has to be pulled off Angie by his son Matt.

Christopher confronts Amy about Jon's script but she is about to fly back to Hollywood. She brushes him off but gets angry when Christopher calls her a D-Girl. Her cool image is shattered.

At AJ's confirmation party Pussy tries to get info about the Philly mob from Tony but they are interrupted. Tony and Carmela catch AJ and his friends smoking marijuana in the garage. AJ goes to his room. Pussy talks to the teenager, saying Tony would take a bullet for AJ.

Christopher finally arrives at the party. Tony gives him one last chance. If Christopher is still there in ten minutes, Tony will assume he is committed to Tony. Otherwise, he never wants to see Christopher again. The would-be movie writer steps outside to contemplate his future. The Sopranos gather for a family photo but Pussy is missing. He is upstairs in a bathroom, sobbing.

Christopher makes his final decision. He goes back inside the house . . .

Deep and Meaningful: The closing scenes show two central characters at a turning point in their lives. Pussy sobs in a bathroom at AJ's confirmation party, as he grasps the scale of his betrayal to Tony. Christopher sits outside the house on the front steps, deciding whether to pursue his Hollywood dreams or stay loyal to Tony and the Family. They speak no dialogue but the quality of the writing leading to these scenes and the acting from Vincent Pastore and Michael Imperioli is eloquence itself.

Mobspeak: At the film set, Christopher suggests replacing the word 'bitch' with 'buchiach' (cunt) in Sandra Bernhard's dialogue. Christopher calls Jon a mezzofinook (half gay, bisexual). Pussy says Tony is a stand-up guy (someone who refuses to rat out the Family, no matter what the pressure or promise).

Mama Mia: Tony says Livia just showed her true colours when she tried to have him killed.

Pussy sends AJ to visit Livia because she has age, wisdom and stuff. She just depresses him even further by saying he shouldn't expect happiness, people will let him down and he will die alone. Life is a big nothing, says Livia.

Bright Lights, Baked Ziti: Skip Lipari reminds Pussy that he had lobster fra diavolo with the Philly mobster Waldemar Wyczchuk in Atlantic City.

Christopher takes Amy and Jon for pizza and soft drinks in New Jersey. Later he takes a New Jersey sandwich to the Soho Grand for Jon but the film star is not to be disturbed.

Livia picks at some scrambled eggs in hospital while talking to AJ.

Jon has ordered some room service food for his meeting with Christopher but the mobster snorts cocaine instead.

When Christopher joins Adriana, Tony and Carmela for dinner, the talk is all about food and weddings. Adriana has ordered some pasta fajioli for Christopher and a plate of antipasto to share. The restaurant has some rare imported salami. Christopher finally rebels when the conversation shifts to caterers. 'I'm so sick and tired of hearing you people talk about food, food, food! That's all anybody ever talks about is prosciutto, cheese, and fucking fava beans. I'm drowning here.'

There's a buffet at AJ's confirmation party.

Mobbed Up: The level of cross-media mentions goes through the roof in this episode as Hollywood comes to *The Sopranos* in a big way. Eyes down for a very full house of pop-cultural references.

Amy Safir used to work for the film director Quentin Tarantino. She's now head of development for the actor Jon Favreau, who wrote and starred in the film *Swingers*. Adriana says Favreau's co-star Vince Vaughn is very cute. Amy says mob-theme stories are always hot.

Christopher says Amy dressed as if she were in *The Addams Family*.

When Christopher visits the film set he recognises Sandra Bernhard from Martin Scorcese's *The King of Comedy* and Janeane Garofalo from *The Truth About Cats and Dogs*, which co-starred Uma Thurman.

Jon recognises an incident related by Christopher as the basis for a scene from *The Godfather*. Christopher says *Swingers* has a 'pussy-assness' to it. He remembers seeing Jon in *Deep Impact*. Jon wants to make a biopic about Joe Gallo but Christopher points out this was already done in the film *The Gang That Couldn't Shoot Straight*. Amy ascribes Christopher's anecdote about the acid-covered transvestite to *The Crying Game*, but Jon tells her this is a real story.

Christopher tells Jon that the acting kind of blew in *Swingers*. He preferred Tom Hanks's acting in *Saving Private Ryan*.

Christopher reads part of Jon's screenplay about Joe Gallo. It's called *Crazy Joe* and is co-written by Ambit Al. Christopher gets angry about the inclusion of his anecdote but Amy refuses to have that sequence removed. She says it has been faxed to the director Oliver Stone and he's agreed to be attached to the project. The scene based on Christopher's anecdote is his favourite thing.

Amy reads in the film industry trade journal *Variety* that the director Robert Rodriguez is to remake *Viva Zapata* for Miramax. She rejects Christopher's script because studios are adopting a wait-and-see attitude on Mafia-related projects because of the weakness of the first weekend foreign-box-office performance of *Mickey Blue Eyes*, a mob comedy starring Hugh Grant.

How Do You Feel?: Tony tells Dr Melfi that his mother is dead to him. The therapist suggests AJ may be feeling intense dread, having realised that death is the only absolute truth. Tony thinks his son may be on to something.

Sleeping With the Fishes: Waldemar Wyczchuk, a Philadelphia mobster blown up in a bomb blast. The FBI are trying to make a connection between the bombing and the Sopranos.

Quote/Unquote: Tony misunderstands when Dr Melfi suggests his son may have stumbled on to existentialism. 'Fucking Internet.'

Amy talks a lot of shit but this line is one of her finest, when she discusses the guns being used by two lesbians: 'The silencers underscore their voiceless place in society.'

Tony tells his son to do what Carmela wants. 'She knows that even if God is dead, you're still gonna kiss his ass.'

Tony shares a significant truth with Christopher. 'When you're married you'll understand the importance of fresh produce.'

Soundtrack: 'Swingtown' by the Steve Miller Band. 'Rhiannon' by Fleetwood Mac. 'Caught My Mind' by Pushmonkey. 'Vedi Maria' by Emma Shapplin.

Surveillance Report: The actors Jon Favreau, Sandra Bernhard and Janeane Garofalo all play themselves. Amy Safir is played by Alicia Witt, who is probably best known for playing Cybill Shepherd's daughter in the sitcom *Cybill*.

Christopher insults Amy by calling her a D-Girl, which is slang for development girl – one of the lowest rungs on the Hollywood ladder.

The Verdict: 'Be a good Catholic for fifteen fucking minutes! Is that so much to ask?' AJ discovers existentialism and has a crisis of faith, while Christopher gets close to his Hollywood dream and has a crisis of loyalty. Pussy is under pressure from the FBI to deliver results.

This is one of the funniest episodes in Season Two, shot through with perfect parodies of Hollywood double-talk. The character of Amy is hardly able to speak without spouting trite pleasantries and borrowed phrases. But the funniest material comes from AJ's brush with various philosophical concepts.

For Pussy, events are starting to spiral out of control. He nearly beats his wife and – against all his instincts – wears a wire into Tony's home. Christopher survives his moment of crisis, choosing to remain with Tony and the Family. That decision could have fatal consequences . . .

21
Full Leather Jacket

US Transmission Date: 5 March 2000
UK Transmission Date: 30 November 2000

Writers: Robin Green and Mitchell Burgess
Director: Allen Coulter
Cast: Saundra Santiago (Jeannie and Joan Cusamano),
Vinnie Orofino (Bryan Spatafore),
Susan Blackwell (Therapist), Joseph Carino (Secretary),
Raymond Franza (Donny K),
Patty McCormack (Liz La Cerva),
Marek Przystup (Stasiu),
Stelio Savante (Gaetano Giarizzo)

Storyline: Hunter Scangarello has been given an early acceptance into Reed College. Meadow wants to go to Berkeley in San Francisco but Tony forbids it.

Christopher cracks a safe, assisted by Matt and Sean.

Carmela can't sleep for worrying about where Meadow gets into college. Great grades aren't enough any more: you need an extra edge to get into the best universities.

Silvio and Paulie visit Richie and ask him to build a ramp to make Beansie Gaeta's home more wheelchair-accessible. Richie refuses.

Carmela approaches her neighbour, Jeannie Cusamano, whose twin sister Joan is regional secretary of the Georgetown University alumni association. Carmela asks if Joan could write a letter of recommendation for Meadow and Jeannie reluctantly agrees to ask her sister.

Richie visits Beansie in hospital and threatens to cripple him further. Beansie knows nothing about the ramp request and wants nothing from Richie.

Christopher forces his way into Adriana's mother's house. He proposes to Adriana with a three-carat diamond ring – she accepts.

Junior is visiting Tony at home when Richie arrives, still complaining about the ramp. Tony says it was his idea. Richie gives Tony a prized possession, a tan leather jacket Richie took off another mobster many years ago in a fight. A bemused Tony accepts the gift but doesn't grasp its significance to Richie, who believes it will help him let go of the past.

Carmela intercepts a letter to Meadow from Berkeley, seeking more information to process her college application. She puts the letter in the trash.

Christopher, Matt and Sean crack another safe. Christopher tells the two wannabe mobsters that Tony's cut from this job will come out of their profits.

Carmela retrieves the letter from the bin and leaves it out for Meadow.

Richie's men go to the Gaeta house to install the ramp.

Matt and Sean are introduced to Richie, who complains that Christopher has an attitude. Richie indicates he is willing to let Matt and Sean work for him.

Jeannie Cusamano visits her sister, who is a lawyer. Jeannie tries to get Joan to write the letter of recommendation for Meadow but she refuses.

Janice and Richie join the Sopranos for Sunday family dinner. Carmela gets a phone call from Jeannie about Joan's refusal.

Next day Carmela visits Joan at her office and politely bullies her into writing the letter for Meadow.

Matt and Sean see Tony at the Bada Bing!. They follow him into the toilets and try to engage him in conversation. Tony storms out after Sean mentions work in a room that could be wire-tapped.

Richie is summoned to Satriale's, where Paulie and Silvio complain that Richie's men did only half the job on Beansie's house. Richie took the men away to make alterations to Livia's house. Tony arrives and Richie asks him about the jacket. Richie proudly tells the others about it.

Jeannie visits Carmela to say Joan has written a letter for Meadow.

Furio and an associate visit Matt and Sean at their apartment to collect Tony's cut from the safe job – $7,500. Furio demands another $1,000 from them, which they meekly surrender.

Christopher and Adriana are living together again. Christopher has stopped taking drugs so he can be completely focused.

Richie takes food to Carmela as thanks for the Sunday dinner. The husband of the Sopranos' maid Lilliana arrives to collect a television set. Richie is shocked to see him wearing the leather jacket.

Matt and Sean realise they are getting nowhere as mobsters. They decide to take drastic action to get ahead.

Carmela and Meadow argue. Carmela almost tells Meadow about her efforts to get the teenager into Georgetown but bites her tongue.

Matt and Sean ambush Christopher. Sean shoots him repeatedly but is killed by a lucky shot from Christopher. Matt runs away while Christopher passes out, bleeding profusely.

Matt goes to Richie for help but is chased away by the furious mobster.

Christopher is in intensive care, surrounded by his family and friends. They do not know if he will survive the night . . .

Deep and Meaningful: Just like Tony, Carmela is determined to do the best for her children. In this episode she shows herself to be just as ruthless as Tony but far more subtle in her methods. Rather than brute force, she uses force of will to get Joan Cusamano to write a letter of recommendation to Georgetown University on behalf of Meadow. Carmela politely bullies Jeannie Cusamano into asking on her behalf, but, when that fails, Carmela uses direct action. Her smiling approach unnerves the highly professional lawyer and gets Carmela the letter of recommendation. She succeeds where Tony would have failed . . .

Mobspeak: Sean wonders how many stockings a company has to sell to pay the nut (the bottom line) on a factory. Matt is surprised that Big Pussy started out chipping safes (cracking a safe by chipping it open with a hammer and chisel). Christopher says Pussy stepped up (went to war) for Johnny Soprano during the unrest of 1983. Matt says it would be an honour to kick upstairs (pay part of the profits from a crime to the boss) to Tony Soprano.

Bright Lights, Baked Ziti: The Sopranos are eating Chinese takeaway for dinner when it is announced that Hunter has got into Reed.

Junior uses grocery shopping as an excuse to visit Tony. Junior's assistant Bacala has a green vegetable, arugala rabe. Tony warns him not to drench the leaves in oil. Bacala says Junior likes to mop the plate with bread afterwards.

Matt tells Sean not to eat burritos before doing a job, because his farts are so noxious as a result.

The Sopranos have a crown roast of meat for Sunday family dinner.

Carmela takes a ricotta cheese pie with pineapples to Joan Cusamano.

Silvio and Paulie have a plate of pastries with their coffee outside Satriale's. Tony joins them and scoffs an almond croissant.

Jeannie Cusamano returns the pie plate to Carmela. She says Joan's family loved the delicious ricotta pie.

Richie takes a plate of tripe and tomatoes to Carmela as thanks for the Sunday family dinner. Richie says he and Carmela must be the only two people who still like tripe. He's probably right.

Mobbed Up: Junior mentions that someone has a bootleg copy of *The Mummy* before it was even in cinemas. Richie says the tapes are real Hollywood-quality broadcast movies, without time codes or blurry pictures.

How Do You Feel?: Tony is bothered about giving Eric Scatino's car to Meadow. He knew she would freak out before he gave it to her. Tony says he spent years shielding

Meadow from certain truths and now he is rubbing her nose in them. Melfi suggests Tony was preparing his daughter for reality and life outside the family home. He denies any suggestion that what he did was noble.

Sleeping With the Fishes: Sean Giamonte, killed by a single shot to the head from Christopher during the ambush.

Quote/Unquote: Tony reveals his sensitivity to gay men when Meadow talks about how many Nobel Prize winners live in San Francisco. 'Nobel Prize for what, packing fudges?'

Tony sees Richie arrive. 'I was wondering why the squirrels went quiet.'

Richie says Christopher's nose is like a natural canopy. 'Did you ever notice he's the only motherfucker who can smoke a cigarette in the rain with his hands tied behind his back?'

Tony says he wants Richie where he can see him, and Carmela agrees. 'That's what we mean when we say family.'

Soundtrack: 'Baker Street' by Gerry Rafferty. 'Dancing in the Dark' by Tony Bennett. 'Fields of Gold' by Sting. 'Up 'N Da Club' by 2nd II None.

Surveillance Report: The title of this episode alludes to a Stanley Kubrick film, *Full Metal Jacket*, about Vietnam and the dehumanising effect of the war.

The roles of the twin sisters Jeannie and Joan Cusamano are both played by the same actress, Saundra Santiago.

Adriana's mother's name is Liz.

This episode breaks the norm of having a song play out over the closing credits. Instead there is just the sound of Christopher's life-support machine, emphasising the uncertain ending.

The Verdict: 'You got to shut one door before another one can open.' Richie tries to reach out to Tony as Christopher puts his life in order – but both suffer major reversals. Carmela uses all her mob-wife charms to improve Meadow's chances of getting into Georgetown University.

This episode is a solid, workmanlike instalment made much more memorable by the attempted hit. 'Full Leather Jacket' gently develops a range of subplots, then creates the show's first true cliffhanger ending. The shooting of Christopher is all the more shocking because the audience knows at the back of its mind that almost every character in *The Sopranos* is expendable, unlike in most television series.

However, the twin irritants of Junior and Livia are conspicuous by their absence in this episode and even the scene with Dr Melfi feels like an afterthought. When Tony questions the value of his session, he seems to be speaking the subconscious words of the viewer …

22
From Where To Eternity

US Transmission Date: 12 March 2000
UK Transmission Date: 7 December 2000

Writer: Michael Imperioli
Director: Henry J Bronchtein
Cast: Brian Agular (Jimmy), Seth Barrish (Doctor),
Michael Cannis (Detective #2),
Tom Cappadona (Daniel King),
Nancy Cassaro (Joanne Moltisanti),
Scottie Epstein (Quickie G),
John Christopher Jones (Kevin Cullen),
Peter McRobbie (Father Felix), Judy Reyes (Michelle),
James Sioutis (Detective #1), Lisa Valens (Felicia Anne),
Gameela Wright (Nurse)

Storyline: Two days after being shot, Christopher is still in intensive care. Tony and his crew plead ignorance when questioned by the police about Matt Bevilaqua. They plan to deal with the surviving assassin themselves. Richie and Janice visit the hospital. Richie says a drug dealer named Quickie G may know something about Matt's hiding place. Gabriella Dante tells Carmela that the mistress of a mobster called Ralph Rutaldo has just given birth to Ralph's illegitimate child.

Tony and Carmela go home but Carmela can't sleep. She says Tony should have a vasectomy to save the family the same shame as the Rutaldos.

Christopher's heart stops. The doctors manage to revive him and operate again to stop internal bleeding. Carmela prays for Christopher's recovery and that God should grant him the gift of vision. Christopher survives the operation, but the surgeon says he was clinically dead for about a minute. Christopher asks to see Tony and Paulie. He tells them about a vision he had of hell. It was an Irish bar where every day is St Patrick's Day. Christopher's father was at the bar, along with Mikey Palmice and Brendan Filone. Mikey gave Christopher a message for Tony and Paulie: 'Three o'clock'.

At a therapy session, Tony says he doesn't believe Christopher will go to hell. He says only the worst people deserve hell, like psychopaths who kill for pleasure, cannibals, child molesters and people like Adolf Hitler. Dr Melfi asks Tony if he is going to hell, but he doesn't believe so. He likens himself to a soldier in a war, following codes and orders. Dr Melfi challenges Tony's belief that he is trying to preserve old Italian values of honour, family and loyalty. He gets angry and accuses her of making a moral judgment on his actions.

Paulie is wide awake at three in the morning, fretting about the cryptic message from Mikey. He visits Christopher in hospital and asks questions about the vision. Paulie decides Christopher visited purgatory instead of hell because it wasn't hot and nobody had horns on their head.

At her own therapy session, Dr Melfi admits to taking pills and drinking alone. She is afraid for herself and her son after passing judgment on Tony.

Pussy meets with his FBI handler, Agent Skip Lipari. Pussy believes Tony is suspicious of him. Skip suggests Pussy try to get into Tony's favour again.

Carmela visits Christopher in hospital. She believes he has been blessed with a second chance and says she will pray for him every day.

Carmela and Tony argue about the vasectomy. AJ drops a plate of food on the kitchen floor and Tony shouts at his son for being fat.

Paulie keeps having nightmares about hell. His goomah suggests he visit a psychic in Nyack.

Quickie G approaches Pussy with word on Matt's hiding place.

Paulie goes to the psychic, who sees the ghosts of all Paulie's victims around the mobster. The psychic talks to Paulie's first victim and Mikey Palmice, who reveal things only they could know. Paulie is shocked. He talks to Tony about what happened, but Tony dismisses it as nonsense.

Tony goes home and apologises to AJ for shouting at him. They are overheard by Carmela, who has a phone call for Tony from Pussy.

Tony and Pussy find Matt and take him to a deserted snack bar. Matt says shooting Christopher was all Sean's idea and that Richie wasn't involved. Tony and Pussy murder Matt.

Paulie confronts his parish priest, demanding answers about what the psychic had to say. The mobster says he should have absolution from all his past sins because of his many donations to the church.

Tony and Pussy share a joke and a meal after the killing.

Tony goes home and volunteers to have the vasectomy, but Carmela has changed her mind. She might want another baby when Meadow leaves for college. Carmela wants Tony to be faithful – they make love.

Deep and Meaningful: Paulie has a long night of the soul in this episode as he tries to make sense of Christopher's message from beyond life. But his religious beliefs seem somewhat simple-minded. He believed he could purchase absolution from his sins until his encounter with the psychic. Afterwards he confronts his parish priest and demands to know why he doesn't have immunity from divine prosecution. He accuses Father Felix of slacking off and leaving him unprotected. For Paulie, even eternal damnation could be avoided by bribery.

Bright Lights, Baked Ziti: Pussy frets about an incident involving six sandwiches – four with ham, salami and cappicola, one with eggplant (aubergine), the other with tomato and mozzarella. Tony claimed to have ordered the eggplant when Pussy knew he had ordered it and Tony had ordered tomato and mozzarella. Tony let Pussy eat the eggplant sandwich. But Pussy believes Tony gave him a suspicious glance as he surrendered the sandwich.

Christopher's mother offers to bring her son some peppers and eggs on round bread for breakfast.

AJ drops food on the kitchen floor. Tony rants at his son for eating again just an hour after dinner.

Paulie worries about what the psychic told him but Tony is unimpressed. Tony says Paulie would go to hell for eating steak in India, which proves religion is meaningless.

Tony brings a pizza to share with AJ when he apologises. Tony doesn't get a chance to eat but AJ scoffs a slice.

After killing Matt, Tony and Pussy eat beef at Duke's Stockyard Inn.

How Do You Feel?: Tony dismisses Christopher's vision as bullshit, a dream combined with morphine. Tony sees himself as a soldier and they don't go to hell for killing other people – it's part of war. He says people like him want to stay Italian and preserve the things that mean something to them – honour, family and loyalty. He is infuriated when Dr Melfi passes judgment on what he does.

How Do You Feel, Doctor?: Dr Melfi is in tears when she relates what happened at her session with Tony. She wonders if she was insensitive, or whether she did it deliberately because she hates Tony. She fears for herself and her son, having told Tony that Jason is a student at Bard. Dr Melfi says she took Tony back as a patient because she felt a professional and ethical responsibility. She didn't want to judge Tony: she wanted to treat him. But now she *has* judged, and she is afraid.

Sleeping With the Fishes: Matt Bevilaqua, shot more than a dozen times in the chest by Tony and Pussy for the attempted hit on Christopher. Christopher Moltisanti was clinically dead for about a minute, but he got better.

I Dream of Jeannie Cusamano: Christopher says he had a vision of hell. He saw a tunnel and a white light. Then he was at an Irish bar called the Emerald Piper, where it was St Patrick's Day every day. Mikey Palmice and Brendan Filone were there playing dice with two Roman soldiers and a bunch of Irish guys, and the Irish were winning every throw. Mikey was wearing an old-fashioned pinstripe gangster's suit. There was a bouncer at the bar who predicted Christopher would be coming to the bar when he died.

Christopher's father was at the bar and he was losing every hand of cards he played. Every night at midnight he is murdered the same way he was murdered in life, and it's painful. Christopher doesn't think it was hot at the bar and nobody had horns or buds for horns, like goats.

Quote/Unquote: Gabriella Dante notices that Adriana has pinned a brooch of Pope John Paul II on Christopher's hospital gown. 'You got his holiness, that's good. He got shot too and survived.'

Paulie is reassured that Christopher's vision can't have been of hell, because it wasn't hot. 'Hell is hot. That's never been disputed by anybody.'

Dr Melfi ponders her situation with Tony. 'I'm living in a moral never-never land with this patient.'

Tony tells Pussy a joke about a poor man who bought his wife a pair of slippers and a dildo. A rich man asks about the choice of gifts. 'And the poor man says, "She don't like the slippers she can go fuck herself." '

Soundtrack: 'My Lover's Prayer' by Otis Redding. 'Used Ta Be My Girl' by the Ojays. 'King Nothing' by Metallica. 'Mona Lisa' by the Starlite Orchestra.

Surveillance Report: Carmela is reading *Memoirs of a Geisha* by Arthur Golden. The book appears in two further episodes this season. Paulie uses the name of the British poet Ted Hughes when he visits the psychic in Nyack.

Hughes was metaphorically haunted by the death of his wife Sylvia Plath, who committed suicide. Gabriella Dante is played by Maureen Van Zandt, the wife of Steven Van Zandt, who plays her screen husband, Silvio Dante. This episode is written by Michael Imperioli, who plays the role of Christopher Moltisanti.

The Verdict: 'He was dead. Science said he was dead.' Christopher has a near-death experience which leaves the Family members pondering the eternal consequences of their actions. Tony and Pussy execute Matt Bevilaqua in retribution for the attempted hit, while Dr Melfi passes judgment on her patient.

The aftermath of Christopher's shooting produces one of Season Two's best episodes. Many of the key characters are brought face to face with the hypocrisy of their beliefs but none are able to change. Dr Melfi is drawn ever closer to the abyss by her sessions with Tony but cannot resolve her dilemma. Unlike so many television series, *The Sopranos* offers no quick solutions or trite morals for its stories, and this episode is a great example.

As this instalment draws to a close, Carmela contemplates having another baby when Meadow goes away to college. Could there be a new mouth to feed in the Soprano household soon? That will have to wait, as a new crisis threatens Tony because of his actions in this episode . . .

23
Bust Out

US Transmission Date: 19 March 2000
UK Transmission Date: 14 December 2000

Writers: Frank Renzulli, Robin Green and Mitchell Burgess
Director: John Patterson
Cast: Susan Campanaro (Mother at Mall),
Janis Dardaris (Karen), Mitch Holleman (Boy at Mall),

Olga Merediz (Fran), Chuck Montgomery (Larry Arthur),
Antone Pagan (Detective Ramos),
Holly Regan (Carol Arthur),
Vince Viverito (Detective Giardina)

Storyline: A concerned citizen, Larry Arthur, identifies
Tony Soprano from a mugshot as one of two men he saw
driving away from the scene of Matt Bevilaqua's shooting.
Arthur picks Tony from a book of mugshots, not knowing
the true identity of who he has linked to the murder.

Tony meets Richie at a mall to discuss business. Richie
complains that Barone Sanitation is overcharging him for
tipping garbage. Tony says he will see about getting Richie
a better rate.

Tony tells Carmela he wants to spend more time with
AJ. Tony thinks his son needs toughening up.

Tony, his crew and Richie have lunch at the Ramsey
Outdoor sports equipment store. Davie Scatino is ordering
large quantities of picnic coolers, mineral water and books
of airline tickets on instructions from Tony – all of it
charged to the store.

FBI Agent Harris and Detective Harold Giardina from
the Essex County Task Force come to Tony's house. They
want him to come to the police station to talk about Matt
Bevilaqua, but Tony declines the invitation.

Pussy meets with Agent Skip Lipari. Skip demands to
know if Pussy was with Tony when he murdered Matt.
Pussy denies all knowledge. Skip says a witness puts Tony
at the scene. He demands that Pussy wear a wire to record
Tony talking about the shooting.

Tony talks with his lawyer about the case. Neil Mink
advises Tony to stall for time and not to give law
enforcement any excuse to arrest him.

Carmela meets with other mothers to plan for the
graduation party for Meadow's class. Afterwards, Christine Scatino stays behind to talk with Carmela. Christine
is picked up by her brother, a decorator called Vic Musto.
Carmela gets his business card because she wants the

dining room redecorated. There is an immediate attraction between Vic and Carmela.

Davie Scatino considers blowing his own head off but is interrupted by Christine arriving home.

Janice and Richie have sex on the couch in Livia's house. Richie holds a gun to Janice's head as he takes her from behind. She talks dirty with him but irritates Richie by saying he should be boss as they fuck. Richie wants to remain loyal but Janice suggests he talk to Junior. They are interrupted by Livia coming down from her bedroom on a stairlift.

Carmela has an erotic dream about Vic. She wakes up feeling guilty but Tony isn't in bed with her.

Tony and Pussy wait for Paulie and Furio at Ramsey Outdoor. Paulie says there's a witness who saw Tony at the crime scene. Tony decides to make preparations in case he has to go on the run.

Carmela and Christine have lunch at Vesuvio. Christine says Davie has a serious gambling problem, but the store is safe because it's in her name. She says Vic is a widower – his wife died of breast cancer.

Tony invites AJ for a trip to the movies but his son wants to go to the mall with his friends. Tony lets him go but is disappointed.

Tony tells Dr Melfi he may be going to prison for a long time. She says he seems scared. Tony doesn't believe he deserves jail.

Paulie and Tony meet that night at Ramsey Outdoor. Paulie hasn't been able to find the witness yet. Tony sends Paulie home, then discovers Davie sleeping in a tent in the store. Davie says some of the airline tickets have arrived. He asks why Tony let him into the card game that got him into debt. Tony says it's his nature to take from others.

AJ comes third in his race at a swimming meet, watched by Carmela. AJ is disappointed Tony didn't attend, breaking a promise.

Tony takes $400,000 to his lawyer for safekeeping. If Tony has to lam it, he wants Mink to make the money available to Carmela.

Tony and Carmela argue about his broken promise. Carmela becomes furious with Tony for shutting her out and attacks him. He throws her on to a sofa and she storms off to the bedroom.

Meadow gets home and finds her father alone, drinking in the dark. Tony says everything he does is for his children.

Vic and his assistant Ramone redecorate the dining room. Carmela takes Vic into a downstairs bathroom to discuss its décor and they kiss passionately. Both excited and embarrassed, they stop and Vic returns to the redecorating.

Richie and Janice visit Junior, bringing him goods from Ramsey Outdoor. Richie tries to talk Junior into killing Tony but Junior won't have it. He warns Richie to be careful of Janice.

Meadow gets letters from the colleges she applied to. She visits Livia to share the good news. Meadow was accepted by Berkeley, NYU and BU and is on the wait list for Columbia, Penn and Georgetown.

Vic phones Carmela to talk about what happened between them. Vic says he has two jobs booked for the next day and he could go to the other job while Ramone finishes the job for Carmela. She suggests Ramone go to the other job so she and Vic can talk over lunch. He agrees.

Larry Arthur's wife sees a newspaper article which mentions that Matt was an associate of the Sopranos and the suspect is a high-ranking Mafia member. Larry is terrified of any reprisal against him.

Vic meets Davie in a bar. Davie says he has gambled away everything – his savings, the business, even his son Eric's college fund. Vic offers to pay for Eric's education. Davie says he can't go to the police because he owes money to the Sopranos.

Paulie calls Tony to say the witness has withdrawn his statement – Tony is in the clear.

Tony tells Dr Melfi about meeting Annalisa in Italy and how she said he brought his troubles on himself. Dr Melfi agreed that was at the root of things.

Tony gives Beansie $50,000 to give to the spinal-cord injury foundation.

Carmela prepares an elaborate lunch for Vic but it is Ramone who comes to finish the decorating.

Liquidators close down Ramsey Outdoor and break up the business. Davie Scatino will be declared bankrupt.

Tony takes AJ out in his boat and lets him steer.

Deep and Meaningful: This episode is packed with moments of Tony under pressure when he is facing a murder charge. But perhaps the most revealing sequence is in the second scene, where Tony is waiting for Richie at the mall. He hears a small boy call out for his mother and Tony flashes back to murdering Matt Bevilaqua. The wannabe mobster cried out for his mother as Tony and Pussy shot him repeatedly. This is one of the first examples shown of Tony being troubled by a specific murder he has committed.

Mobspeak: Paulie says the FBI have an eyeball witness (someone who is willing to testify they saw Tony at a crime scene). Tony tells Davie he is not the first guy to get busted out (bankrupted by mobsters ordering goods through a legitimate business but never paying the bills).

Mama Mia: Livia overreacts when Janice suggests buying a second television set for Livia to have in her bedroom. 'Listen to her. Like Rose Kennedy with all our money to throw around.'

Livia complains to Meadow that Janice never locks the front door. Livia doesn't trust that new mailman.

Bright Lights, Baked Ziti: Tony and his crew order cases of Ramlosa mineral water through the books of Ramsey Outdoor. They charge takeaway to the store, including four pizzas and a chicken-and-peppers sandwich for Richie.

When Carmela and Christine go to Vesuvio for lunch, Artie offers to make them a special tasting menu. He also suggests they try some Ramlosa mineral water, on which he got a great deal.

Carmela makes sandwiches for Vic and Ramone. Vic says he is hungry for a home-cooked meal – his late wife was a gourmet cook.

Janice takes Junior some salami and eggs.

Livia is watching an infomercial for kitchen equipment when Meadow visits. The equipment enables the user to make homemade sausage, pasta and even chocolate pasta for children.

Carmela invites Vic for lunch. She offers to cook a chicken, and serve it with salad and a nice bottle of Barollo. Next day Carmela is cooking up a storm when Ramone arrives instead of Vic.

Mobbed Up: Junior is watching a daytime soap opera when Janice and Richie visit. Junior says one character is a whore who fucked an arson investigator in a previous episode.

Tony watches a show about General Patton on the History Channel.

How Do You Feel?: Tony is sad that his son would rather go to the mall than be with his father. Dr Melfi asks Tony how he feels about the idea that he could be sent to prison. Tony says he wants to stay around until his children have grown up and left the house. After that he doesn't care if the government gives him the electric chair. He doesn't know how he feels. Dr Melfi says he seems scared.

When the witness recants his testimony, Tony feels relieved. He recalls meeting Annalisa and says she was right – he brings his troubles on himself. But Tony is feeling so good about avoiding the murder charge he waives the rest of the therapy session.

I Dream of Jeannie Cusamano: Tony has a brief flashback to murdering Matt Bevilaqua, triggered by a small boy calling for his mother at a mall.

Carmela has an erotic dream about Vic. She mentions the dream to his sister Christine, but says Vic was wallpapering her dining room. (Never heard it called that before!)

Quote/Unquote: Vic says he would never get involved with a married woman like Carmela Soprano because he respects the wedding ring. His sister agrees: 'Especially that ring. Probably came off a dead person's finger.'

Tony mentions a mobster who ended up in Elvis country. Furio doesn't understand, so Paulie explains: 'Anywhere there are no Jews or Italians.'

Paulie says it is difficult getting information from inside the FBI, especially compared with local law enforcement. 'Local cops, you buy them a Christmas tree, they'll give you their grandmother.'

Tony sums himself up quite neatly by alluding to a fable. 'It's my nature. The frog and the scorpion, you know?'

Soundtrack: 'Cast Your Fate to the Wind' by the Vince Guaraldi Trio. 'Wheel in the Sky' by Journey. 'Con Te Partiro' by Andrea Bocelli. 'Still the One' by Shania Twain.

Surveillance Report: Tony quotes Junior's line about Virginia ham from 'The Happy Wanderer' but Richie doesn't understand. Later Janice quotes Sun Tzu to Richie, a writer Dr Melfi previously suggested Tony read if he wanted to be a better gangster.

While Carmela is preparing lunch for Vic, she listens to Shania Twain sing 'Still the One' – a song about fidelity.

The Verdict: 'Sometimes . . . we're all hypocrites.' Tony and his crew bankrupt Davie Scatino through his sporting-goods store, while Carmela gets the hots for Davie's brother-in-law. Tony contemplates spending the rest of his life in prison.

This episode proves how much the viewer empathises with Tony Soprano. He murdered Matt Bevilaqua in the previous instalment and now faces imprisonment for his actions, yet the audience wants him to get off the hook. When it happens, the sense of relief is palpable. This just shows the strength of the writing and James Gandolfini's acting.

'Bust Out' is another fine episode as Season Two builds to its climax. The script concentrates on the impact of Tony's actions, both on his own family and how it affects other people. This is what *The Sopranos* does best.

24
House Arrest

US Transmission Date: 26 March 2000
UK Transmission Date: 21 December 2000

Writer: Terence Winter
Director: Tim Van Patten
Cast: Will McCormack (Jason La Penna),
Patricia Marand (Helen Barone),
Jennifer Albano (Connie),
Vito Antuofurmo Sr (Bobby Coniglio),
Sabine Singh (Tracy), James Biberi (Maître D'),
Ilene Kristen (Woman Smoker), George Xhilone (Man),
Gary Perez (Agent Marquez),
Ron Lee Jones (Michael McLuhan),
Louis Petraglia (Sanitation Worker),
Remy K Selma (Siraj), Janet Busher (Nurse),
Robert McKay (Orderly),
Amy Hart Redford (ER Doctor),
Roy Thinnes (Dr Baumgartner), Frank Adams (Guest #1),
Alan Levine (Guest #2), Paul Borghese (Guest #3),
Russ Brunelli (Guest #4), Gary Lamadore (Chucky),
Mary Louise Wilson (Catherine)

Storyline: Richie is causing problems with the way he runs
his routes on the garbage business. His men dump a load
of rubbish outside a delicatessen that complained about the
service.

Tony retrieves his bag of cash from his lawyer's office.
Neil Mink says Tony needs to stay away from criminal
activities and spend time at one of his legitimate businesses
– otherwise he runs a greater risk of being caught and
prosecuted by the FBI.

Junior goes into hospital to have a small operation.

Dr Melfi drinks vodka in her office when she realises her
next session is with Tony. He complains about being bored
and admits to being behind on his medication. He can't
take part in the things that normally give him pleasure.

Junior meets an old school friend as he prepares to leave hospital. Catherine Romano was married to a cop and her son is now a detective. She suggests they could have coffee but Junior says he can't leave his house for medical reasons.

Tony takes his lawyer's advice and spends some time at the offices of Barone Sanitation. He admires the new secretary, Connie Desapio, who is a born-again Christian. The manager complains that Richie's drivers are selling cocaine on their garbage routes.

In therapy with her own shrink, Dr Melfi admits her drinking is worse. She says she talked Tony out of giving up therapy.

Junior is fitted with a breathing mask to help him sleep better and prevent strain on his heart. Catherine visits but Junior politely sends her away.

At a party for New Jersey's garbage bosses Tony corners Richie. He orders him to stop selling cocaine on the routes because it risks getting the FBI and the Drug Enforcement Administration interested in their business. Tony blacks out after talking to Richie. In hospital, preliminary tests show no physical reasons for the blackout. Tony has developed a rash on his arm.

Junior is washing up when Bacala brings round some shopping. Something gets stuck in the garbage-disposal unit and Junior tries to get it out. Just after Bacala leaves, Junior gets his hand stuck down the kitchen sink.

Tony turns down the chance to join his crew at the docks, where a big shipment of World War Two memorabilia has arrived.

Dr Melfi takes her son out for dinner and gets into a fierce argument with a woman smoking at the next table. The maître d' asks Melfi to leave. Her son walks out, deeply embarrassed.

Richie and Janice visit Junior, whose hand has been trapped in the garbage disposal for six hours. Richie helps Junior get his hand out of the plughole. Richie gives Junior his money from the garbage routes but the envelope is light, thanks to Tony's intervention about selling drugs.

Tony is back in office at Barone Sanitation, bored and listless. He scratches his rash so hard it starts bleeding.

Dr Melfi tells her therapist about what happened in the restaurant. She denies being an alcoholic. Dr Kupferberg prescribes a drug called Luvox, which he uses to treat patients with compulsions.

Tony meets Junior at his doctor's office. They argue about the drug sales but Tony's rule is law as boss. When Junior gets home he decides to give Catherine Romano a call.

Tony sees a doctor about his rash, who prescribes some cortisone cream. He suggests Tony talk to someone about stress management.

Tony manages his stress by banging Connie from behind while she bends over his desk at Barone Sanitation.

Junior and Catherine share a coffee and conversation at his house.

Carmela and Tony go house hunting with Richie and Janice, who are engaged to be married. Richie nearly brings on another of Tony's blackouts.

Livia phones Junior and badmouths Catherine. Junior hangs up on his sister-in-law, then takes a drink down to Catherine in the basement. He admits to being under house arrest and shows her the electronic tag around his ankle. She doesn't mind and volunteers to bring him food.

Dr Melfi tells Tony about a condition where antisocial personalities crave ceaseless action to avoid thinking about the abhorrent things they do. When they are not distracted, they crash – just as Tony has been doing.

Tony returns to Satriale's and his crew. Christopher is out of hospital and on the mend. Otherwise, not much else is happening. A car crash draws them outside. FBI Agent Harris visits and introduces a new agent. Harris and Tony talk about recent sports results, like two long-time acquaintances . . .

Deep and Meaningful: Season Two introduced scenes of Dr Melfi talking with her own therapist about problems in her life. Treating Tony is taking a heavy toll on the psychiatrist, who has started drinking during the day. This episode allows the viewer to see an example of Melfi's disintegration at first hand, rather than see it related afterwards to her therapist.

Melfi is having a meal with her son Jason, who is at college. She is not up to date on what courses he is currently taking and tries to make a joke, which falls flat. Melfi gets into an argument with a woman smoking at the next table and finally is asked to leave the restaurant by the management. Her son walks out on Melfi and she is left feeling humiliated and ashamed. Her actions are spiralling out of control . . .

Mobspeak: Tony asks Richie if he has any blow (cocaine). Catherine asks if her cop husband was ever on the take (receiving payments from mobsters).

Mama Mia: Livia phones Junior because she's heard he is keeping company with Catherine Romano. Livia says her husband Johnny said Catherine let him feel her up behind the Sons of Italy hall. Junior hangs up on Livia.

Bright Lights, Baked Ziti: Catherine brings Junior a plate of manicotti. Bacala eats most of it, to Junior's irritation.

Carmela says the finger food at the garbage managers' party is better than the previous years. Tony eats peanuts just before he passes out.

Bacala goes shopping for Junior. The shop has sold out of lady fingers so he gets Entenmann's crumbcake instead.

Tony eats ham when Silvio calls him about the memorabilia.

Melfi takes her son out for dinner at a restaurant. They both have pizza.

The doctor examining Tony's rash asks if he is allergic to shellfish. Tony says he eats shrimp all the time.

Junior offers Catherine a jar of vinegar eggplant but she declines, because she can't handle the acidity.

Paulie is cooking sauce in the office at Satriale's when Tony arrives.

Mobbed Up: Tony shares a joke with his lawyer about being home alone, like Macauley Culkin in the film of the same name.

Tony talks to Dr Melfi about seeing a film with Brad Pitt and Gwyneth Paltrow. She prompts him for the title, hopefully suggesting *Sliding Doors*. He says it was the serial-killer hit *Seven*. Tony thought it was a good film but he lost interest halfway through it.

Pussy does a passable imitation of Sergeant Schultz from the 1960s sitcom *Hogan's Heroes* when the crew play with the World War Two memorabilia.

Junior snores loudly while Catherine watches *Diagnosis Murder*, a whodunnit TV series starring Dick Van Dyke.

How Do You Feel?: Tony tells Dr Melfi the therapy is starting to feel like a waste of time. He is bored and thinks everything is just a series of distractions until you die. He is behind on his medication and doubts its usefulness.

How Do You Feel, Doctor?: Dr Melfi says she is afraid and repulsed by what Tony might tell her, but she can't help herself from wanting to hear it.

At a session after the incident in the restaurant, Melfi is in tears at how she embarrassed her son. She denies being an alcoholic and then tries to make bargains about when she will drink in future. Dr Kupferberg says her continuing treatment of Tony is a compulsion and he prescribes a drug designed to treat obsessive compulsive disorders.

Quote/Unquote: Junior is underwhelmed when Bacala suggests he try using a bedpan. 'I'm not a cat. I don't shit in a box.'

Richie just stares at Tony after being forbidden to sell cocaine on any garbage routes. 'Don't give me your fucking Manson lamps, just fucking stop.'

Tony has a laugh while Junior is being refitted with a breathing mask that makes him look like an ageing fighter pilot. 'How many MiGs you shoot down last week?' Tony asks.

Tony says America is the only country where the pursuit of happiness is guaranteed, but Dr Melfi notes only the pursuit is guaranteed – not the happiness. 'Always a fucking loophole, right?' Tony says.

Soundtrack: 'Space Invader' by the Pretenders. 'Gotta Serve Somebody' by Bob Dylan. 'Disco Inferno' by the Trammps. 'More Than a Feeling' by Boston. 'Can't Put Your Arms Around a Memory' by Johnny Thunders.

Surveillance Report: Melfi makes a very Livia-like gesture when Tony makes a joke and then questions her sense of humour.

Tony's face when he is told the secretary at Barone Sanitation is a born-again Christian is a picture – he obviously considers Connie's religious beliefs an extra challenge to overcome, which he does. Tony hadn't used his office at Barone Sanitation for eight years.

Carmela and her reading group discuss *'Tis* by Frank McCourt.

The doctor who treats Tony's rash is played by Roy Thinnes, best known for playing the architect David Vincent in the 1960s sci-fi TV series *The Invaders*.

Media rumours in circulation before Season Two aired suggested the character of Catherine was an old flame of Tony!

The Verdict: 'Where's my happiness, then?' Tony is having blackouts again, thanks to agita from Richie and pretending to be a legitimate businessman. Junior is caught in his own home but gets a new flame in his love life.

This episode is all about being trapped. Junior gets stuck in the garbage disposal for six hours. The terms of his house arrest are proving very restrictive and even his own body is becoming a prison as he gets older and his health declines. Tony feels trapped by the need to avoid illegal activities, which stops him having fun with his Family. Dr Melfi feels compelled to continue treating Tony, even though his revelations terrify and repulse her. The consequences of this are now bleeding into her relationship with her son.

This episode is light on plot but rich in character moments. Like other Terence Winter scripts, it's packed with great lines, which the actors deliver with relish. In terms of story, 'House Arrest' is the calm before the storm of the final two episodes. But it's still a great appetiser for the main event . . .

25
The Knight In White Satin Armor

US Transmission Date: 2 April 2000
UK Transmission Date: 3 January 2001

Writer: Robin Green and Mitchell Burgess
Director: Allen Coulter
Cast: Jason Cerbone (Jackie Aprile Jr),
Richard Maldone (Albert Barese),
Andy Blankenbuehler (Richie Aprile Jr),
Alla Kliouka (Svetlana)

Storyline: Tony helps Janice begin moving furniture into the house she is buying with Richie. Richie's son, Richie Jr, is ballroom dancing around the house – he's ranked in the world top ten. Also visiting is Jackie Aprile Jr, son of the late boss and Richie's nephew.

Tony has sex with Irina and then dumps her. She threatens to commit suicide unless he comes back.

Tony meets with Larry Boy Barese's cousin Albert, Richie, Jackie Jr and Dick Barone to divide up lucrative garbage contracts. Tony takes away one of Richie's contracts as punishment for continuing to sell cocaine on the routes.

Junior meets with his lawyer, who wants an extra $400,000 for litigation against the wiretaps that could send Junior to jail. Junior gets home to discover Tony has cut off another of his cash supplies. Richie wants to whack Tony but Junior suggests he seek support from Albert Barese first.

Pussy tries to present a gift to his FBI handler, Agent Skip Lipari. Pussy is now ridiculously co-operative and imagines a future where he could tour police departments giving lectures about organised crime. He gives Skip an airline ticket from the Scatino bust-out. Skip wants Pussy to wear a wire to the engagement party for Janice and Richie, which the Sopranos are hosting.

Carmela smells CK One on a shirt of Tony's in the laundry basket. It is his Russian lover's favourite scent.

At the engagement party Pussy tries to get information from Tony on tape, but Tony is obsessed with Richie. Carmela is cold and distant with Tony. When Janice gives a speech about how Richie is her soulmate, Carmela leaves the room and bursts into tears.

Tony gets a phone call from Irina's friend Svetlana: Irina is in hospital after getting drunk and taking twenty sleeping pills. Tony visits Irina and agrees to pay her medical bills.

Carmela helps Janice choose a wedding dress. Carmela says Janice will have to accept that Richie will have a mistress within a year. Janice doubts any mistress would let Richie fuck her with a loaded revolver held to her head. She says he usually takes the ammunition out.

Skip and his boss, Agent Frank Cubitoso, discuss Pussy's conversion to gung-ho informant. Cubitoso warns Skip not to get too close with Pussy.

Carmella finds Victor Musto in a decorating store and thanks him for not getting involved with her.

Tony asks Dr Melfi for a psychiatrist for Irina. He says he is dumping the mistress because he's supposed to – and it's not fun any more.

Richie reports Albert Barese's reluctance to Junior. After Richie has gone, Junior decides he is better off with Tony – nobody respects Richie.

Pussy visits Christopher at the stock brokerage in search of fresh information for Skip. Christopher invites Pussy along on a planned raid on a truck loaded with Pokémon trading cards. Pussy phones Skip with this news but the FBI agent warns him not to get involved in violent crime.

Tony tries to give the therapist's number to Irina but she refuses it.

Richie tells Janice to stop spending on the new house, as money may be tight, thanks to Tony's rulings. Janice says Tony stopped AJ seeing Richie, turning Richie further against Tony.

Pussy follows Christopher on his way to the hijack but has to swerve to avoid another vehicle. Pussy collides with a cyclist and crashes his car into another. He limps away from the scene.

Irina calls Tony at his home but he hangs up on her. Carmela confronts Tony about his mistress. Afterwards, Carmela wishes Tony were more like Victor Musto, but Gabriella Dante tells Carmela that Victor stayed away from her because he feared Tony – not out of any noble respect for Carmela.

Junior tells Tony that Richie plans to whack him. Tony increases Junior's income by 50 per cent in gratitude. Junior wonders how much influence Janice has over Richie in this matter.

Tony orders Silvio to whack Richie.

Janice and Richie argue at Livia's house about whether Richie's son is gay. Richie punches Janice in the face and then goads her. She gets a gun and shoots him twice, killing Richie. Janice phones Tony for help. He arrives to find her having a cigarette by the body. Tony calls his crew for assistance.

Skip confronts Pussy at the hospital where he is being treated. He tells the mobster he will never be able to join the FBI. Pussy sulks.

Christopher and Furio take Richie's body to Satriale's Pork Store, where they chop it into small pieces for easier disposal.

Livia comes downstairs just as Tony arrives to take Janice to the bus station – she is going back to Seattle. Mother and son argue, then Tony storms out. He trips and falls as he leaves – Livia laughs at him.

Silvio gives Irina $75,000 from Tony for her future.

When Tony finally gets home, he hints to Carmela what has happened to Richie. She says she is going to Rome for three weeks with Rosalie Aprile after Meadow graduates. Tony will have to look after the children when she's away.

Deep and Meaningful: Yet again, Janice proves herself to be cut from the same cloth as her mother. Janice cold-bloodedly murders Richie but has slipped into Livia-style self-denial mode by the time Tony arrives to clean up her mess. Janice claims it was an accident and she didn't mean to do it.

By the time Tony takes Janice to catch the bus back to Seattle, she is rewriting recent history in her own head. Tony jokes about burying Richie on a hill overlooking a little river and Janice believes it for a moment. She says she loved him so much – yeah, but that didn't stop you shooting him twice to make sure he stayed dead? Nope.

Mama Mia: When she hears that Richie is missing, Livia says he probably jilted Janice and it's the story of her daughter's life. Livia denies ever nagging Janice about her weight or calling her a tramp. The old woman reveals her philosophy of child rearing: 'Babies are like animals. They're no different than dogs.' Livia sobs and whines one of her beloved catchphrases about giving her life to her children on a silver platter. She calls Tony cruel when he won't kiss her goodbye, then laughs at him when he trips and falls.

Bright Lights, Baked Ziti: Carmela serves finger food on trays at the engagement party for Richie and Janice.

Tony sends Frank Cubitoso a large deli tray of cold meats, bread and cheese with balloons for the FBI agent's birthday.

Junior is eating a sandwich for lunch when Richie reports that Albert Barese wouldn't support a hit on Tony. Junior loses his appetite.

Janice cooks Richie his last supper, pasta with tomato sauce.

Christopher cuts up Richie's body using the equipment at Satriale's. He says it will be a while before he eats anything from the pork store again.

Mobbed Up: Tony asks if Richie Jr is still 'Flying Down To Rio', a ballroom-dancing reference to the first film to feature Fred Astaire and Ginger Rogers. Tony asks Junior if he's become a secret agent like Matt Helm, who was played by Dean Martin in four films.

How Do You Feel?: Tony says he is ending the relationship with Irina because he thinks that's what he's supposed to do and that's what Dr Melfi has been telling him to do all the time. The therapist denies passing judgment on a patient's sex life. Tony admits he is dumping Irina now because it's not fun any more.

Sleeping With the Fishes: Richie Aprile, shot twice by Janice for punching her in the face and taunting her. He had already been marked for death by Tony, so Richie was not long for the world, anyway. Janice just got her retaliation in first.

I Dream of Jeannie Cusamano: Livia says she had the strangest dreams all night long. People were coming and going but she couldn't get off her bed. In fact, Janice had given her mother two Nembutals to keep Livia quiet.

Quote/Unquote: Irina tells Tony she is reading *Chicken Soup for the Soul* but he suggests a different book. 'You should read *Tomato Sauce For Your Ass* – it's the Italian version.'

Melfi asks Tony if he feels responsible for Irina's suicide attempt. He says he was banging Irina for two years. 'Was that a hardship for her?' Melfi asks.

Carmela is upset with Tony's reason for the perfume on his shirts. 'You're putting me in a position where I'm feeling sorry for a whore who fucks you?'

Carmela sums up Richie and Janice's fatal attraction. 'That . . . that was not a marriage made in heaven.'

Soundtrack: 'I Saved the World Today' by the Eurythmics. 'The Memory Remains' by Metallica.

Surveillance Report: There's a bizarre use of subtitles in this episode for some of Irina's dialogue – even though she's speaking English. Her accent is thick but not so thick it can't be understood. The subtitles are reminiscent of scenes from the David Lynch TV series *Twin Peaks*.

When Richie and Albert discuss whacking Tony, Richie calls Larry Boy Barese the king of dermabrasion, a reference to a recent facelift. At the end of this scene a sound like machine-gun fire breaks in from the next scene. The picture changes to show the sound coming from a paint mixer at a DIY store. This clever transition was also used in the film *The Usual Suspects*.

Christopher pronounces Pokémon as 'Pokey-Man'.

Irina retells the story about her friend Svetlana's prosthetic leg falling off in a Gap store and her boyfriend carrying her out. Irina previously told this story to Tony over the phone in the 'College' episode during Season One. Irina creates this episode's title by combining the romantic notion of a knight in shining armour with the song title 'Knights In White Satin' by the Moody Blues.

Livia laughs when Tony trips outside her home. This echoes dialogue from a first-season episode in which he recalled his mother laughing when his father fell over.

This episode introduces Jackie Aprile Jr (played by Jason Cerbone), who will become a significant recurring character in Season Three.

The Verdict: 'All and all, though, I'd say it was a pretty good visit.' Richie tries to organise a hit on Tony but meets his own death at the hands of an unexpected killer. Tony dumps his Russian mistress but not without difficulty. Junior allies himself with Tony for the foreseeable future.

All the agita between Richie and Tony finally pays off in this gripping episode. Rather than meet the audience's expectations of having Tony pull the trigger, it's Janice who does the deed. She might put up with being fucked by a man holding a loaded pistol to her head, but she won't stand for being punched in the face by her fiancé. But, with Janice leaving town, who'll look after Livia?

As that plotline reaches its bloody conclusion, the FBI informant Pussy is becoming increasingly unstable. The groundwork has been laid for the finale of Season Two, but it won't be what viewers expect . . .

26
Funhouse

US Transmission Date: 9 April 2000
UK Transmission Date: 4 January 2001

Writers: David Chase and Todd A Kessler
Director: John Patterson
Cast: Ajay Mehta (Sundeep Kumar),
Dan Grimaldi (Patsy Parisi),
Robert Lupone (Bruce Cusamano),
Barbara Andres (Quintina),
David Anzuelo (Flight Attendant), Ray Garvey (Guard
#1), David Healy (Vice Principal), Jay Palit (Indian Man),
Kathleen Fasolino (Meadow's Friend)

Storyline: Tony meets with Livia and Barbara to decide where Livia should live. Tony gives his mother illegally obtained airline tickets from the Scatino bust-out for Livia and her sister Quintina to go and stay with Aunt Gemma in Tucson.

Tony and Pussy have an Indian meal at a restaurant and collect a fat envelope of cash from the owner. They go on to Vesuvio, where Tony gives Silvio a cut of the money. They have another meal with Silvio and Furio. Patsy Parisi – identical twin brother of the late Philly Parisi – arrives with a sable coat for Tony.

Tony goes home and presents the coat to Carmela. They make love with Carmela wearing just the coat. Tony falls asleep and starts having a series of surreal dreams. He wakes up and realises he's about to vomit. Tony just makes it to their en suite bathroom in time.

Pussy meets with Skip Lipari and has to hand over nearly all his cut from a telephone calling-card scam.

Tony has another dream, including a section where he thinks he wakes up and has a session with Dr Melfi. Artie Bucco arrives to finalise the menu for Meadow's graduation party. Tony accuses Artie of giving him food poisoning but Artie blames the Indian food Tony had already eaten by the time he got to Vesuvio. Tony runs for the bathroom again. Artie calls Pussy but he only had a touch of diarrhoea, so Tony's illness can't have been caused by the shellfish he shared with Pussy at Vesuvio.

Livia and her sister are arrested at the airport for presenting illegally obtained airline tickets.

Tony has another dream about Dr Melfi. The Sopranos' next-door neighbour, Dr Cusamano, visits and thinks Tony has food poisoning. It will pass. Tony dreams that Pussy is a fish who confesses to working for the feds.

Tony gets out of bed and gets dressed. He and Silvio visit Pussy, not giving their friend enough time to put on his wire. Tony invites Pussy to help him decide whether to buy a new boat. Tony fakes another stomach cramp and goes through Pussy's things while Pussy and Silvio have a coffee downstairs. Tony discovers the wire and tapes from a recording device – there can be no doubt that Pussy is a rat.

Tony, Pussy and Silvio are met at the docks by Paulie. They take the boat out to sea when Pussy is confronted with the truth. He claims to have given the feds disinformation and titbits, nothing substantial. He's been a rat for eighteen months. Pussy asks not to be shot in the face. His friends gun him down, wrap his body in a black tarpaulin, weight it and throw it overboard.

Livia calls Tony from the airport to say she has been arrested. FBI Agents Harris, Cubitoso and others arrive to arrest Tony. They've already found more illegal airline tickets in his four-wheel drive. They are taking Tony away in cuffs just as Meadow gets home with her friends.

Tony is soon bailed out by his lawyer, who says the charges are relatively minor. Tony is angry with himself for giving the tickets to his mother.

Dr Melfi senses Tony is full of sorrow about something but is covering it up with rage. She feels she hasn't confronted Tony enough in therapy because she was frightened of him. Tony walks out, waving goodbye and singing.

Meadow graduates. Afterwards, Tony tells Christopher he is recommending him to become a made man. Tony talks to Davie Scatino, who has split from Christine and is moving near Las Vegas to become a cowboy. He invites Tony to visit him.

The Sopranos host a graduation party for Meadow, with guests from the family and the Family. Tony smokes a cigar. At the seashore, the sun sets and the waves keep rolling in . . .

Deep and Meaningful: The murder of Pussy is the moment of truth for Tony, Paulie and Silvio. Killing a rat is one thing, but killing one of your best friends is something else. Paulie shows no hesitation. He has murdered many men before and was ready to kill Pussy during Season One. He seems almost eager.

Silvio shows the most reluctance. He walks out on to the deck of the boat while Tony and Paulie are confronting Pussy in the cabin below. Silvio blames his hesitancy on the swell of the sea, making him feel sick. Tony doesn't accept this and brings Silvio back down into the cabin.

Once he has proof that Pussy is a rat, Tony shows no hesitation. He will do what has to be done. When Pussy brags about bedding a 26-year-old acupuncturist in Puerto Rico, Tony shatters the illusion by asking if the girl even existed. At that moment, Pussy knows he is already dead to Tony. Less than a minute later, he *is* dead.

Mobspeak: Tony tells Christopher he is proposing him for his button (becoming a made man, a full member of the Mafia).

Mama Mia: Livia whines that Tony won't accept food from his own mother. She says she never conspired with Uncle Junior. Livia refuses to go back to Green Grove but Tony says the retirement community has already refused to take her back because she was abusive to the staff.

After she gets arrested Tony denounces his mother as a goddamn idiot and a fucking demented old bat.

Bright Lights, Baked Ziti: Livia tries to get Tony to eat some eggplant.

Tony and Pussy have a meal at an Indian restaurant. Tony has chicken vindaloo, which gives him food poisoning. The pair go on to Vesuvio, where they order zuppa di mussels and zucchini (courgette) flowers stuffed with melted dry ricotta cheese. Tony says Artie should put the flowers on the menu for Meadow's graduation party, for which Artie is doing the catering.

After he starts vomiting, Tony wonders if the chicken vindaloo was actually cocker spaniel in disguise.

Artie visits the Sopranos to finalise the party menu. He denies Tony's claim that the mussels caused the food poisoning. Artie picks every piece of shellfish himself and Tony had top-of-the-line Prince Edward Island mussels. Artie talks about Indian cooking's use of clarified butter and how it is also used to light funeral pyres, like the one for Indira Gandhi.

In one of his dream sequences Tony joins the rest of his family for a dinner of Chinese takeaway food.

When he gets arrested Tony tells Agent Cubitoso not to expect any more deli trays to arrive for his birthday.

There is a massive cake at Meadow's graduation party along with all of Artie's delicious food.

Mobbed Up: In one of Tony's dreams Silvio repeats his impersonation of Al Pacino as Michael Corleone in the *Godfather* films: 'Our true enemy has yet to reveal himself.' Tony sings the theme tune to the TV sitcom *Gilligan's Island* as he dreams, to the bemusement of Carmela and Dr Cusamano. Pussy the dream-sequence fish alludes to *The Godfather* when he says the fish on either side of him on the stall are asleep.

How Do You Feel?: Tony pretends to sob in a mocking manner when Dr Melfi suggests his mother inflicted serious psychic injuries on him as a child. The therapist tries to get past his rants about Indian food and his mother because she suspects there is something else that is causing him sorrow. Tony refuses to be drawn and walks out, waving his fingers at her and singing.

Sleeping With the Fishes: Salvatore 'Big Pussy' Bonpensiero, shot repeatedly by Tony, Paulie and Silvio for being a rat. They abide by his last request not to shoot him in the face. The trio dump Pussy's body at sea.

I Dream of Jeannie Cusamano: This episode goes for the record of most dream sequences, although the 'Isabella' episode from Season One might run it close. But, where those dreams were drug-fuelled fantasies, these dreams are brought on by food poisoning. Here's a full list of the surrealisms – can you say fish?

In the first dream sequence, Tony is walking along a snowy, deserted boardwalk by the sea. He meets Paulie, Hesh, Christopher, Pussy, Silvio and one of the Parisi brothers on the boardwalk. They are all waiting for someone who hasn't arrived yet. Tony has been diagnosed with a terminal disease and has decided to set fire to himself, rather than put everyone through the agony of his illness. The crew praise his bravery. Tony thanks Parisi for the sable coat, thinking the brother is Patsy. But it is Philly, who turns to reveal the gunshot wound in the side of his head. Tony gets impatient and decides to go ahead with the burning. He pours a can of petrol over himself. Pussy has disappeared. Philly is getting a shoeshine from Gigi Cestone, the man who killed him. Paulie lights a Zippo and hands it to Tony. Christopher asks what if the doctors are wrong? As Tony thinks about this, he is engulfed in a fireball.

In the second dream sequence, Tony is walking on the boardwalk again but the snow is gone. Junior looks at him from the broken window of an abandoned building. Silvio talks to him and imitates Al Pacino. Tony smiles widely. He looks through a viewer out to sea, but the view is of the inside of a huge, empty terminal. Tony sees himself playing cards with Paulie. He pulls out a gun and shoots Paulie in the chest.

Tony wakes up and hears Carmela's voice. He goes to a session with Dr Melfi and talks about his dream. Melfi turns into Annalisa, the mob boss he met in Italy. She speaks with her own voice, then with the voice of Dr Melfi. Tony realises this is all still part of the same dream.

In the third dream sequence Tony gets into a red car with Adriana in the driver's seat and Christopher in the back. Tony asks where Pussy is but gets no response. Somebody hands him a roll of toilet paper from the back of the car – Furio is now sitting beside Christopher in the back. They all drive away in the car – a tiny, bright-red bubble car.

In the fourth dream sequence Tony sits in Dr Melfi's waiting room. She calls him in and he follows, his trousers bulging with a massive erection. They talk about his penis, the dream about the duck stealing his penis, pussy and Pussy. Tony gets understandably confused and knows he's in a dream. Melfi says she finds Tony immensely attractive, even though he goes out of his way to repulse her. He fucks Dr Melfi on her desk.

In the fifth dream sequence, Tony has a conversation with Pussy, who is represented by a talking fish on a stall at the seaside. Pussy admits to being a rat and says he gave the feds a lot of information. He jokes that the fish on either side of him are asleep. Tony tips the fish stall over in anger.

In the sixth and final dream sequence, Tony arrives at a typical Soprano family dinner. He announces that he bought a boat today. Meadow announces that she has decided on going to Columbia University. Everyone is happy.

Quote/Unquote: Tony reveals his sensitive side to Dr Melfi: 'I got pussy on the brain, I always do.'

The dream-sequence version of Pussy proudly says he now weighs only eight pounds and reveals how he got so thin: 'Swimming. The best exercise. Works every muscle group.'

Meadow gets tough after seeing her father arrested and led away by the FBI. 'My friends don't judge me. And fuck them if they do, I'll cut them off.'

Christopher is surprised and overjoyed when told he will become a made man at last. 'I fucking deserve it. Got no spleen, Gene.'

Soundtrack: 'Thru And Thru' by the Rolling Stones. 'Free Fallin'' by Tom Petty. 'Baubles, Bangles and Beads' by Frank Sinatra. 'Ain't Too Proud To Beg' by The Temptations. 'Diamonds and Rust' by Joan Baez.

Surveillance Report: In Tony's first dream sequence, the Parisi brother says he is Philly and shows his gunshot wound to the head. In the episode where Philly was shot, he was played by Ian Grimaldi. Yet the credits for this episode mention only Patsy Parisi, played by Dan Grimaldi. Patsy does appear earlier in the episode but doesn't speak and only speaking parts are mentioned in credits.

In Tony's final dream sequence he imagines Meadow announcing that she has chosen to go to Columbia. In Season Three she does exactly that, making Tony's dream eerily prescient.

The final sequence for the season shows shots of everyone celebrating at Meadow's graduation party intercut with scenes of the many activities controlled by the Soprano Family – pornography, garbage collection, the stock brokerage, the telephone calling-card scam, the motel and others. The final image is of the sea rolling in as waves on to the beach while the sun sets.

The Verdict: 'Not in the face, OK? You give me that? Keep my eyes?' Tony contracts food poisoning and realises Pussy is a rat. Tony, Paulie and Silvio execute their friend at sea. Meadow graduates from high school.

The FBI finally manage to arrest Tony, in connection with illegally obtained airline tickets. But they lose a significant informant with the 'disappearance' of Pussy, who is left sleeping with the fishes. This brings sadness for Tony, but it is balanced by Meadow's graduation.

This episode ties up two long-running plot threads with the revelation that Pussy is a rat and Christopher finally becoming a made man. But, unlike the finale to Season One, this episode does not paint the series into a corner for future instalments. Instead it sets up several new plots for the coming year, such as Meadow going to college, Tony's feelings about having to execute his friend and the FBI tightening the net around Tony. Season Three should make for very interesting viewing, but one very significant character will be absent . . .

Season Three
(2001)

Company Credits

Created by David Chase
Producers: Martin Bruestle, Henry J Bronchtein,
Terence Winter (27–30), Todd A Kessler (27–33)
Executive Producers: David Chase, Brad Grey,
Robin Green and Mitchell Burgess
Co-Executive Producer: Ilene S Landress
Supervising Producer: Terence Winter (31–39)

Regular Cast:

James Gandolfini (Tony Soprano)
Lorraine Bracco (Dr Jennifer Melfi)
Edie Falco (Carmela Soprano)
Michael Imperioli (Christopher Moltisanti)
Dominic Chianese (Corrado 'Junior' Soprano)
Steven Van Zandt (Silvio Dante)
Tony Sirico (Peter 'Paulie Walnuts' Gualtieri)
Robert Iler (Anthony Soprano Jr, also known as AJ)
Jamie-Lynn Sigler (Meadow Soprano)
Drea De Matteo (Adriana La Cerva)
Aida Turturro (Janice Soprano, also known as Parvati)
Federico Castelluccio (Furio Giunta, 27–30, 32–33,
35–36, 38–39)
John Ventimiglia (Arthur 'Artie' Bucco, 28–29, 31,
34–36, 39)

Steven R Schirripa (Bobby 'Bacala' Baccalieri Jr, 28–29, 31–33, 36–37, 39)
Robert Funaro (Eugene Pontecorvo, 28–29, 31, 34, 36, 38–39)
Katherine Narducci (Charmaine Bucco, 28, 31, 36, 39)
Joe Pantoliano (Ralph 'Ralphie' Cifaretto, 28–32, 34–35, 38–39)

Recurring Cast:

Jerry Adler (Herman 'Hesh' Rabkin, 27–28, 34–36)
John Fiore (Gigi Cestone, 27–32, 34, 36)
Dan Grimaldi (Patsy Parisi, 27–29, 32–34, 36, 38–39)
Katalin Pota (Lilliana Wosilius, 27–28, 30)
Matt Servitto (Agent Harris, 27, 31, 39)
Frank Pelligrino (Agent Cubitoso, 27, 31, 39)
Frank Pando (Agent Grasso, 27–28, 39)
Ari Gaynor (Caitlin Rucker, 27, 32, 34, 37)
Matthew Breiner (Rob, 27, 35)
Tommy Savas (Xavier, 27, 35)
Ian Group (Colin, 27, 35)
Mark Karafin (Egon Kosma, 27, 35, 39)
David Mogentale (Coach Goodwin, 27, 29)
Gary Evans (FBI Tech #1 in 27, 30–31, FBI Tech #2 in 28)
Glenn Kessler (FBI Tech #2, 27, 30–31)
Alla Klioka (Svetlana Kirilenko, 28–29)
Patrick Tully (Noah Tannenbaum, 28–29, 32)
Tom Aldredge (Hugh DeAngelis, 28–29, 31–35, 37)
Suzanne Shepherd (Mary DeAngelis, 28–29, 31–35, 37)
Joseph R Gannascoli (Vito Spatafore, 28, 31–32, 34, 39)
George Loros (Raymond Curto, 28–29, 36)
Ralph Lucarelli (Cozzerelli, 28, 39)
Maureen Van Zandt (Gabriella Dante, 28, 30, 32, 36, 38–39)
Jason Cerbone (Jackie Aprile Jr, 28–32, 34–39)
Sharon Angela (Rosalie Aprile, 28–30, 32, 34–35, 38–39)
Peter Riegert (State Assembleyman Ronald Zellman, 28, 30–31)

Gregalan Williams (Rev. James Jr, 28, 34)
Vincent Curatola (Johnny 'Sack' Sacrimoni, 28–31, 34, 39)
Marie Donato (2–4, 7–9, 28, 31, 39)
Richard Maldone (Albert Barese, 28–29, 38)
Vincent Pastore (Pussy Bonpensiero, 28, 36)
Raymond Franza (Donny K, 29, 34)
Max Casella (Benny Fazio, 29, 34–35)
Kevin Janicelli (Roy Del Guerico, 29, 38)
Andrew Davoli (Dino Zerilli, 29, 34–35, 38)
Oksana Babiy (Irina Peltsin, 29–30, 37)
Peter Bogdanovich (Dr Elliot Kupferberg, 30, 34)
Denise Borino (Ginny 'Sack' Sacrimoni, 30, 34, 39)
Will McCormack (Jason La Penna, 30, 35)
Igor Zhivotovsky (Igor Parnasky, 30, 36)
Frank Santorelli (Georgie, 32–33)
Ariel Kiley (Tracee, 32, 34)
Kelly Madison Kole (Debbie, 32, 36)
Toni Kalem (Angie Bonpensiero, 33, 38)
Annabella Sciorra (Gloria Trillo, 34–35, 37–39)
Turk Pipkin (Aaron Arkaway, 34–36)
Annika Pergament (Newscaster in 34, 36)
Daniel Oreskes (Principal Cincotta, 35, 39)
Emad Tarabay (Matush, 35, 38)
Louis Crugnali (Carlos Renzi, 35, 38)
Frank Ciornei (Slava Malevsky, 36–37)
Vitali Baganov (Valery, 36–37)
Lewis Stadlen (Dr Fried, 38–39)

STOP PRESS: No UK transmission dates have been listed for Season Three in this first edition of *Bright Lights, Baked Ziti*. As this book was going to press it was announced that the first UK broadcast would be on the digital channel E4, beginning on Sunday, 24 June 2001. If E4 broadcasts an episode a week, the season finale will screen on Sunday, 16 September 2001 – after this book is published. Reports in the British media indicate Season Three of The Sopranos will receive its first UK terrestrial broadcast on Channel 4 in Autumn, 2001.

27
Mr Ruggerio's Neighborhood
US Transmission Date: 4 March 2001

Writer: David Chase
Director: Allen Coulter
Cast: Louis Lombardi (Skip Lipari),
Saundra Santiago (Jean Cusamano),
Michelle De Cesare (Hunter Scangarelo),
Erica Leerhsen (Birgit Olafsdottir),
Albert Makhtsier (Stasiu Wosilius),
Robert Bogue (Ed Restuccia),
Anthony Dimaria (Ruggerio's Son),
Jesse Doran (Judge Lapper),
Gary Perez (Agent Marquez), Brian Smyj (Agent Smyj),
Colleen Werthmann (Agent Malatesta),
Jay Christanson (Agent Jongsma),
Dennis Gagomiros (Agent Theophilus),
Neal Jones (Agent Tancredi),
John Deblasio (SET Lineman),
Anthony Indelicato (SET #1), Murphy Guyer (SET #2),
Frank Deal (R&D #1), Katie C Sparer (R&D #2),
Etan Maiti (Jason)

Storyline: Fade-up on a new day at the Soprano household. Tony collects his morning paper from the end of the driveway. The front-page lead is about mob competition for garbage contracts heating up – violence is feared.

A team of FBI agents review their ongoing investigation into Tony's illegal activities. A missing informant, Pussy Bonpensiero, is written off as 'compost', which torpedoes efforts to prosecute Tony for stock fraud over the Webistics scam. Agent Cubitoso says the stolen airline tickets could lead to charges, but only if Livia Soprano is willing to testify against her son. The other agents consider this unlikely. They decide to concentrate on Tony's garbage business. The FBI believe Richie Aprile was whacked by his fellow mobsters. To get evidence, the feds need to get a bug into Tony's house. Skip Lipari suggests placing one in the basement, because that's the only place Tony will talk business. He believes the noisy air-conditioning ducts make the room safe from effective bugging. The FBI get a warrant to enter the Soprano household and place a surveillance device in the basement.

Two agents sit outside Tony's house in a County of Essex Mosquito Abatement utility vehicle. Tony leaves for work but pauses to tell them where he's going today, to save them the trouble of tailing him. He is obviously aware of the constant surveillance of his activities.

The FBI decide to enter the house on a Tuesday afternoon, when everyone is usually out of the house. Tony is at work, AJ is at school, Carmela is having tennis lessons and their maid Lilliana is having English lessons with her husband. Meadow now lives in a dorm at Columbia University in New York City. Agents will have to follow everyone who has a key to the Soprano house, to make sure nobody catches the federal invaders.

Next Tuesday the FBI prepare to move in. By 12.12 p.m. nearly everyone has left the house. The FBI have given the Soprano family nicknames – Tony is Bada Bing!, Carmela is Mrs Bing, AJ is Baby Bing and Meadow is Princess Bing. The house is codenamed the Sausage Factory.

Tony arrives at the Bada Bing! strip club, where all his crew (Paulie, Silvio, Christopher, Hesh, Furio, Gigi and Patsy) are having lunch in the back office. Paulie is washing his hands and gives an extended rant about how urine gets on to your shoelaces in men's public toilets. He is paranoid about getting a disease from touching his own shoes. Patsy Parisi has joined Tony's crew, having been one of Junior's men. Patsy is unhappy because today is his 51st birthday. It would also have been his twin brother Philly's birthday, but Philly was whacked a year ago. Patsy misses his brother, who was known as Spoons. Tony tells Patsy to leave the morbid shit back with Junior's crew. Patsy stares at Gigi, who executed Philly on orders from Tony.

The feds carefully enter the Sausage Factory after disabling the phone lines and alarms and picking the locked doors. They switch on the air conditioning and take sound readings in the basement. They also use a video camera to film the interior of the basement.

Carmela is joined at her tennis lesson by Adriana, who has never played before. Carmela's tennis coach is leaving but introduces his replacement, Birgit.

AJ and his friends turn truant, cutting assembly to leave the school grounds. AJ admires a shirt worn by his friend Egon Kosma, who is trying out for the school's American football team.

At the Columbia University dorms, Meadow is woken by the return of her roommate Caitlin. Caitlin has been out all night drinking to celebrate the end of Frosh Week, the US equivalent of Freshers Week at a British university. The wall above Caitlin's bed is covered with ads for Absolut Vodka.

The Soprano's maid, Lilliana Wosilius, has a picnic lunch with her husband Stasiu after their language class. He is bitter about driving a cab, having been an engineer with twenty employees and a state grant for autonomous research when they lived in Poland. Lilliana steals cutlery and glasses from the Sopranos.

The FBI agents review the videotapes taken in the basement. They note that the Sopranos' 120-gallon water tank is probably going to rupture in the next six months. The FBI decide to put the bug into a battered lamp on a table beneath the air-conditioning ducts. At FBI headquarters in Quantico, Virginia, technicians put a listening device into a lamp like that in the Sopranos' basement. The new lamp is distressed to resemble the one it will replace.

Next Tuesday the Sopranos go about their usual routine. At the Bada Bing! Gigi tells Tony that Patsy has been drinking heavily and claiming he knows who ordered the hit on his twin brother. Tony brought Patsy over from Junior's crew to keep an eye on him. He considers having Patsy whacked, but decides to bide his time.

Everyone has left the Sausage Factory except Lilliana. The Feds move closer to find out why and hear her call out in anguish. Carmela gets a phone call at her tennis lesson and rushes away. Tony leaves the Bada Bing! in a hurry and heads for home. The FBI realise something is wrong and hurriedly pull the team away from the property. The agents wonder what happened.

In the basement Tony and Carmela are knee-deep in water – the predicted water-tank blow-out happened early. The local plumber, Mr Ruggerio, arrives to sort out the mess.

Next day the FBI send agents to stake out the house, hoping to learn what went wrong. They see a drunken Patsy standing in Tony's back yard, pointing a gun at the house. Patsy can't bring himself to pull the trigger. Instead he urinates in Tony's swimming pool and stumbles away. Eventually the FBI learn about the water tank. The insurgent team have to wait a week to try again.

The following Tuesday the FBI try again and finally succeed in planting the bugged lamp in the basement. At Columbia, Meadow is visited by her old school friend, Hunter Scangarello. Caitlin is acting strangely, seemingly freaked out by life in New York. She's been prescribed anti-anxiety drugs.

Tony talks to Patsy in the office at Satriale's Pork Store. He makes Patsy attest to having put his grief about Philly behind him. Tony invites Patsy to visit the house and bring his son to hang out with AJ – they could swim in the pool! At school AJ is trying out for the football team.

Next day two FBI technicians sit in a van, listening to transmissions from the Sausage Factory. They get excited when they hear Tony saying he has a job for someone, which might get a little messy. It turns out he wants Stasiu to rig a draining system should the water tank ever burst again. It may be some time before the bug in the basement bears fruit for the FBI ...

Deep and Meaningful: Before this episode Patsy Parisi had appeared in only a single episode, delivering a sable coat to Tony. Now he gets his own showcase moment as he draws a gun and points it at Tony. FBI agents look on bewildered as the meek made man sobs and shakes with impotent fury. Patsy had to get roaring drunk to summon the courage to come this far, but he cannot pull the trigger. Instead he pisses into Tony's swimming pool, the greatest act of rebellion he can muster. He stumbles off, cursing himself and his boss . . .

Mobspeak: Judge Lapper describes the FBI application to enter and bug the Soprano household as a 'sneak-and-peak warrant'. Tony talks to Patsy about his dead twin brother Philly and says '*buon' anima*' (rest his soul). On the FBI pinboard showing the structure of the Soprano Family, Tony is labelled as underboss (second in command to the boss). The FBI technicians talk about minimisation – they are allowed to listen to conversations for only forty seconds. If there is no mention of organised crime, they must switch off. They are allowed to check back in two minutes later.

Mama Mia: The FBI do not believe Livia would testify against Tony in exchange for immunity over the stolen airline tickets. They obviously weren't paying attention to the wiretaps that proved she was happy to coerce Junior into ordering a hit on Tony in Season One!

Tony tells Carmela that he has got a Russian girl moving in with Livia to look after his mother. He claims to have found the carer through an agency. In fact, the FBI have a recording of Tony telling Pussy that the woman is a cousin of his former mistress, Irina.

Tony Soprano, Paper Boy: The opening episode of each season has included a scene of Tony in his bathrobe walking to the end of his driveway in the morning to collect his morning newspaper, the *Star-Ledger*. This episode has him slob out to the front gate four times over several weeks to collect the paper.

Bright Lights, Baked Ziti: The FBI agents pick at their lunches while meeting to discuss how best to get a bug into Tony's home. The following Tuesday Agent Harris eats a filled roll while he monitors movements at the Soprano household.

Tony joins his crew for lunch at the Bada Bing!. There is plenty of pasta, salad, bread and wine. Tony tries to persuade Patsy to have some brasciole, but he has no appetite. Paulie says the average women's public bathroom is so clean you could eat maple walnut ice cream from the toilets.

AJ and his friends discuss how useful skateboards would be in the school cafeteria. One of the truants says the food 'tastes like ass'.

Lilliana has a picnic lunch to share with her husband. He finds a jar of Italian capers among the food. She says the Soprano children don't like capers.

The Sopranos store preserved and tinned food in their basement. The FBI agents joke that the large quantity of food is just for AJ.

Silvio eats nuts while watching golf at the Bada Bing! office.

Tony eats cereal for breakfast at home. He is visited by Gigi, who has brought some fresh Italian pastries, which Tony enjoys.

Carmela tells Tony that Lilliana is preparing a leg of lamb for Meadow to take back to Columbia. Tony complains that a new brand of coffee acted like a laxative on him. Carmela says he needs more roughage in his diet.

Mobbed Up: Agent Harris talks about the Soprano's plumber, saying the area is Mr Ruggerio's neighbourhood. This is a reference to an American children's TV show about kindly Mr Rogers and his neighbourhood.

I Dream of Jeannie Cusamano: Gigi has a brief flashback to murdering Philly Parisi in #14, when Patsy is talking about his brother's execution.

Quote/Unquote: FBI Agent Skip Lipari comes to terms with the disappearance of Pussy. 'I think at this point it's time to consider Bonpensiero compost.'

Judge Lapper tells the FBI to limit entrances to only the basement of the Soprano household. 'It's not a *Better Homes and Gardens* tour.'

Tony cracks wise to Patsy after Paulie's rant about urine and footwear. 'You want to commit suicide? Tie your shoes and have a bite of brasciole.'

Tony tells Gigi to log off the Internet in case the FBI use the connection for surveillance. 'That cookie shit makes me nervous.'

Soundtrack: 'Sad-Eyed Lady of the Lowlife' by Alabama 3. Tony sings along to Steely Dan's 'Dirty Work' in his car. 'The Peter Gunn Theme' by Henry Mancini is mixed with 'Every Breath You Take' by the Police during many of the FBI sequences. Caitlin sings some of 'New York, New York', along with what sounds like an old cheerleading chant. 'Hotel California' by the Eagles. 'High Fidelity' by Elvis Costello and the Attractions.

Surveillance Report: In America HBO launched Season Three by screening #27 and #28 one straight after the other. This episode faded out before the closing credits. A caption labelled 'Episode 2' appeared before #28 was shown in its entirety. That was followed by another screen caption, introducing the closing credits for #27. The double-header debut also introduced widescreen broadcasts as HBO gave viewers a choice of watching the episodes in conventional ratio on HBO Plus or in widescreen on its main channel.

Lilliana's husband Stasiu is played by Albert Makhtsier. When the character appeared previously in the Season Two episode 'Full Leather Jacket', he was played by a different actor, Marek Przystup.

The Verdict: 'We've had every one of Tony's phones bugged for four years. But the guy says less than Harpo Marx.' The FBI go to great lengths to place a listening device into the Sopranos' basement. Tony is having problems with a new crew member, Patsy Parisi, unaware of the efforts to ensnare him . . .

Season Three hits the ground running with this opening episode, unlike the first instalment of the previous season. 'Mr Ruggerio's Neighborhood' cleverly uses the FBI's point of view to update viewers quickly on what's been happening since the end of Season Two. In terms of plot, not much actually happens, but the viewer hardly notices.

This is one of *The Sopranos*' funniest ever episodes. It's packed with wisecracks and visual humour, while the seamless mix of 'The Peter Gunn Theme' with the Police's ode to stalking is a hilarious sound gag. *The Sopranos* is back and it's still one of the best things on television . . .

28
Proshai, Livushka
US Transmission Date: 4 March 2001

Writer: David Chase
Director: Tim Van Patten
Cast: Nancy Marchand (Livia Soprano),
Nicole Burdette (Barbara Giglione),
Peter McRobbie (Father Felix), Tim Gallen (Mr Zachary),
Marcia Haufrecht (Fanny),
Vito Antuofurmo Sr (Bobby Zanone),
Dimitri De Fresco (Young Man),
Ed Vassallo (Tom Giglione), Carlos Lopez (FBI Tech #1),
Michael Strano (FBI Agent)

Storyline: Late at night a garbage truck is blown up. Next day the *Star-Ledger* reports that this is the second explosion in a sanitation war, with further retaliation expected. A copy of the paper lies on the breakfast bar in the Sopranos' kitchen. Lying on the floor is Tony, who has collapsed. Carmela comes home with groceries and discovers him on the floor and asks what happened.

Everything does a fast rewind back to Tony coming downstairs. He finds Meadow rewinding a videotape of the 1931 gangster film *The Public Enemy*. She brought a classmate home to watch it because someone stole the VCR at Columbia. Her black classmate emerges from the bathroom and introduces himself to Tony as Noah Tannenbaum. While Meadow goes upstairs to get a CD, Tony asks about Noah's background. Noah is half Jewish, half African American. His father is an entertainment lawyer in Los Angeles. Tony warns Noah to stay away from Meadow in future. Noah and Meadow go back to Columbia. Tony gets food out of the fridge, opens a kitchen cupboard and then collapses.

Back to real time and Carmela warns Tony not to play the race card against Noah: it will only backfire on him. She will talk to Meadow about Noah.

Tony visits Livia at her home. Svetlana has shifted in to be Livia's carer. Tony asks his mother not to testify against him about the illegal airline tickets, but Livia doesn't respond. Tony walks out, frustrated and angry.

That night Tony is watching *The Public Enemy* on video. Meadow comes home and demands to know what her father said to Noah. Carmela calls her upstairs. Tony goes outside to smoke a cigar. When he comes back in, Carmela, Meadow and AJ are all waiting for him in the dining room. Svetlana called – Livia has died in her sleep. Tony and Carmela go to Livia's house.

Svetlana says Livia died of a massive stroke. She did not suffer.

At the Sopranos' home, AJ is struggling to understand a poem by Robert Frost. Meadow explains that snow symbolises death. When she leaves, AJ hears noises in the house. He calls out to see if it is Livia, but nobody replies.

Tony calls his sister Barbara with news of their mother's death. She volunteers to call Janice in California. Tony suggests they meet at Cozzerelli's Funeral Home the next day but Barbara says Livia did not want a service. Tony says they'll pick an urn instead. Tony, Carmela and Svetlana toast Livia.

When Tony and Carmela get home Tony's crew are waiting for him. Everyone says they're sorry and Tony tells them his mother didn't suffer. Carmela's parents arrive as Tony gets a call from Barbara that Janice is refusing to come home. Tony phones Janice and demands she return to New Jersey. He offers to pay her airfare. He tells her that everyone believes her dead fiancé, Richie Aprile, has disappeared into the FBI's witness protection programme.

That night Tony can't sleep. He gets up to watch more of the old film, which shows a gangster's happy relationship with his mother.

Next day more of the Family come to pay their condolences. Tony takes Ralphie Cifaretto, Albert Barese and Gigi outside. He demands to know who gave the order to torch one of Albert's garbage trucks. Ralphie says it was retaliation for Albert lighting up two of his dumpsters. Ralphie talks about his crew, but Tony points out that Ralphie hasn't been made captain of Richie Aprile's old crew yet. The dispute is over who will get an upcoming garbage contract for Reardon township. Ralphie says the Reardon recycling manager, Mr Zachary, is threatening to bust them all with the Environmental Protection Agency and Albert backs this up. Tony tells Ralphie to fix Zachery but forbids anyone from starting any more fires.

Tony, Barbara and Janice gather at Cozzerelli's. Tony says Livia didn't want a service, Barbara wants a priest to be there and a tearful Janice worries about how it will look if they don't have a service. Tony eventually agrees to having the works and paying for it himself, just to shut everyone up. Janice wants a time for people to share remembrances at Livia's wake but Tony rejects the idea as California bullshit.

Mobster Raymond Curto meets with his FBI handler. He volunteers to wear a wire to Livia's funeral.

At Livia's house Janice is tapping the basement walls looking for loot when Tony arrives. Janice has been going through their old possessions. Livia kept all of Tony's stuff, a baby shoe and communion certificate of Barbara's, but nothing from Janice's childhood.

Everyone prepares for the funeral in a different way. Silvio has a temper tantrum because he will have to miss the Jets' first home game to attend. Furio, Christopher and Adriana smoke and snort various drugs.

The funeral home does a brisk trade in people coming to pay their respects to Livia and her family. The FBI's

Newark office has sent a sympathy wreath. Junior arrives, all out of sorts. He is accompanied by Bacala, who says his own father is very ill too. State Assemblyman Ronald Zellman makes an appearance, as does Reverend James Jr. Junior tells Tony that Ralphie wants a bump up to captain. Junior says Ralphie has been a top earner since taking over Richie's crew, pulling it into shape.

Ralphie watches as his men beat Mr Zachary.

After Livia is buried, Janice tells Svetlana to vacate Livia's house by the weekend. The Russian woman says Tony told her she could stay longer. Janice demands the return of Livia's record collection, which Svetlana claims was given to her as a present. Janice says the records are worth a fortune to the right collector.

At Livia's wake Carmela is hitting the booze heavily. When Tony opens a mirrored cupboard in a hallway, Pussy Bonpensiero is reflected in the mirror for a moment. Tony stops and looks around, as if he caught the ghostly apparition out the corner of his eye. Paulie and Furio are standing near Tony at the time, but they do not notice.

Janice gathers everyone to share remembrances and feelings about Livia. They all stand or sit, silent and awkward. Hesh says the dead woman didn't mince words. Livia's best friend, Fanny, says she would always call with news if someone they knew had died or gone into hospital. Tony walks out in disgust when a guest says that at least Livia didn't suffer.

Outside Tony talks with his old friend Artie Bucco, who is catering the wake. Artie has been remembering Livia telling him that it was Tony who had the original Vesuvio restaurant burned down. Artie threatens to share this secret with the gathering. Tony follows him inside but before Artie can say anything Carmela speaks her mind. She says the wake is a crock of shit and describes Livia as terribly dysfunctional. Carmela's mother tries to hush her but Carmela's father Hugh demands to have his turn. He says they suffered for years under the yoke of Livia, who spoiled numerous family events and holiday gatherings. Barbara's husband endorses this view. After a painful silence, Artie invites everyone to try some of the desserts.

When everyone has left or gone to bed, Tony watches the end of *The Public Enemy*. He cries as the film finishes – but for whom is he crying?

Deep and Meaningful: The whole remembrance scene is excruciatingly awkward and cringe-making in its accuracy. Almost nobody has a good thing to say about Livia but some manage to concoct a few platitudes. Janice uses the occasion to be the centre of attention and act the role of grieving daughter. It takes a half-cut Carmela to unleash a little truth. Pray your wake isn't like this!

Mobspeak: Tony has a clutch of slang expressions to describe black people including ditsoon, charcoal briquette, mulignan and butterhead. Junior talks about Richie going into the programme (witness protection programme).

Mama Mia: Livia makes her final appearance as a CGI apparition, with her head cut from previous episodes and grafted on to the body of a double. Her dialogue in the short scene with Tony is also culled from the archives and sounds like a selection of Livia's greatest moans. She wishes the Lord would take her now. She supposes she should have kept her mouth shut, like a mute. She doesn't like swearing, it upsets her. Livia also manages to roll her eyes or her head half a dozen times, gets in three dismissive hand gestures and a couple of hankie waves.

Bright Lights, Baked Ziti: When Tony regains consciousness after collapsing, his first words are 'Uncle Ben', referring to a brand of rice the Sopranos have in their kitchen cupboard. It was the last thing he saw before passing out. Just before that, he got a packet of capiccola sausage slices out of the fridge to eat.

Carmela's father Hugh brings a box of pastries when he and his wife come round to offer their sympathies for Livia's death.

Tony watches the famous scene in *The Public Enemy* where James Cagney pushes a grapefruit into his girlfriend's face.

Next morning Tony is eating cereal straight from the box when members of the Family arrive to sympathise. Tony tells Vito Spatafore to eat a Shfiadell pastry while the others go outside to talk business.

Outside the funeral home Tony says people can drink, eat some Gorgonzola cheese and yak about Livia at the wake.

At the wake Artie remembers visiting Livia in hospital and taking her some food from his restaurant. Artie caters the food at the wake, which includes a finger buffet and desserts by Vesuvio's new pastry chef. Janice says everyone could take a break from eating for five minutes. Carmela berates her own hypocrisy at 'evading, smiling and passing out Cheese Puffs' at the wake.

Mobbed Up: Nearly half a dozen scenes from *The Public Enemy* are shown during this episode. Tony says it's a great movie. Noah credits the director, William Wellman, with inventing the gangster film genre, rather than Howard Hawks, whose film *Scarface* was released a year later. Noah says Cagney exemplified barbarity in *The Public Enemy*. Noah and Meadow are studying the film as part of a course entitled 'Images of Hyper-Capitalist Advancement in the Era of the Studio System'.

At the wake Furio talks with Paulie about the TV reality game show *Survivor*, which was a big hit on US television in 2000.

How Do You Feel?: Tony complains that Dr Melfi offers no condolences for the death of his mother, but then says it is a relief she hasn't – everyone else is all bullshit about it. Tony says he is glad Livia died. In fact, he had wished for it. He says relief flooded into his veins when he heard the news, because she could have testified against him in court. Now he feels guilty, because no good son should wish his mother dead.

He calls his mother a fucking demented old bat and a selfish, miserable old cunt who ruined his father's life. Dr Melfi says Tony is still letting his mother off. Tony is hopeful that the death of his mother means his therapy is done, but Dr Melfi doesn't agree.

Sleeping With the Fishes: Livia Soprano, killed by a massive stroke in her sleep. Dead at last, but definitely not forgotten . . .

I Dream of Jeannie Cusamano: Artie Bucco has a flashback to the day he visited Livia at the Green Grove nursing unit (#13, 'I Dream of Jeannie Cusamano'), when she told him Tony had Vesuvio torched.

The ghostly appearance of Pussy reflected in a mirror happens so quickly that most viewers in America caught it only on repeated viewings of this episode. Does Tony notice? He pauses for a moment after it happens, as if unnerved by what he saw in the mirror . . .

Quote/Unquote: Carmela warns her husband against playing the race card, as it will only drive Meadow into Noah's arms. 'Not if I cut off those fucking arms,' Tony says.

AJ is befuddled by Robert Frost's use of snow as a metaphor for death. 'I thought black was death.'

Tony dismisses Janice's fears about being implicated in the disappearance of Richie Aprile. 'Jesus, that case is colder than your tits.'

Carmela's father, Hugh DeAngelis, demands his wife Mary give him a chance to speak his mind at Livia's wake. 'Goddammit, who are you – the Minister of Propaganda?'

Soundtrack: 'I'm Your Captain' by Grand Funk Railroad. 'If I Loved You' from the musical *Carousel*. 'I'm Forever Blowing Bubbles' by Les Paul and Mary Ford.

Surveillance Report: 'Proshai, Livushka' is Russian for 'Goodbye, Little Livia', according to Svetlana. She uses the phrase to toast Livia's memory.

Marcia Haufrecht returns as Fanny, the friend Livia ran over way back in #02, '46 Long'. Fanny had her hip broken in the auto accident – now she attends Livia's wake in a wheelchair. Also returning in this episode is Father Felix (played by Peter McRobbie), the priest Paulie berated for failing to secure him divine immunity in #22, 'From Where To Eternity'.

The Public Enemy uses the song 'I'm Forever Blowing Bubbles' as its theme tune. The song was subsequently adopted by fans of London's West Ham United football club.

Watch out for the mystery man who appears on the stairs behind Tony during the remembrance sequence, then disappears back upstairs again. This detail caused endless speculation on the Internet as hardcore fans tried to discern the identity of this individual, who looks a little like Uncle Junior. Eventually someone from the show's production team said the mystery man was merely an extra who wandered into shot, decided to avoid the sharing of remembrances and retreated back upstairs again.

Ralphie Cifaretto is played by Joe Pantoliano, who has starred in the hit films *The Matrix*, *The Fugitive* and *Bound*. He was Guido the Killer Pimp in the 1983 film *Risky Business* with Tom Cruise. State Assemblyman Ronald Zellman is played by Peter Riegert, who starred in *Local Hero* and *The Mask*.

The Verdict: 'I wish the Lord would take me now.' Livia finally gets her wish and everybody else has to deal with the fallout. Meanwhile, Tony's racist attitude and comments alienate his daughter, driving her away from the family.

This episode was necessitated by the death of the actress Nancy Marchand, who played Livia Soprano in Seasons One and Two. Alas, the CGI sequence just doesn't work. The special-effects company that did the work said it cost a six-figure sum – David Chase should ask for his money back. It is easy to say in retrospect, but the show would have been better served if Tony had had the same conversation with Livia over the telephone.

Despite this glitch, the episode is an inspired effort as Tony wrestles with his feelings for his dead mother. Several significant characters get their introduction and crucial plotlines for the rest of the season are begun.

29
Fortunate Son

US Transmission Date: 11 March 2001

Writer: Todd A Kessler
Director: Henry J Bronchtein
Cast: Joseph Siravo (Johnny Boy Soprano),
Rocco Sisto (Young Junior Soprano),
Tony Lip (Carmine Lupertazzi),
Laila Robins (Young Livia), Peter Byrne (Security Guard),
Megan Curry (Punked-Out Co-ed),
Steven Grillo (Pizza Customer #1),
Mario Lavanderia (Male Student),
Steve Mellow (Bill Owens),
Peter Napoliello (Football Dad),
Sal Petraccione (George Piocosta),
Frank Savino (Operator #1), Paul Reggio (Operator #2),
Jessica Ripton (Pizza Customer #2),
Johnny Spanish (Junkie),
Brian Anthony Wilson (Warren Dupree),
Lou Bonacki (Francis Satriale),
Mark Damiano II (Young Tony Soprano),
Juliet Fox (Young Janice), Elxis McLaren
(Young Barbara)

Storyline: It's football season, the busiest time of year for the Family. Christopher gets a call to prepare for the ceremony where he will become a made man. He tells Adriana this means she will have to quit her job as a hostess at Vesuvio restaurant. Paulie and Silvio collect the very nervous Christopher and take him to the ceremony. Tony performs the ceremony on Christopher and another prospective Mafia member, Eugene Pontecorvo. During the ritual Christopher is perturbed by a blackbird, which appears at a window.

When the ceremony is completed the Family hold a celebration meal. Paulie gives Christopher his sports betting business. All Christopher has to do is give Paulie one-tenth of his take every week, with a minimum payment of six thousand dollars. Tony talks with the New York Family man Carmine Lupertazzi, who asks about the progress of a riverfront esplanade project planned for Newark, New Jersey. Tony says his man in the State Assembly reports that the matching funds are very close. The development agency has added plans for a City of Newark Museum of Science and Trucking. Johnny Sack is hovering in the background, trying to listen to their conversation. Carmine asks how Tony is doing with his panic attacks and psychotherapy. Tony is unhappy that everyone seems to know about his health problems.

Tony and Janice discuss her nineteen-year-old fiancé Drew, who is still in California. Janice plans to stay in New Jersey until Livia's estate is settled. Tony suggests she move back into Livia's house. He says Svetlana is moving soon.

Christopher and his associate Benny Fazio go to the Ooh-Fa Pizza Restaurant, where they run into Jackie Aprile Jr and Dino Zerilli. Dino congratulates Christopher on being made, which Jackie reluctantly endorses. He is thinking of dropping out of Rutgers University. Dino says they are planning to hit a coffee house on the campus. Jackie gets into a shouting match with a customer who bumps into him.

Tony tells Dr Melfi he wants results from the therapy or it ends. She says the next step is for him to consider cognitive behavioural therapy. They trace his latest anxiety attack to his taking some capiccola sausage from the fridge.

Christopher takes a heavy loss on the points spread from a football game. The betting-parlour manager, Warren Dupree, says Paulie used to offload some of the action on to other bookies, to spread the risk. Christopher has a tantrum – he's going to struggle to pay Paulie the six-thousand-dollar minimum.

Tony barbecues meat for a big Sunday family dinner. Tony asks Christopher to look out for Jackie. The guests include Carmela's parents Mary and Hugh, Christopher and Adriana, plus Ralphie Cifaretto and Rosalie Aprile. Ralphie is dating the wife of the late Jackie Aprile Sr. Jackie Jr is also meant to be at lunch but he phones and rudely tells his mother he won't be coming. Carmela says she'll ask Tony to have a heart-to-heart with Jackie Jr. Meadow phones from Columbia but doesn't want to speak to her father.

Christopher gives four thousand dollars to Paulie – only two-thirds of what he owes. Paulie taxes him another two thousand dollars, so Christopher has to find another four thousand in the next two days.

Tony has a lunch meeting with Jackie Jr at Vesuvio. He tells the surly youth that Richie was a rat who has gone into the witness protection programme. Tony says Jackie's dad never wanted the mob life for his son, and Tony feels the same way about AJ.

Tony goes to see AJ play at a school football game. AJ comes on as part of the defensive line in the closing minutes of the final quarter and grabs a crucial turnover by jumping on a fumbled ball. Tony is very proud.

Janice shifts into Tony's old room at Livia's house because Svetlana is sleeping in Janice's former room for a few more days. Svetlana still won't give Livia's records to Janice. She says possession is nine-tenths of the law.

Christopher is stressed out, shouting at Adriana and fretting about how he will pay Paulie. He believes the bird sitting outside on the windowsill at his ceremony was a curse. Adriana says a bird inside the house symbolises death, not bad luck.

Svetlana wakes up. Her artificial leg is missing and so is Janice. She calls Tony to come round. When he arrives, his old mistress, Svetlana's cousin Irina, is at Livia's house. Tony doesn't want to talk to Irina but agrees to contact Janice about the missing leg. He gets some capiccola from the fridge and it triggers a memory from his childhood.

He recalls seeing his father and Uncle Junior demand payment from Francis Satriale, the original owner of Satriale's Pork Store. Johnny Boy Soprano chopped off one of the butcher's fingers with a meat cleaver. That night Tony's father says what he saw was a lesson – a man honours his debts. Johnny and Livia have an amorous moment when she gets the roast meat out of the oven. When the meat is being carved, young Tony faints in the kitchen – his first anxiety attack.

Tony tells Dr Melfi what he has remembered. She recalls that the attack that led Tony to begin therapy happened when he was cooking meat. She says his very first attack happened when he short-circuited after witnessing his parents' sexuality, the violence and blood associated with the food he was about to eat, and the thought that someday he would have to bring home the bacon like his father. Melfi relates this to an experience of the writer Marcel Proust, which inspired a seven-volume classic. She says understanding root causes will make Tony less vulnerable to future attacks. The therapist asks Tony to keep a log of any further thoughts he has about all this.

AJ and Tony are watching football at home while Carmela prepares a care package to take to Meadow. AJ goes with her but Tony stays at home on Carmela's advice so he doesn't further alienate Meadow.

At Columbia Meadow and Noah are waiting for Carmela and Tony to arrive. Meadow knows what her father said to Noah and wants to confront him about it in front of Noah. Carmela tries to placate Meadow.

Svetlana's boyfriend Bill Owens helps her move out of Livia's house as Janice is moving in. Janice claims to know nothing about the disappearance of Svetlana's leg. The Russian woman swears vengeance on Janice.

Christopher and Benny visit Jackie Jr at the pizza restaurant. Dino has been arrested for possession. Jackie says they were going to rob a benefit concert for Amnesty International at Rutgers University. Christopher and Benny adopt the plan with Jackie as getaway driver.

At dinner AJ says he doesn't want to go to college. He was perturbed by his visit to the Columbia campus and doesn't think he's smart enough to attend.

Christopher and Benny rob the concert box office, while Jackie stays in the car. He pisses his pants because he dares not leave the car to urinate.

Next day, Christopher gives Paulie the four thousand dollars. He talks about Jackie helping him. Christopher is finding being a made man a lot tougher than he expected.

Paulie gives Tony his weekly cut and reports about Jackie helping Christopher at the Rutgers robbery. Tony says newly made guys are subject to strip searches for surveillance wires.

At football practice the coach makes AJ defensive captain of the team. The teenager passes out, just like his dad . . .

Deep and Meaningful: There are two very insightful moments in this episode. Dr Melfi and Tony make a breakthrough in tracing his panic attacks back to an incident from his childhood. In Season Two Tony discovered that his father had suffered from the same problem. As this episode ends, AJ is unexpectedly given a position of responsibility and leadership. He reacts in the traditional Soprano male fashion – by passing out . . .

Mobspeak: Tony wants to know why Jackie Jr is hanging out with a mortadella (loser) like Dino Zerilli.

Mama Mia: Tony says the only time you could count on his mother being in a good mood was when the weekly meat delivery from Satriale's showed up, or sometimes when fresh vegetables came from Fusco's. He says it was probably the only time his father got laid.

Bright Lights, Baked Ziti: Adriana is making cheese dogs when Christopher gets the call about his ceremony. After he has been made, there's a vast buffet laid on for all the mobsters. Tony and Carmine help themselves to the food.

Janice is eating crisps and drinking a beer when she and Tony talk.

The manager of the Ooh-Fa Pizza Restaurant orders a free large OF pizza and soft drink of choice for Christopher to celebrate his being made.

Tony barbecues various meats for the Sunday family dinner. Carmela serves roast pumpkin and string beans with Parmesan cheese.

Tony and Furio have lunch at Vesuvio. Tony tells Artie
that Meadow is always coming home from Columbia to
haul food away.

After the football Tony takes AJ to have some hotdogs.
That night Tony, Carmela and AJ eat a roast dinner at
home together.

Tony asks Svetlana if Janice has put any food in Livia's
fridge yet. Svetlana says Livia's weekly meat delivery is still
coming. Tony eats some capiccola sausage from the fridge,
triggering his flashbacks.

Dr Melfi says Marcel Proust's inspirational flashbacks
were triggered by eating a Madeleine, a kind of tea cookie.

AJ and Tony eat crisps while they watch football on TV.
Carmela is taking Meadow some of her homemade brasciole.

Tony, Carmela and AJ have a meal including pasta,
salad and bread.

Tony is having steak for lunch at Vesuvio when Paulie
arrives.

Mobbed Up: Adriana is worried that Christopher will be
whacked instead of being made, as happened to Joe Pesci's
character in *Goodfellas*. Christopher says she's seen too
many movies. When Christopher arrives at the ceremony
unscathed, Silvio accuses him of sitting on one ass cheek
for the whole journey. Tony uses the same line Christopher
used on Adriana.

Janice watches a TV show that mentions how Jayne
Mansfield broke into Hollywood with a single phone call.

Christopher and Benny wear masks from the film
Scream as disguises when they rob the benefit concert's box
office.

How Do You Feel?: Tony says it wasn't traumatic seeing
his father cut off Satriale's finger – it was a rush for him to
witness the violence. When Dr Melfi makes the connection
between meat, violence and his parents, Tony says he
doesn't want to think about any of this. He protests that
his head is spinning when the therapist starts talking about
Marcel Proust.

I Dream of Jeannie Cusamano: Tony has two consecutive flashbacks to the late 1960s, which show his first anxiety attack and how it relates to meat.

Quote/Unquote: The New York mobster Carmine Lupertazzi confuses religion with shame when discussing psychiatry with Tony. 'There's no stigmata these days.'

Janice extols the virtues of her young fiancé Drew. 'He's nineteen, actually, and he can go all night.'

Carmela tells her daughter that Tony is outside. 'Burning a cross?' Meadow replies.

Dr Melfi explains how Marcel Proust was inspired to write a seven-volume classic by biting a tea cookie, which unleashed tidal waves of memories. Tony is not impressed. 'This sounds very gay.'

Soundtrack: 'Shaking That Ass' by Groove Armada. 'It's All Good' by De La Soul. 'Rock and Roll' by Led Zeppelin. 'The Happy Organ' by Dave 'Baby' Cortez. 'The Good, The Bad and The Ugly' by Hugo Montenegro. Johnny Boy Soprano sings 'All Of Me' to Livia in flashback. 'Sally Go Round the Roses' by Jaynetts. 'Since I Met You, Baby' by Ivory Joe Hunter. 'Ain't Talking 'Bout Love' by Van Halen. 'Where's the Money' by Dan Hicks and His Hot Licks.

Surveillance Report: Joseph Siravo (Johnny Boy), Laila Robins (Livia) and Rocco Sisto (Young Junior) all reprise the roles they first played in the first-season episode 'Down Neck'. But the young Tony and Janice are played by different child actors in this episode.

Also returning are Sal Petraccione as George Piocosta (last seen in the first-season episode 'Meadowlands') and Tony's former mistress, Irina, played by Oksana Babiy.

The Verdict: 'Take away Tony Soprano, he's a zero with shoes.' Christopher finally gets his wish and becomes a made man, but soon finds it brings much greater stress and responsibility. As he gets on the wrong side of Paulie, Janice riles Svetlana and Tony alienates Meadow with his racism.

Several significant stories begin or develop here that will resonate through the rest of the season, such as Jackie Jr's attraction to the mob life and AJ struggling with adolescence. This episode shows many of the show's younger characters having problems coping with the onset of adult responsibility.

Season Two episodes suffered from the sidelining of Livia and Tony's sessions with Dr Melfi. Livia's death could have made matters worse but it has actually freed the show from its past and enabled the creative team to move forward into fresh territory . . .

30
Employee of the Month
US Transmission Date: 18 March 2001

Writers: Robin Green and Mitchell Burgess
Director: John Patterson
Cast: Richard Romanus (Richard La Penna),
Shaun Toub (Arouk Abboubi),
Traci Godfrey (Edwina Fowley),
Zabryna Guevara (Clerk), Stephen Kunken (ER Doctor),
Jill Marie Lawrence (Detective Piersol),
Mario Polit (Jesus Rossi), Bobby Rivers (News Reporter).

Storyline: Irina calls Tony at home. She wants to see him again and uses Svetlana's missing leg as an excuse for phoning. He tells her never to call him at home again.

Dr Melfi has taken her estranged husband Richard back into her life. At home they argue about Melfi having a mobster as a patient. She says Tony made a real breakthrough recently. Richard works for the National Italian American Foundation, fighting against negative depictions of Italian Americans in the media. His latest campaign is against a TV film called *Gangster*. Richard urges Melfi to drop Tony as a patient.

At her next session with Tony, Melfi is disappointed to discover he has not been thinking about the recent breakthrough at all. The therapist suggests involving Carmela in their sessions but Tony doesn't like the idea. Melfi accuses him of not trying but Tony changes the subject.

Melfi tells her own therapist, Dr Kupferberg, that Richard was right – she has been charmed by a sociopath. She agonises about her relationship with Richard and accidentally discloses Tony's name to her therapist. Dr Kupferberg suggests it's time to hand Tony over to a behavioural therapist.

Janice is searching the basement of Livia's house with a metal detector, looking for loot. Tony arrives and tells his sister to give Svetlana's leg back, instead of holding it for ransom against Livia's record collection. He warns her not to fuck with the Russians.

Ralphie and Jackie Jr have dinner at Vesuvio. Rosalie is seeing Ralphie and wants him and Jackie to get along. Ralphie notes Jackie's interest in Meadow Soprano and tries to build a bond with the surly 23-year-old. After dinner Ralphie takes Jackie when he goes to confront a late-paying garbage collector, Arouk Abboubi. Jackie gives Arouk a beating at Ralphie's behest. Ralphie gives Jackie a cut of the proceeds.

Tony visits Johnny Sack, who has bought a palatial house in New Jersey. Tony is upset that the New York Family man has moved into Soprano Family territory, but Johnny insists there is no hidden agenda.

Tony meets with Ralphie and says he is installing Gigi Cestone as captain of the Aprile crew. This is partly as punishment for involving Jackie Jr in the beating of Arouk. Tony admits Gigi is there to spy on the Aprile crew, but says that shouldn't be necessary – Ralphie makes it necessary. Ralphie protests that he is busting his ass for Tony, but to no avail.

Dr Melfi tells Tony he's ready to move on to behavioural therapy with another psychiatrist. Tony apologises for his attitude at the last session and accuses her of giving up on him.

Afterwards Dr Melfi walks down a stairwell to her car in the building's basement, talking to Richard on her cellphone. A man in a red cap passes her going up the stairs. Melfi rings off as she enters the basement and goes to her car. The man in the red cap grabs her from behind and threatens to stab her. Melfi tries to escape but her assailant is too fast and too strong. He drags the therapist into the stairwell and rapes her.

Melfi is being treated at hospital when Richard arrives. Melfi's face is bruised and her left leg is badly sprained. A man matching her attacker's description has been caught with Melfi's palm pilot in his possession. He denies the rape and says he found the palm pilot on the street. The man in custody is Jesus Rossi, a 28-year-old with no previous convictions. Richard is startled to hear that Rossi has an Italian name, because he had been told the attacker was Puerto Rican. He wrings his hands in anguish. Their son Jason arrives. He is furious that his mother was attacked and vows to kill the rapist.

Melfi phones the Soprano household to cancel Tony's next appointment. The therapist tells Carmela she hurt her leg in a car accident. When Carmela tells Tony, he worries that Melfi will have a scar on her leg. Carmela seems unimpressed by his concern. Tony quickly changes the subject by asking if Carmela would get involved in his therapy sessions. She agrees.

Melfi is waiting at home for the police to call so she can pick her assailant from an identity parade. Richard arrives home and phones the police. The detective on the case has been transferred to another department and Jesus Rossi has been released. The police had to let him go on a technicality after mishandling the chain of custody and misplacing forensic evidence for a while. Richard threatens to sue the police. Melfi and Richard argue about who is to blame and accuse each other of being culpable. Melfi is especially upset about Richard's reaction to Rossi having an Italian surname, as if any misdeed by an Italian might damage his self-esteem.

Tony and his crew are hanging out at the Bada Bing!'s back office. They are swapping jokes about how fat Johnny Sack's wife Ginny is when Johnny Sack walks in. He tells them to watch the news for once. On TV, State Assem-blyman Ronald Zellman announces that the first $25 million of state and federal matching funds have been approved for the New Jersey project. The Museum of Science and Trucking alone will cost $100 million. The mobsters all raise a toast – they stand to make a fortune, as Zellman is in Tony's pocket.

Melfi and Richard apologise to each other – they realise their argument was born of frustration. Richard says he could kill Rossi with his own hands, but then he'd end up in jail.

Christopher visits Tony at home and they talk business in the basement. Christopher apologises for involving Jackie in the box-office heist. Tony repeats that he doesn't want Jackie involved in the mob.

Melfi goes back to work with the aid of a cane. She has to use the stairwell and go past the spot where she was raped. Tony is shocked when he sees her appearance at their session. She lies about how she got her injuries. Melfi gives him some notes on behavioural therapy to read. Her cane falls over and she almost jumps out of her chair, clearly terrified. Tony is worried and asks her if everything is all right. She appreciates his concern.

Jackie is at the Soprano house borrowing a samovar for his mother when Tony comes home. Meadow arrives and asks Tony for money. She and Jackie flirt in front of Tony.

Melfi is buying her lunch from a sandwich bar when she sees the face of the rapist on the wall, enshrined as employee of the month. The therapist drops her drink on the floor and walks out.

Two burly Russian men break into Livia's house and start beating Janice. She takes them to a bowling alley where she has Svetlana's leg hidden in a locker. Janice surrenders the leg meekly.

Melfi dreams about a Rottweiler dog attacking her rapist, Jesus Rossi.

Melfi discusses the dream with her therapist. Melfi realises the dog represents Tony, a violent creature whom she could unleash on Rossi. By comparison, Richard is employing a $300-an-hour attorney to seek some legal recourse. Melfi reassures her therapist that she will not break the social compact by using Tony as a weapon of vengeance.

Tony goes to see Janice, who is being treated at an emergency room in hospital. She has three broken ribs. Janice says she has hit bottom and now feels born again in the Lord. 'I give myself up totally to God.' Tony says Janice has done this before with a variety of gods and it only spells trouble.

Johnny and Ginny Sack have a house-warming party. Tony's crew wonder how much the huge house cost. Gigi ponders the level of property taxes and says you actually have to pay them. Tony notices Ralphie deep in conversation with Johnny Sack.

Tony tells Dr Melfi he is ready to move on to behavioural therapy with another doctor. She is shocked and begins sobbing. Tony hugs and comforts her. He asks if there is something she wants to say to him. Dr Melfi says no.

Deep and Meaningful: The crucial moment in this episode is not the rape, but stems from its aftermath. Dr Melfi knows she can tell Tony what really happened to her and he would deliver a swift and terrible vengeance upon Jesus Rossi. As the episode is ending, he gives her a chance to do just that. There is a long, long pause as the therapist decides whether to tell Tony. The silence lasts for nine seconds, but it feels like forever. Finally, she rejects the chance to get revenge by using one of her patients. Melfi stays true to herself and her beliefs.

Mobspeak: Richard calls the TV film *Gangster* a stereotypical goombah fest (a goombah is a guy who hangs around and does things for mobsters, as Bacala does for Junior). Silvio says Tony cut off Ralphie's gotsies (short for stugots, the testicles).

Bright Lights, Baked Ziti: Richard and Dr Melfi prepare dinner together. Richard chops herbs and prepares chicken for cooking, while Melfi crushes garlic and sets the table.

Tony is looking for food in the fridge when Carmela takes the phone call from Dr Melfi. He wants to know who ate the last piece of cake. Tony munches on a stick of celery instead, a healthier alternative.

When Tony's crew are cracking jokes about Ginny Sack, Silvio offers this gem: 'She's so fat, her blood type is ragu.'

Meadow invites Jackie Jr to visit her in New York so they can have sushi.

Dr Melfi orders a chicken avocado wrap at Wrap Nation sandwich bar. She is shocked when she sees her rapist's photo on the wall as employee of the month and walks out, leaving her lunch behind.

In Melfi's dream she puts two pieces of dried pasta into a vending machine instead of coins. One of the pieces reappears in the coin-return slot.

Mobbed Up: Richard whines about the US television network ABC producing the film *Gangster*. He says it is full of stereotypes and it tries to give Mafia sociopaths the tragic grandeur of Al Pacino.

Ralphie quotes dialogue from the film *Gladiator*: 'What we do in life echoes in eternity.' Silvio says Ralphie is fucking obsessed with the movie.

How Do You Feel?: Tony is unable to answer when Dr Melfi asks if he is happy. She accuses him of not trying in therapy but he changes the subject. Without a hint of irony, he says AJ shies away from anything that requires real effort. Tony believes his son picks that up from him.

Tony is genuinely concerned for Melfi when he sees her after the rape, even though he doesn't know what has really happened.

How Do You Feel, Doctor?: After her dream, Melfi tells Dr Kupferberg that she felt a sense of relief. She felt safe for the first time since being raped. She realises the Rottweiler dog represents Tony. Like him, it has a big head and massive shoulders. (Rottweilers were used by Roman armies to guard camps.) Melfi says no feeling has ever been so sweet as to see her rapist beg, plead and scream for his life. She admits to feeling a certain satisfaction in knowing she could have Rossi squashed like a bug if she wanted.

I Dream of Jeannie Cusamano: Dr Melfi dreams she is working in her office late at night. She hears footsteps outside her door and the sound of a car being unlocked by remote. the back of her office door has a sign which says: DANGER! HIGH VOLTAGE! NJG&E (New Jersey Gas and Electric). Melfi opens the doors to her office.

Next she is standing by an Acme Cola vending machine in her office. She puts two pieces of dried pasta into the coin slot but no can of drink is dispensed. Melfi crouches down and puts her arm deep into the machine but can't get her drink. A single piece of pasta appears in the coin-return slot. Melfi is now stretched out on the floor, her arm completely caught inside the vending machine. A black Rottweiler dog appears and barks at her menacingly.

Jesus Rossi appears in the doorway. He stands over Melfi and then takes hold of her legs. The dog attacks Rossi, who screams in pain and anguish. Melfi wakes up with a start.

Quote/Unquote: Janice sums up Irina, Tony's ex-mistress: 'Miss Petrograd Carburettor Works from 1987?'

Johnny Sack welcomes Tony to his new home: 'Look who's here – the guinea welcome wagon!'

Tony delivers the best of the jokes about the obese Ginny Sack. 'When Ginny hauls ass, she has to make two trips.'

Christopher busts Tony's balls about trying to keep Jackie away from the Family. 'The life's good enough for me but not for Little Lord Fuckpants?'

After her beating Janice has an epiphany. 'I think there's only one trajectory for me – God.'

Tony is less than convinced by her revelation. 'All this soul-searching, Janice, it's always on my fucking dime.'

Soundtrack: 'Speedo' by the Cadillacs. 'Americano' by the Brian Setzer Orchestra. 'Oops, I Did It Again' by Britney Spears. Janice tries to play the Rolling Stones' 'Satisfaction' on electric guitar. 'Love Rollercoaster' by the Ohio Players. 'I Don't Make Promises (I Can't Break)' by Shannon Curfman. 'Fisherman's Daughter' by Daniel Lanois.

Surveillance Report: The film director Peter Bogdanovich returns as Dr Melfi's therapist, Dr Elliot Kupferberg. Also reprising their respective roles are Richard Romanus and Will McCormack as Dr Melfi's husband Richard and son Jason.

The rape of Dr Melfi was kept a complete surprise until this episode was first broadcast in America. Trailers for the episode hinted that something shocking and dramatic would happen but gave no other clue. Few other TV series would have been able to keep the storyline under wraps and some might even have been tempted to use it as a way of gaining publicity and higher ratings. *The Sopranos*' cast and crew pride themselves on maintaining a code of silence about future plot developments and it paid off in this episode.

The episode sets up a comparison between the law-abiding Richard and the brute strength of the lawless Tony. There's a scene of Richard talking about how he could kill the rapist with his own hands but can't because he would be sent to jail. The action cuts to Tony towering over the camera, hefting an axe and cutting wood with practised ease. This just reinforces the impression of Richard as a weak, hand-wringing liberal.

The Verdict: 'Who could I sic [let loose] on that son of a bitch to tear him to shreds?' Dr Melfi is raped but her assailant gets off after the police bungle procedures. Despite this, the therapist resists the urge to have Tony intervene for her.

Watching this episode is like being suddenly punched in the stomach – unexpected, shocking and painful. The rape scene is unflinching without being gratuitous, while the aftermath is adroitly handled. When Melfi is denied justice, viewers watching the final scene are likely to find themselves shouting at her to involve Tony. Instead she stays true to herself and her ideals.

The rape and its fallout dominate this episode but several significant developments take place. Ralphie is fast emerging as a dangerous individual, while Jackie Jr twice shows interest in Meadow Soprano. Watch this space . . .

31
Another Toothpick

US Transmission Date: 25 March 2001

Writer: Terence Winter
Director: Jack Bender
Cast: Burt Young (Bobby 'Bacala' Baccalieri Sr),
Richard Portnow (Attorney Hal Melvoin),
Brian Tarantina (Mustang Sally),
Paul Schulze (Father Phil), Vanessa Ferlito (Tina),
Sheila Gibbs (Receptionist),
Charles S Dutton (Officer Wilmore),
Vincent Orofino (Bryan Spatafore),
Michael Variano (Petey),
Michael Martochio (Carlos),
Eric Weiner (Manager)

Storyline: Tony and Carmela have their first joint therapy session with Dr Melfi but it does not go well. They both become very angry. Tony drives home too fast while Carmela cries. She says the therapist took his side. Tony is pulled over for speeding by a black cop. He tries to gently bribe the cop without success.

Two workers from Spatafore Brothers Construction drive to a sandwich shop to get lunch for the team. Bryan Spatafore stays with the car so it doesn't get a ticket. A couple sitting in a parked car start arguing. The woman gets out and asks Bryan for a lift. He declines – he doesn't want to get involved in a domestic argument. The man emerges from the car and attacks Bryan, viciously beating him with a golf putter.

Tony and Paulie visit the comatose Bryan in hospital. The brain-damaged builder is the nephew of Vito Spatafore, one of the Aprile crew. Vito and the rest of the crew – their captain Gigi, Eugene and Ralphie – are all at the bedside, along with Jackie Jr. Ralphie tries to make jokes but nobody finds them funny. Vito has told the police nothing but he knows the culprit was a gangster called Mustang Sally. Vito wants bloody vengeance and Jackie Jr volunteers to help. Tony sends Jackie Jr out of the room. Ralphie is giving Gigi agita – he's obviously still bitter that Tony passed him over to give the captaincy to Gigi. Gigi says Mustang Sally will be brought under control with extreme fucking prejudice.

Father Phil leads a funeral for Carmela's uncle, Febby Viola, who has died of cancer. Uncle Junior arrives partway through the service, accompanied by Bobby 'Bacala' Jr and his father, 'Bacala' Sr. The old man coughs almost constantly into a handkerchief. He has come back after nearly a decade of retirement in Miami to visit his grandchildren. Junior looks unhappy and out of sorts, as he has done for weeks. After the funeral Carmela and Father Phil share an awkward moment outside the church. Tony tells Bacala Sr about the planned hit on Sally – Bacala Sr was Sally's godfather. The old man has lung cancer.

The Vesuvio restaurant has a great night's business. Artie wants to celebrate with Adriana but she resigns as hostess. Christopher doesn't want her working now he's a made man.

Uncle Junior and Bacala Jr try to play draughts ('checkers' in the US), but neither has his mind on the game. Bacala Jr is upset because Tony has approved having Bacala Sr whack Mustang Sally. He asks Junior to intervene.

Junior and Tony meet in the office of Junior's lawyer. Tony refuses to change his decision about the hit. Using Bacala Sr was Gigi's idea – if Tony changes that, it will seem he's undermining the new captain. Tony also believes using the old man is a smart move. Sally has been hiding but approached Bacala Sr for help. He can get close to Sally without suspicion.

Tony and Christopher are the last dinner customers at Vesuvio when Artie emerges drunkenly from the kitchen. He calls Christopher a cocksucker for insisting Adriana quit work and jokes about poisoning the newly made mobster. Christopher throws Artie against a wall and threatens to poke his eye out with a fork. Tony rescues Artie by pulling Christopher away and sending him outside. Artie confesses that he's in love with Adriana and says his wife Charmaine is a cunt. Tony tells him to sober up – he has a business opportunity for Artie.

Tony talks to State Assemblyman Zellman, demanding to know when his speeding ticket will be sorted out.

Junior tells Bacala Jr he decided not to intervene with Tony. Bacala Sr arrives, coughing up blood. Junior urges him to consult Dr John Kennedy, the head of oncology at a local hospital. Junior is angry about Bacala Sr being used for the hit, but the old man says he wanted the job. It makes him feel useful. He doesn't care if it goes wrong – he's dead already.

Artie and Charmaine argue about Artie's plan to launch a line of Italian sauces in a business with Tony called Satriale's. She insists it will become a front for the mob and a guaranteed disaster.

Tony, Paulie, Gigi, Ralphie and Johnny Sack meet over a meal at Vesuvio. Johnny says Junior asked him to get Tony to reconsider using Bacala Sr. Ralphie needles Gigi about the decision. Tony says the matter is closed.

Tony goes to a garden centre to buy piping. He encounters the cop who stopped him. The cop says he has been transferred to the property room and is no longer eligible for overtime – hence the weekend job. Afterwards, Tony feels sorry for the cop and tries to get him reinstated.

Bacala Sr whacks Mustang Sally and an associate called Carlos. Driving home, the old man has a coughing fit. He passes out and crashes his car into a pole, dying as a result of the collision.

Bacala Jr tells Junior about his dad's death. Junior wants to know whether the crash or the cancer killed Bacala Sr. The dead man's son says he doesn't know. Junior smashes up a room in his own house.

Charmaine is working reception at Vesuvio but is no match for the charming and beautiful Adriana in Artie's eyes. The couple argue and Artie insists he is going into business with Tony. He pushes Charmaine into seeking a divorce. She pledges to keep their children and walks out.

Tony meets with Junior at Dr Schreck's office. Junior says he has cancer of the stomach. He had his first test the day before Livia's funeral. Tony realises that's why Junior has been acting so weird lately. Junior won't know how bad the cancer is until surgeons operate in a fortnight. Junior believes cancer deaths come in threes – first Jackie Aprile Sr, then Carmela's uncle, then Bacala Sr. But the last of the trio was killed by a car crash, so Junior believes the cancer will get him instead to complete the threesome. Junior makes Tony promise not to tell anyone about the cancer.

Tony immediately phones Janice to tell her. They have a drink and talk about death. Janice asks whatever happened to Pussy. Tony says he went into the witness protection programme. Since that's the same place he says Richie went, Janice knows Pussy is actually dead.

Meadow comes home to do her laundry. Her bike was stolen from outside the college library by a black guy, which gives Tony reason to smirk. Meadow attacks his racist attitudes and storms out, taking a lamp from the basement. She says the lighting at college gives her headaches.

Artie and Adriana have a secret dinner. Artie says he will miss her and invites her to join his business with Tony as a vice president. He asks if she's sure about marriage and keeps trying to hold Adriana's hand. She excuses herself to go to the bathroom.

Zellman, Tony and Johnny Sack have a meal at Vesuvio to decide who gets to control which workers on the multimillion-dollar Newark project. Tony gets plumbing and electrical unions, while Johnny Sack gets the steel workers and bricklayers. Zellman offers to have the black cop reinstated but Tony, still smarting from Meadow's remarks, decides the cop got what he deserved.

FBI Agent Harris tells his boss that the wire in the Soprano basement has been neutralised, because Meadow took the lamp away to college.

Junior doesn't want to go to Bacala Sr's funeral. He tells Bacala Jr that he has cancer.

Tony returns to the garden centre to buy an ornament. Tony tries to give the cop some extra cash but he refuses to accept it and walks away . . .

Deep and Meaningful: Junior is distraught when he hears that Bacala Sr has died in the car crash. He demands to know the cause of death. Bacala Jr is mystified and asks why Junior cares about the details. Junior agrees that everyone should show respect for the dead man. Then he loses control, smashing up his room before rushing away. Junior almost never loses control, usually bottling up his feelings. The truth behind this scene is revealed later in the episode. Junior has cancer but hoped he would survive it if Bacala Sr was killed by the disease, ending a cycle of three cancer-related deaths.

Mobspeak: Tony tells Zellman to straighten (resolve) his speeding ticket. Ralphie calls Gigi 'my man Googoots' (stupid person). Junior says he is playing the big casino (cancer). He makes Tony promise to dummy up (keep quiet) about his medical condition.

Mama Mia: Janice says Livia always used to call people who died from cancer 'another toothpick'. Janice recalls that her mother hated giving or taking compliments, in case they invoked the wrath of God.

Bright Lights, Baked Ziti: Bryan Spatafore sends Petey into the sandwich store to get the construction workers' lunches. Bryan says Freddy wants peppers and eggs on one of the sandwiches.

Paulie brings a box of chocolates to the hospital. Vito promises he can keep his mouth shut but Ralphie says that is unless there's a salami sandwich around. When Tony and Paulie have left, Vito opens the chocolates and everybody has one.

Junior puts the remains of his lunch down the garbage disposal but it jams on a fruit stone. Bacala Sr arrives with a shortcake from a bakery.

Artie and Charmaine carry fresh produce into the kitchen at Vesuvio as they argue about Artie launching a food business with Tony. Artie says she knows how people love his sauce. The first Vesuvio restaurant was opened by Artie's grandfather in the 1930s.

Tony, Paulie, Gigi, Ralphie and Johnny Sack have a dinner of pasta, bread and wine at Vesuvio.

Tony brings Junior the last of the sweetcorn from his garden when they meet at Dr Schreck's office.

Artie takes Adriana out to a very expensive restaurant as thanks for her work at Vesuvio. She goes to the bathroom just as their main courses of elaborately constructed cuisine arrive.

Junior is trying to have a sandwich when Bacala Jr arrives to take him to Bacala Sr's funeral.

Mobbed Up: Ralphie praises the quality of DVD as 'fucking incredible'. He quotes *Gladiator*: 'In this world or the next, I shall have my revenge.' Ralphie says that, with a flat-screen TV and surround sound, it's like the chariots are going through the fucking house.

Tony mocks the black cop at the garden centre. 'Oh, it's *Shaft*!'

Junior tries to watch a film starring Frank Sinatra, but struggles to see around the bulky body of Bacala Jr.

How Do You Feel?: Tony, Carmela and Dr Melfi sit in a resounding 25-second-long silence at their first joint therapy session. The only sound is Tony's stomach rumbling.

How Do You Feel, Carmela?: Carmela says she feels concerned and helpless when Tony passes out. She is also frustrated at Dr Melfi's inability to help him.

Sleeping With the Fishes: After four episodes with only one death (and that from natural causes), this episode suddenly opts for a pile-'em-high approach. Carmela's uncle dies from cancer off screen. Bacala Sr murders Mustang Sally and his friend Carlos with a handgun, before dying himself in a car crash. Four for the price of one – now *that's* value for money!

Quote/Unquote: Carmela reveals her hypocritical side when Tony gets a ticket for speeding. 'Makes me sick. You think they'd be out arresting dope dealers.'

Junior is dismissive when Bacala Jr asks him to intervene so Bacala Sr will not have to come out of retirement. 'Fuck that – we're in the navy?'

Artie parrots market research findings: 'Product brandings of things beginning with the letter V make people think of vagina – it's a turn off.'

Johnny Sack comments on a scale model for the new waterfront development. 'Fucking Newark. They got little hookers giving little blow jobs?'

Soundtrack: 'Jim Dandy' by Laverne Baker and the Gliders. *Concierto de Aranjuez* by Rodrigo. 'Sister Golden Hair' by America. Meadow sings along to 'Breathless' by the Corrs as she's doing her laundry. 'Shuck Dub' by RL Burnside.

Surveillance Report: Tony uses the name Mr Spears when he is contacting State Assemblyman Zellman.

There are pumpkins for sale on the counter at the garden centre, indicating that Hallowe'en is fast approaching. That dates this episode as taking place around October.

When Bacala Sr crashes his car, a sign falls from a lamppost which reads YOUR AD HERE. Some viewers took this as a swipe by the show's creators against product placement on television.

The Verdict: 'All this goddamn morbidity!' Junior reveals he has stomach cancer, Tony has a close encounter with a black cop and Bacala Jr's dad comes out of retirement for one last job. Meanwhile, Artie and Charmaine Bucco's marriage is coming apart at the seams.

This episode is relentlessly downbeat. Any humour that crawls from the human carnage is bleak at best. Four people die, Uncle Junior faces a medical death sentence and divorce seems certain for the Buccos. Artie is playing a very dangerous game by declaring his love for Adriana and goading Christopher.

In the midst of all this, Tony's attitude to the black cop flip flops back and forth between anger and sympathy. The subplot seems out of place in what is otherwise a grim but gripping episode.

32
University

US Transmission Date: 1 April 2001

Teleplay by: Terence Winter and Salvatore J Stabile
Story by: David Chase, Terence and Todd A Kessler,
Robin Green and Mitchell Burgess
Director: Allen Coulter
Cast: Michael Garfield (Len Tannenbaum),
Daniel Booth (Waiter),
Yvette Mercedes (Homeless Woman),
Richard Verdino (Police Officer),
Michette Ardente (Mandee),
Luiza Liccini (Stripper #1),
Marie Athanasiou (Stripper #2)

Storyline: Tony is approached by Tracee, one of the topless dancers at the Bada Bing!. She wants to thank him for suggesting she take her child to a doctor. Tracee has baked Tony some bread, which he politely refuses. She wants to be friends but Tony doesn't think that's a good idea since she is seeing Ralphie.

Ralphie and Rosalie join the Sopranos and Carmela's parents for Sunday lunch. Jackie Jr turns up to collect house keys from his mother after locking himself out of their house. He ignores Ralphie, who is dating Rosalie. Jackie asks after Meadow, who is spending Sunday at Columbia.

Meadow and Noah are spending a lot of time together and becoming much closer. They are kissing passionately in Meadow's dorm room when Caitlin walks in and interrupts them. Caitlin is pulling her own hair out and is on medication from the university medical centre. Noah leaves to write a paper and Meadow soon follows him. She joins Noah in his room. He advocates patience with Caitlin. Meadow is impressed with his sensitivity. They have sex for the first time.

Meadow goes home to visit. She is full of joy but still blanks her father.

There is a VIP room at the Bada Bing!. Georgie is the bouncer. He allows the dancers inside only if they give him fifty bucks and a blow job later. Tony is in a sideroom getting a blow job. Ralphie arrives and starts winding everyone up. He kisses Gigi on the mouth and hassles Georgie for never having seen *Gladiator*. Silvio and Paulie warn Ralphie to behave but he ignores them. Ralphie pokes Georgie with a pool cue, then starts swinging a chain above his head. It strikes Georgie in the eye socket, injuring him badly. Tony emerges and orders Ralphie to take Georgie to a hospital.

Meadow returns to her dorm room after spending the night at home. Caitlin is more clingy and obsessive than before. Meadow goes to see Noah. He suggests taking Caitlin out for her birthday. Noah and Meadow have sex.

Tracee approaches Tony at the Bada Bing!. She wants to show him the braces on her teeth. Silvio gets her up on stage to dance. He lent her $3,000 to get her teeth fixed.

Meadow and Noah take Caitlin out on the town. She wants to give money to a homeless woman, but the baglady drops her pants to reveal she has pages of the *Daily News* up her butt.

In a sideroom at the Bada Bing! Ralphie fucks Tracee from behind while she sucks a cop's penis.

Caitlin is still in shock from the baglady incident and starts drinking vodka. Noah leaves to meet a friend with whom he is going away for the weekend. He lies about having previously told Meadow about the trip.

Meadow goes home and talks with Carmela about Noah. Meadow indicates she is sleeping with Noah but will not elaborate.

Tracee approaches Tony outside the Bada Bing!. She is pregnant with Ralphie's baby and wants advice. He suggests she have an abortion.

Noah is working on an important paper in his room when Caitlin arrives, looking for Meadow. She talks her way into stopping in his room.

Silvio discovers Tracee has been off sick from work for three days. He goes in search of the dancer.

Noah is pissed about getting a C minus on his paper and blames Caitlin. This will lower his grade point average and hurt his chances of making law school.

Silvio tracks Tracee to Ralphie's place. He drags her out and slaps her face when she talks back to him. Ralphie stays inside, laughing.

Noah and Meadow have a meal with Noah's father, Len Tannenbaum. He's an entertainment lawyer and quite jaded about his clients. He asks what Meadow's father does for a living. Later Noah and Meadow go to see a film. Meadow feels guilty for not including Caitlin but Noah says his father is getting a restraining order against her. Meadow thinks this is a joke but Noah says Caitlin is ruining their lives.

At the Bada Bing!'s VIP room Tracee criticises Ralphie in front of the other mobsters. He follows her outside and they argue. He teases her by suggesting he'll support her and the baby. Tracee spits in his face and punches him. Ralphie punches her back, so Tracee taunts Ralphie. He beats her to death. Ralphie goes back inside and plunges his knuckles into a bucket of ice. He says Tracee fell while they were arguing. Tony and his crew go outside, where they find her corpse. Tony has Ralphie brought outside. Ralphie says it's not his fault Tracee was a klutz. Tony starts beating Ralphie and has to be pulled away by the others. Ralphie is furious at Tony – a made man does not lay hands on another made man without permission. The crew clean up the crime scene.

Noah and Meadow are studying in the college library. Noah dumps Meadow. He says she is too negative and there's an underlying cynicism about her. He returns to studying, leaving her quite stunned.

Carmela and Tony have another joint therapy session with Dr Melfi, but Tony says almost nothing. Eventually, he explains this by saying a young man working at Barone Sanitation has died.

Meadow comes home in a foul mood. She slams doors in the kitchen before stomping upstairs to her room.

At the Bada Bing! the dancers discuss what happened to Tracee. They agree it's better not to know. The dancers go on stage and life goes on . . .

Deep and Meaningful: Ralphie shows his dark side in this episode. Up to now he has been obnoxious and a jerk, but his behaviour has been acceptable in the context of his world. However, beating to death a young woman pregnant with his own child puts Ralphie into a category all of his own. She humiliated him, so Ralphie kills her. Afterwards, he shows absolutely no remorse. He claims that she was clumsy and fell, when the truth is obvious to everyone. He does not even bother to rationalise his actions as being part of upholding a code of honour or protecting the Family. Ralphie is a true sociopath.

Mobspeak: Meadow slips into euphemism when Noah's dad asks what Tony does for a living, saying her father is in environmental clean-up.

Bright Lights, Baked Ziti: Tracee bakes a date-and-walnut breakfast bread for Tony as a gesture of thanks. He tips it into a bin when she's gone.

The Sopranos, Carmela's parents, Rosalie and Ralphie have roast meat and vegetables for Sunday lunch.

Carmela has just baked a cake for a fundraising event when Meadow comes home from college full of joy. She says it smells delicious. Tony comes into the kitchen and eats ham from the fridge.

Christopher complains about having to work so hard now he's made. If he had wanted eighteen-hour days, he could get a job at a Denny's Restaurant.

Carmela cooks AJ waffles for breakfast. He says the family are out of syrup. Meadow says that's because he uses a whole gallon at a time.

Tracee heats up a poptart for Ralphie to eat.

Rosalie and Ralphie have Tony, Carmela, Silvio and his wife Gabriella over for dinner. They eat a cake baked by Rosalie for dessert. Everyone compliments the cooking.

Tony is eating cereal for breakfast when Meadow comes home from college after being dumped by Noah. She slams doors to cupboards and the fridge before shouting that there is nothing to eat in the house.

Mobbed Up: Ralphie and AJ discuss several ultra violent scenes from the film *Gladiator* during Sunday lunch at the Soprano house. Carmela's mother, Mary DeAngelis, says she prefers *Erin Brockovich*, which was a nice movie. Her husband Tom says he didn't care for it. When Jackie Jr turns up, Tony hails him as the 'Fresh Prince of New Jersey', a reference to the TV comedy *The Fresh Prince of Bel Air*, starring Will Smith.

Caitlin is upset after seeing the 1932 film *Freaks*.

Ralphie quotes *Gladiator* twice in the Bada Bing!'s VIP room. His favourite line of the day: 'I have come to reclaim Rome for my people!'

Ralphie watches *Spartacus* after having it recommended to him by Christopher as a great gladiator movie. Ralphie is unhappy with Kirk Douglas's hair – they didn't have flat-tops in ancient Rome.

Len Tannenbaum complains about having to listen to five hours of whining by the actor Tim Daly on the flight from Los Angeles. Len did the deal for Daly to star in the new TV series of *The Fugitive*. Len never watches his client's films if he can help it. He is in town to meet with Dick Wolf, producer of the TV series *Law and Order* and *SVU*.

Noah and Meadow go to the cinema to see *Dementia 13*, a 1963 film directed by Francis Ford Coppola – one of his arliest works.

How Do You Feel?: Tony says he is saddened by the 'work-related death' of the 'young man' in his employ.

How Do You Feel, Carmela?: Carmela says she and Tony seem to talk more since the first joint session.

Sleeping With the Fishes: Tracee, beaten to death by Ralphie with his bare hands behind the Bada Bing! strip club.

Quote/Unquote: Caitlin pinpoints one possible cause for her homesickness: 'I think I miss my ferrets.'

Silvio says most of his dancers want money for fake tits but Tracee only needed her teeth fixed. 'Kid's a thoroughbred but Madonn', those choppers – fucking train wreck.'

Caitlin refuses to go back to the university medical centre for help and opens a bottle of vodka instead. 'No more drugs,' she vows.

Tony thinks Tracee should get an abortion. 'Believe me, with Ralphie as the father, you'll be doing this kid and the next three generations a favour.'

Soundtrack: 'I'll Remember April' by Bobby Darin. 'You Shook Me All Night Long' by AC/DC. 'Taking Care of Business' by Bachman Turner Overdrive. 'Powder Your Face With Sunshine' by Dean Martin. 'Livin' On a Thin Line' by the Kinks. 'The Dolphin's Cry' by Live. 'Emily' by Frankie Valli. 'Everybody's Jumpin'' by the Dave Brubeck Quartet. 'Inside My Love' by Minnie Riperton.

Surveillance Report: This episode sets a record for having the most writers' names attached to it – seven in total. It generated a lot of controversy with the brutal murder of Tracee. During the first two seasons of *The Sopranos*, violence was almost always directed at men. But Season Three changed that with the rape of Dr Melfi and the slaying of Tracee. The show's creator, David Chase, says in interviews that this was a deliberate move to show what Mafia life is really like.

Rumours circulated before this episode aired that the homeless woman would be seen with a specific page of the *Daily News* up her butt, featuring an image of a newspaper columnist who had leaked Season Three plot details. Like most rumours, this proved groundless.

The scene where Noah dumps Meadow raises some intriguing questions. Why did he dump her? Was Meadow too negative, as he suggested? Did Noah's father pressure him to dump Meadow because she was the daughter of a mobster? Or did Noah decide he had got what he wanted from Meadow – deflowering an apparent virgin – and then cast her aside once the novelty had worn off, once the chase was over? Certainly, by dumping her when he did, Noah remained in control and did not risk getting hurt or involved.

One more question to ponder: did Noah sleep with Caitlin? In the scene where she joins him in his room, the image fades to black as she comes in. According to Noah they spent six hours together while he worked on his paper. He subsequently got only a C minus for the paper and his father was trying to get a restraining order on Caitlin. Could all this be because he had sex with her?

The Verdict: 'Watch those braces, honey.' Ralphie shows his true colours and Meadow's boyfriend Noah proves to be no saint.

Young women suffering at the hands of men is the focus of this episode. Meadow gets a harsh lesson from Noah, seemingly surrendering her virginity only to be dumped soon afterwards. The topless dancer Tracee suffers far more. She gets pregnant by Ralphie, who just considers her a cheap whore. When she wants more from him, he beats her to death.

Tracee reaches out to Tony for help but he spurns her. When she is murdered, he feels guilt and remorse for what has happened. But that won't bring her back. Worse still, Tony has broken a Mafia code of conduct by striking another made man without permission. There will be a price to pay . . .

33
Second Opinion

US Transmission Date: 8 April 2001

Written by: Lawrence Konner
Director: Tim Van Patten

Cast: Sam McMurray (Dr John Kennedy),
Frank Wood (Dean Ross), Mike Nichols (Dr Krakower),
Ilene Landress (Dr Laurens), Ismail Bashey (Dr Mehta),
Peter Davies (Paxton), John Fiske (FBI Man),
John Freudiger (Chooch), Lorenzo Gregorio (Miles),
Tony Hale (RN Collins), Zachary Knower (Dr Enloe),
James Shanklin (Anaesthesiologist)

Storyline: Junior goes under the knife to remove his cancer. His surgeon, Dr John Kennedy, is in a rush to complete the operation. Afterwards he tells Tony and Bacala that he removed a tumour the size of a fist from Junior's stomach. Tony offers Dr Kennedy a favour but the surgeon brushes it off.

In the back office at the Bada Bing!, Christopher beats Paulie at pool but Paulie refuses to pay the agreed stake. Christopher bitches about having to pick up the tab for Paulie too often. Paulie takes umbrage and demands the recently made man strip naked so he can be checked for wires.

Carmela's parents, Hugh and Mary, join the Sopranos for Sunday dinner. AJ is trying to get out of a school trip to Washington but his parents insist he go. Tony is called away on business and AJ goes to his room to finish homework before the trip. Mary criticises Tony after he has gone and chides Carmela for not marrying a more respectable husband. Carmela reminds her parents that both of them have done well financially thanks to Tony's efforts.

Tony arrives at the Bada Bing! and finds a novelty mounted fish called Billy Bass on his desk, which Georgie brought in. The fish starts singing and reminds Tony of having to whack his friend Pussy. Tony beats Georgie with the fish.

Carmela has a solo therapy session with Dr Melfi – Tony has decided not to attend. Dr Melfi thinks the joint sessions have stirred up Carmela's feelings and recommends a colleague who may be able to help Carmela.

Dr Kennedy tells Junior there may still be some malignant cells that the surgery missed. He recommends Junior have another operation and rushes him into making a decision. Junior is like a humble peasant, accepting whatever Dr Kennedy says as gospel.

Angie Bonpensiero deliberately bumps into Carmela in a supermarket. Angie pleads poverty since Pussy's disappearance and says her poodle Cocoa needs a $1,200 operation that she can't afford. Tony usually helps her with money but Angie says it isn't enough for emergencies.

Christopher brings home two bags of stolen designer shoes for Adriana, but they are the wrong size. He complains about his treatment by Paulie. Christopher is holding back from giving Paulie a full share of his profits.

Tony arrives home late for dinner. Carmela is unhappy with him. She says the Dean at Meadow's college has invited them to lunch. Tony thinks the college just wants a donation from them and refuses to attend. Carmela mentions Angie's money troubles, pushing Tony into a rant about Pussy joining the witness protection programme.

Paulie and Patsy Parisi visit Christopher and Adriana at home at two in the morning. Paulie confiscates the designer shoes as part of his payment and begins searching the apartment. Christopher sees Paulie sniffing a pair of Adriana's panties.

Carmela visits Meadow in the dorms. She brings laundry and home-cooked food. Carmela wants to know how Meadow is doing after being dumped by Noah. Meadow blames Tony for what happened with Noah.

Junior is making a tuna-fish milkshake at home but only succeeds in spraying himself and the kitchen in milk and fish. Tony arrives, sneaking in through the basement so as not to endanger Junior's bail conditions. Tony is shocked to hear about the need for another operation. He suggests his uncle get a second opinion, but Junior doesn't want chemotherapy. Bacala arrives with shopping. Junior finally agrees to let Tony arrange for a second opinion.

Tony visits Angie. He sees that she has a new-looking Cadillac in the drive – hardly the sign of a poor woman.

Tony attacks the car with a baseball bat and warns Angie not to use Carmela to get more money from him again.

Carmela has lunch with Dean Ross. He praises Meadow's work and asks for a donation of $50,000 towards a new student centre for the college. Carmela and Tony discuss the amount that night in bed. Tony offers just $5,000, which he plucks from a wad in his trouser pocket.

Tony takes Junior to see a doctor at a hospital in New York reputed to be the best cancer-treatment centre in the world. The doctor suggests chemotherapy, but says there's no guarantee further surgery will not be needed. He says the case should go before a team of doctors for further discussion. Junior is unimpressed, still preferring the opinion of Dr Kennedy. Junior had a great fondness for the doctor's namesake, the assassinated US President John F Kennedy. Tony says Junior should not make life-and-death decisions just because of a man's name.

Carmela has a sly cigarette outside the Sopranos' household. The therapist recommended by Dr Melfi returns Carmela's call and arranges an appointment for her. Tony finds Carmela outside. They start arguing and Carmela throws the phone at Tony. AJ returns home from his school trip. Once he goes inside, husband and wife start arguing again. Tony still refuses to donate $50,000 to Meadow's college.

Christopher complains to Tony about Paulie's actions. Tony tells Christopher to act like a man and stop whining.

At the medical meeting to discuss Junior's case, Dr Kennedy is sulking about his patient seeking a second opinion at a famous New York hospital. After threatening to wash his hands of Junior's treatment, he reluctantly agrees to arranging chemotherapy for his patient. Junior starts the treatment but can't get Dr Kennedy to answer his calls.

Tony talks to Paulie about harassing Christopher and Adriana.

Tony visits Junior at home. His uncle is having an adverse reaction to the treatment and has to keep vomiting. Junior and Bacala complain that Dr Kennedy never returns calls or messages. Tony decides to get involved.

Paulie approaches Christopher and warns him not to go whining to Tony.

Tony tracks Dr Kennedy to a golf course. Backed up by Furio, he frightens the surgeon into giving Junior better treatment in future.

Carmela has a traumatic therapy session with Dr Krakower. He pulls no punches and offers no sympathy. If she wants to feel good about herself, she has to leave Tony and take only the children – what's left of them. The therapist refuses to accept any of her 'blood money'. He dismisses psychiatrists who allow patients to blame their present situation on some incident from their childhood. Dr Krakower makes sure Carmela understands exactly what he means. What she does now is up to her.

At Junior's next chemotherapy session Dr Kennedy turns up, all attentive and helpful. He even gives his home phone number to Junior.

Tony comes home and finds Carmela sleeping on the sofa. She seems very down and he suggests she try going to therapy on her own. Carmela insists Tony donate $50,000 to the college and he agrees to placate her. Tony takes her out to dinner.

Deep and Meaningful: Carmela gets both barrels from the unforgiving Dr Krakower. He tells her exactly what she has to do to purge her sins and find some inner peace. But she cannot bring herself to do it now. Just saying out loud what Tony does for a living is difficult enough. When the therapist translates her phrase 'organised crime' into a single word, 'Mafia', Carmela squirms in shame and embarrassment. But the real moment of revelation comes in the final scene. Tony suggests she try therapy on her own, little realising her depressed mood is caused by the truths presented to Carmela in a single session. She cannot cope with what Dr Krakower had to say. Instead, she says she hasn't got time for therapy – an excuse to save her from further harsh truths.

Mobspeak: Tony says the Dean's request for a $50,000 donation is a shake-down (to blackmail or try to get money from someone).

Mama Mia: Junior hears the voice of Livia among many when he is semiconscious and being wheeled to the operating theatre.

Carmela tells Dr Melfi she hoped Tony would be better after Livia died, but it hasn't happened yet.

Carmela's mother Mary seems determined to take on the role of nag now vacated by the late Livia. She complains about the example Tony sets when he leaves in the middle of the Sunday family dinner. 'The man's got two speeds – moping and yelling.' Mary compares Tony to a more respectable man who was dying to marry Carmela. He now runs a chain of drugstores.

Bright Lights, Baked Ziti: Tony gnaws on a chicken drumstick during Sunday family dinner. He has to leave before the meal can be completed. Mary asks her daughter what is the secret ingredient in the cooking. Carmela says it is balsamic vinegar. Carmela's father Tom says all cooks seem to be obsessed with balsamic vinegar, but his mother had never heard of it.

Bacala asks Dr Kennedy how long it will be before Junior can return to a regular diet. Junior glares at him for asking a food-related question.

Tony arrives home too late for a meal with Carmela, so he eats it cold. He praises the food, especially the pecorino cheese. They discuss Pussy, and Tony says Angie should look for her husband at any TGI Friday's – Pussy loved the wings at the restaurant chain.

Carmela takes Meadow a container of home-cooked ziti with the sweet sausage she likes. Meadow is hungry and scoffs the baked pasta down cold.

Junior tries to make a tuna-fish milkshake, so he can get some nutrition. Bacala returns from shopping. Junior accuses him to stopping to eat White Castle mini-burgers, which have a distinctive smell.

Mobbed Up: Adriana tells Christopher she once gave head to the television magician Penn, the tall guy from Penn and Teller.

How Do You Feel, Carmela?: Carmela bursts into tears when she attends a solo session with Dr Melfi. She says she's frustrated that Tony has been out of sorts for so long and there's nothing she can do about it. Dr Melfi suggests Carmela seek therapy for herself and recommends Dr Krakower.

He proves to be no solace and instead reduces her to tears again. Carmela admits to feelings of shame and guilt. Dr Krakower says she will never feel good about herself until she leaves Tony and his blood money.

I Dream of Jeannie Cusamano: Junior slips into a dream when he is given a pre-op sedative. He imagines the FBI offer him a deal – give evidence against Tony in exchange for a total cure from cancer. The front page of a newspaper spins to a halt on screen. The headline screams SOPRANO WINS FREEDOM: INDICTS NEPHEW. Underneath, another heading says STAR WITNESS WEDS ANGIE DICKINSON and there is a photo of Junior with the film and television actress. This refers back to a comment by Junior in #13, 'I Dream of Jeannie Cusamano', when he told the FBI he wanted to fuck Angie Dickinson.

Tony has a brief flashback to a dream from #26, 'Funhouse', when he imagined Pussy as a talking fish.

Quote/Unquote: Junior displays his faith in Dr Kennedy with a scatological example. 'You tell me to take a crap on the deck of the *Queen Mary*, an hour later they're hosing it down with disinfectant.'

Tony tries to joke his way out of being late for dinner. 'That's why they invented microwaves – for inconsiderate husbands.'

Junior remonstrates with Tony. 'If you're going to lie to me, tell me there's a broad waiting in the car to tongue my balls.'

Junior worries that his nephew has a hidden agenda. 'Anthony is a cunt hair away from owning all of New Jersey – I am that cunt hair.'

When Carmela throws a phone at Tony, he asks for her reasons. 'I'll write you out a list,' she replies.

Furio sums up golf: 'Stupid-a fucking game.'

Soundtrack: 'Mysterious Ways' by U2. The Billy Bass fish sings Al Green's soul stunner, 'Take Me To The River', and the Village People's camp classic 'YMCA'. A Muzak version of Billy Joel's 'Just The Way Your Are' plays in the grocery store where Carmela and Angie meet. 'Goldberg Variations' by Glenn Gould. 'Black Books' by Nils Lofgren.

Surveillance Report: When Carmela is sitting in Dr Melfi's waiting room, the scene is set up to resemble exactly the very first scene of the very first episode – the nervous patient seen through the legs of a statue of a woman. Just as that image began Tony's journey into therapy, so Carmela begins her own such journey from the same position.

For the second episode running, the Bada Bing! barman Georgie gets a beating. This time Tony does the hitting, using a Billy Bass singing fish. Poor Georgie is still wearing an eye patch from last episode's violence.

The Verdict: 'One thing you can never say, that you haven't been told.' Carmela tries solo therapy and gets a rude awakening. The trouble between Christopher and Paulie continues to escalate while everybody wants money from Tony.

This episode could have been called 'The Trouble With Doctors'. Junior is having a tough enough time coping with cancer, but his beloved Dr Kennedy proves himself to be no saint. Carmela has her first and final session with the therapist Dr Krakower and is forced to face some harsh truths. Her injuries are not fatal but, like Junior, she finds the cure tougher than the illness.

In the midst of all this, the sparring between Paulie and Christopher offers some welcome comic relief – as does the scene where Tony goes to bat on Angie's Cadillac. At least Angie's dog got out of the episode unscathed . . .

34
He Is Risen

US Transmission Date: 15 April 2001

Written by: Robin Green, Mitchell Burgess and Todd A
Kessler
Director: Allen Coulter
Cast: Carl Capotorto (Little Paulie Germani),
Anne Asante (Caterina Cella),
Kieran Campion (Epsilon Zet),
RJ Reed (Epsilon Zet #2), William Da Ruffa (Joe),
Michael Hogan (Dov Ginsberg),
Margo Singaliese (Lisa Cestone).

Storyline: Meadow and her roommate Caitlin attend a
1960s theme party at Columbia's Epsilon Zet frat house.
Caitlin gets high on ecstasy supplied by Jackie Jr, who is
also at the party. He is affiliated to Epsilon Zet at Rutger's.
Meadow tries to buy ecstasy from Jackie but he gives it to
her for free.

Ralphie and the rest of the Aprile crew are having a
good night at a private casino when Tony and Paulie
arrive. The crew pay their respects but Ralphie does so
very reluctantly. He turns down Tony's offer of a drink.
Ralphie is still bitter that Tony punched him, a made man,
over the murder of Tracee.

Meadow and Jackie Jr have gone to Meadow's dorm
room. Jackie wants to fuck Meadow but she says no before
passing out. He resists the urge to rape her, just sneaking
a peak at Meadow's breasts before leaving.

Tony and Silvio discuss the problem with Ralphie after
dinner at Vesuvio. Silvio says Ralphie has a legitimate
grievance. Tony has only two choices: make nice or make
Ralphie disappear. Ralphie will become a captain only
over my dead body, Tony says.

In another restaurant Ralphie is bitching about Tony.
He is not looking forward to having Thanksgiving dinner
at the Soprano household.

Rosalie Aprile asks Jackie Jr if he will be coming to the Sopranos' dinner with her and Ralphie. Jackie wants to know if Meadow will be there. Carmela phones Meadow to find out if her daughter will be attending Thanksgiving dinner. Meadow is reluctant to come unless Jackie Jr will be there. Rosalie phones Carmela about the dinner and the two mothers realise their children are romantically involved. Tony comes home and asks Carmela to cancel the dinner invitation to Rosalie and Ralphie.

Tony arrives at Dr Melfi's office to discover he is double-booked with Gloria Trillo, an attractive Mercedes sales rep. They flirt for a few minutes until Dr Melfi comes out. Tony volunteers to let Gloria have the appointment – he will come back later for a 7 p.m. session.

Carmela calls Rosalie and cancels the dinner invitation by lying that her father is unwell.

At his rescheduled therapy session, Tony praises the strategy in a book recommended by Dr Melfi – *The Art of War* by a Chinese general, Sun Tzu. He asks about Gloria Trillo, wondering why she needs a shrink. Dr Melfi says she cannot discuss her patients. When the session ends it is dark outside. Tony offers to walk Melfi to her car but she says she has work to do.

The Sopranos' extended family gather for Thanksgiving dinner. Janice brings Aaron Arkaway, a narcoleptic man from her prayer group. Tony tries to make peace with Meadow, who is close in age to the dead stripper Tracee.

At the Aprile house Ralphie is in a foul mood. Rosalie turns to matchmaking, suggesting Jackie Jr see if Meadow wants to go to a movie. He arrives to find the Sopranos still around the dinner table. Jackie Jr takes Meadow out. Later they kiss outside Hunter Scangarello's house. Jackie Jr wants to sleep with Meadow but she asks for some time. Jackie Jr roars off in his car, sulking about being rejected.

Tony and Carmela discuss the budding romance between Jackie Jr and Meadow. Tony watches a Mercedes ad on TV. He is thinking about Gloria.

Tony meets with Gigi at the Bada Bing! to discuss Ralphie. Gigi is stressed by his new role as captain of the

Aprile crew, along with the cost of house renovations and sending his children to college soon. Tony says Gigi is doing a good job. Silvio comes in as Gigi leaves. Silvio says all this stress is killing Gigi.

Ralphie visits Johnny Sack at home, complaining about Tony's attitude. Ralphie threatens to whack Tony but Johnny Sack dissuades him. Ralphie asks if he could switch Families, give his allegiance to New York. Johnny says that would jeopardise the long-standing ties between New York and the Sopranos. Ralphie blames murdering Tracee on cocaine. Johnny tells Ralphie to apologise, then Tony will make things right.

Johnny Sack and Tony meet at Vesuvio. Johnny suggests making Ralphie a captain but Tony rejects the idea. He is unhappy at Johnny's intervention in New Jersey business. Johnny phones Ralphie and says Tony wants a meeting. Afterwards Ralphie offers to help Jackie Jr get regular supplies of ecstasy to sell.

Ralphie meets with Tony at Vesuvio and apologises for his recent actions. He blames events on the coke and swears the problem will not happen again. Tony does not apologise for punching Ralphie.

Gigi arrives at a card game for members of the Aprile crew. He complains that his bowels are clogged by Thanksgiving turkey.

Johnny Sack watches a TV news report about work starting on the New Jersey esplanade project. The mob will need its own bulldozer to take away all the money it will make from the project. Ralphie storms in, furious about Tony. Johnny tries to calm him down.

Gigi is on the toilet, straining against constipation.

Tony visits Junior and they discuss the Ralphie problem. Junior says there are no easy answers when you're the boss.

Vito and the rest of the Aprile crew discover Gigi dead on the toilet.

At the funeral home, Tony discusses the situation with Paulie and Silvio. A new captain has to be appointed for the Aprile crew and Ralphie is the only obvious candidate.

Later, Tony has a meeting with Ralphie at Vesuvio. He makes Ralphie captain but refuses to have a drink with the newly elevated mobster.

Meadow goes out with Jackie Jr. When he refuses to give her a lift, she pinches his car keys and tries to drive off. Meadow crashes the car outside but escapes unscathed. Jackie Jr says he doesn't care about the car – it's stolen – he only cares about her. She agrees to sleep with him.

Tony visits the Mercedes dealership where Gloria works. They flirt and then take a test drive together. The pair go to Tony's boat, the *Stugots*, where they have sex. Gloria phones Dr Melfi to cancel an appointment for later that day. Dr Melfi thinks she hears Tony's voice in the background . . .

Deep and Meaningful: Tony embarks on an affair with Gloria after two brief moments earlier in the episode. He watches a TV ad for Mercedes and tells Carmela he is thinking about getting one. She says he should, not realising the subtext of what her husband is saying – he is thinking of sleeping with a Mercedes sales rep. Later, Tony gets a second, unwitting approval from Junior. His uncle says a boss has to find his pleasures where he can.

Mobspeak: Silvio talks about living through the walyo (Italian) version of Thanksgiving dinner.

Bright Lights, Baked Ziti: Turkey, turkey and more turkey – the big bird dominates this episode as part of the Thanksgiving dinner tradition. Ralphie complains about eating with Tony. 'Fuck him and his turkey. I ought to shove a drumstick up his ass.'

Reverend James Jr visits the Bada Bing!, where Tony and his crew discuss the coming feasts. The priest says everyone has to love eating turkey, sweet potatoes and pumpkin pie. The mobsters disagree. The Italian-American version is much bigger, beginning with major antipasto, then soup, meatballs, baked manicotti and finally turkey with all the trimmings. Christopher delivers a truck of stolen frozen turkeys to the Bada Bing!.

Carmela unloads food shopping as she discusses Thanks-giving dinner with Rosalie Aprile. Carmela is counting on Rosalie for her almond torte. Tony brings home a massive frozen turkey from the Bada Bing!.

At Thanksgiving Janice reveals she was a waitress at a Kenny Rogers restaurant. When Tony sees Meadow carrying a plate of food to the table, he remembers Tracee giving him date-and-walnut bread.

At the Aprile house, Ralphie picks disconsolately at his turkey dinner. Jackie Jr compliments his mother on the food. When Jackie arrives at the Soprano house, everyone is still at the dinner table, picking at fruit and cheese. Jackie Jr turns down turkey sandwiches.

When Ralphie first visits Johnny Sack at home, he also turns down leftover turkey, this time offered by Ginny Sack.

Johnny and Tony eat pasta at Vesuvio when they discuss Ralphie.

Jackie Jr has a bowl of cereal while Ralphie is on the phone with Johnny.

Tony eats pasta at Vesuvio while Ralphie apologises.

Gigi brings a brown bag filled with turkey sandwiches when he joins the rest of the Aprile crew for the card game. Vito Spatafore hungrily examines the sandwiches. Gigi complains that the turkey is clogging his bowels.

Tony takes Junior a bag loaded with leftover turkey, stuffing and manicotti but his uncle turns it down. Food is going right through him, unlike the unfortunate Gigi.

Mobbed Up: Junior is watching a daytime soap opera, *The Bold and the Beautiful*, when Tony comes to visit.

Tony, Silvio and Paulie discuss famous people who died on the toilet. Silvio talks about a Hollywood guy called Don something who had a similar fate. Silvio thinks he was the producer of *The Simpsons*. In fact, he's referring to Don Simpson, producer of the films *Top Gun* and *The Rock*.

How Do You Feel?: Tony complains about having prob-lems sleeping, due to a 'management' problem with an underling.

How Do You Feel, Doctor?: Dr Melfi tells her therapist that she feels like shouting at her own patients to stop whining. She is still recovering from the trauma of being raped but feels that no one is listening to her feelings. She just wants to say she hurts and be heard. Melfi relates the moment where Tony offered to escort her to her car. She says she almost fell into his arms crying.

Sleeping With the Fishes: Gigi Cestone, dead of a heart attack after straining too hard on the toilet. Not a very dignified way to die.

I Dream of Jeannie Cusamano: Tony has a fleeting flashback to dead stripper Tracee when he sees Meadow carrying a plate of food.

Quote/Unquote: Silvio sums up the Ralphie problem for Tony: 'Make him disappear or make nice – you only got two choices.'

Tony sums up the Ralphie problem for Hesh in a different way: 'He refused a drink because he's a despicable fuck that I bitch-slapped in a moment of very justified anger.'

Gloria tells Tony why she is seeing a therapist: 'Serial killer. I murdered seven relationships.'

Janice feels a chill when she see Jackie Jr taking Meadow out to a movie. ' A Soprano and an Aprile . . .'

Soundtrack: 'Rag Doll' by the Four Seasons. 'Ghost Riders in the Sky' by the Ramrods. 'Whoa' by Black Rob. 'The Captain' by Kasey Chambers.

Surveillance Report: This episode was first broadcast on Easter Sunday in America, so the title 'He Is Risen' is a sly pun on the resurrection of Jesus Christ while actually referring to Ralphie's elevation to captain.

Sales of the book *The Art of War* by Sun Tzu surged dramatically after Tony endorsed its strategic value in this episode.

The Verdict: 'Have you heard the good news? He is risen.' The conflict between Tony and Ralphie escalates towards gunfire until an unexpected death provides a solution. Meanwhile, Meadow gets it on with Jackie Jr and Tony begins a new affair with a Mercedes sales rep.

The Tony and Ralphie war of words seems to be building towards a major conflict but is defused by the all too convenient death of Gigi Cestone. This episode wraps up many of the plot threads from the first half of this season, such as the captaincy of the Aprile crew and the fallout from Ralphie's murdering Tracee. But it also brings two new relationships centre stage, where they will remain for the rest of the season.

Meadow and Jackie Jr become a couple, while Tony finds a fresh mistress in Gloria Trillo. But he should have paid more attention to her joke about being a serial killer who murders relationships . . .

35
The Telltale Moozadell

US Transmission Date: 22 April 2001

Written by: Michael Imperioli
Director: Daniel Attias
Cast: Joe Bacino (Little Joe),
Frank Bongiorno (Guiseppe),
Charles Trucillo (Cop #1), David Warshofsky (Cop #2),
Cyndi Ramirez (Girl),
Richard Petrocelli (Rocco De Trollio),
Gregory Russell Cook (Club Kid), Jay Boryea (Bouncer),
David Ross (Janitor).

Storyline: Tony gives Carmela a ring with an enormous sapphire surrounded by diamonds for her birthday. AJ gives his mother *The Matrix* on DVD while Meadow turns up with a voucher for Carmela to be treated to a day of pampering at a New York beauty parlour. Meadow is also booked in so they can go together – all charged to Carmela's credit card.

The Lollipop Club in New Jersey gets new owners after Rocco De Trollio runs up gambling debts with the Soprano Family. Furio and Christopher take over as silent partners.

The extended Soprano family gather for Carmela's birthday. Jackie Jr turns up and presents Carmela with a bottle of wine. AJ asks if he can spend the night at the home of his friend Egon and his parents agree.

Christopher presents the club to Adriana – she will be manager with Rocco now reporting to her.

Carmela suspects Tony's motives for the extravagant gift and asks if he has something to tell her. She notes that he never bought a Mercedes. Tony says he didn't like the car. Carmela says her neighbour, Jeannie Cusamano, calls them mid-life-crisis cars. Carmela worries about Meadow dating Jackie Jr. She wants her daughter to take advantage of all the opportunities living and studying in New York can offer. Tony reassures her, saying Jackie Jr is a good kid. He agrees to talk to Jackie Jr about Meadow.

Meadow gives Jackie Jr a paper on Edgar Allan Poe she has written for him. They have sex in Jackie's car.

AJ and friends break into the swimming pool at his school, Verbum Dei. They open an office and throw a desk and chair into the pool. One of the teens smashes the pool's trophy display case and throws awards into the water.

Meadow asks her parents for a car but they are unconvinced by her arguments. Tony points out that Meadow turned down a car last year.

The school principal is shocked by the vandalism at the pool. The janitor finds a pizza box amid the debris, two slices of pie still inside.

The police use the box to trace its origins to the La Pizza store. The manager says the pie is a custom-made special which only one person orders.

Carmela confronts AJ, who has been sent home from school after being busted for the vandalism. A sleepy Tony enters and is shocked by the news. He slaps AJ in the head and warns him that a promising football career is fast going down the drain. They all have to see the Verbum Dei principal.

Carmela and Rosalie Aprile have lunch at Vesuvio. Rosalie is very happy that Jackie Jr and Meadow are dating. Rosalie is shocked that Charmaine Bucco has hired a lawyer as a first step to divorcing Artie.

Tony visits Gloria at her workplace and brings her a gift. She refuses to take the afternoon off but arranges to see Tony at the zoo.

Tony meets with Jackie Jr in the back office at Satriale's Pork Store. He warns Jackie to be very careful in how he treats Meadow. Jackie boasts that he has just got an A on his English literature, but neglects to mention that Meadow wrote the paper for him.

Opening night at Crazy Horse, formerly known as the Lollipop Club. Adriana introduces the first band to perform there, the Miami Relatives. A drug dealer called Matush is selling ecstasy in the men's room. He is caught by a bouncer and violently ejected from the club.

Tony meets Gloria at the zoo. She talks about some of her Buddhist beliefs. They go into the reptile house and fuck in front of the snakes, fully dressed and standing upright.

Matush and his friend Carlo Renzi come to Jackie Jr for help. Matush used to sell drugs at the Lollipop but he was banned by the new management. Carlo understands that the Soprano made man Christopher Moltisanti is involved and asks Jackie to intervene. Jackie agrees to help.

The Verbum Dei principal, Cincotta, tells Tony and Carmela that the school has a zero tolerance policy towards vandalism, which means immediate expulsion. But the school is going to suspend this sentence for AJ, in views of his academic performance and extracurricular activities. He is not going to be kicked off the football team either. The principal suggests Tony and Carmela punish AJ. Afterwards Carmela is furious – it's clear the school has let AJ off because he's too valuable to the freshman football team. She accuses Tony of being complicit in the white-wash.

Gloria has a session with Dr Melfi and says it's been a wonderful two weeks. She lies to the therapist about the man's voice Dr Melfi heard during a phone call the previous week. Melfi does not believe her and Gloria pretends to be offended.

Jackie Jr approaches Christopher at the Bada Bing!, seeking permission for Matush to deal ecstasy at the Crazy Horse. Christopher refuses – the drug is now federal territory and too much trouble. Jackie scampers away when he sees Tony coming towards them.

Jackie tells Matush he can deal at the club, but only outside. He also demands a weekly payment for his involvement in brokering the deal.

Carmela and Tony lay down the law to AJ. He is denied video games, DVDs, skateboards and computer access for a month. He will also have to do more chores around the house, such as clearing the gutters and drainpipes.

Outside the Crazy Horse Matush is caught dealing drugs and gets a severe beating from Furio and friends. Jackie Jr visits Matush in hospital, but is mostly worried that his name has been mentioned by the drug dealer. Worried for his own safety, Jackie Jr gets a gun from Ralphie for his protection.

Tony and Gloria meet in an expensive hotel room. Gloria says she expects nothing from Tony, except kindness.

At Tony's next therapy session, he quotes one of Gloria's Buddhist sayings. Dr Melfi recognises the source of this new wisdom. Tony is feeling very positive about therapy and gives the therapist a cash bonus with his monthly payment. She can always give it to her favourite charity, Tony says. Dr Melfi's son calls from college – he needs cash to buy a couple of expensive textbooks. She looks down at the extra money Tony has just given her.

Tony visits the casino and sees Jackie Jr at the tables gambling. He confronts Jackie and sends him away.

Next morning Carmela says she has changed her mind about Jackie Jr. He seems to be the perfect gentleman. Tony keeps his own counsel. Leaves fall past the window as AJ struggles to clean out the guttering and drain-pipes . . .

Deep and Meaningful: Tony gets his first hint that all is not well with Gloria Trillo when they are at the zoo. He complains that she plays mind games. 'Poor you,' she says in mock sympathy – just as his mother Livia used to. The moment jolts Tony to his senses for a moment. But the pair are soon humping in the reptile house, watched by snakes. Talk about your Adam-and-Eve symbolism . . .

Bright Lights, Baked Ziti: There's a large birthday cake for Carmela's special day. Tony later eats a slice of the cake in bed, sharing a forkful with Carmela.

Tony eats a bowl of cereal for breakfast when Meadow asks for a car.

The custom-job pizza features double meatballs, pepperoni, sausage, peppers, onions and extra mozzarella cheese. It proves to be AJ's downfall.

Artie serves Carmela and Rosalie a special dish of cheese and string beans at Vesuvio to go with their ham starter. He specially imported the cheese from Italy via FedEx. It is more subtle and smooth than mozzarella with an almost nutlike flavour. Artie says the crispness of the beans contrasts with the smoothness of the cheese. Rosalie is unimpressed and says the cheese still tastes like mozzarella. She wants hot antipasto.

Ralphie shows Jackie Jr the best way to finish cooking sauce and macaroni. You should put a spoonful of sauce and some butter in with the cooked pasta and then reheat it for forty-five seconds. That way the pasta absorbs the flavour, instead of just being coated with it.

In the final scene Tony gets some of the previous night's cannoli out of the fridge for a snack.

Mobbed Up: AJ gives Carmela *The Matrix* on DVD. She has never seen it. The birthday gift is plainly a present AJ has really bought for himself. One wonders if either of them will notice Ralphie (actor Joe Pantoliano) appearing as a traitorous character.

Tony lies on bed watching WC Fields in the 1934 film *It's A Gift*.

How Do You Feel?: Tony is very happy after a very good week. He thinks all the therapy sessions are paying off now. He says he visited the zoo. 'Sometimes you've got to stop and smell the gorilla shit.' He skirts attempts by Dr Melfi to discover if he is seeing Gloria.

How Do You Feel, Gloria?: Gloria tells Dr Melfi that she has not been having the usual nightmares. Gloria lies about not having a social life. Dr Melfi tries to get to the truth but Gloria acts offended. The therapist says she asked because Gloria was referred to her after attempting suicide when a relationship broke up.

How Do You Feel, Doctor?: Dr Melfi tells her son that she hates all her patients. They all lie to her face. She says quitting doesn't sound like a bad idea.

I Dream of Jeannie Cusamano: Gloria tells Dr Melfi she had a wonderful dream about lighting the big torch at the Olympic Games.

Quote/Unquote: Janice's prayer-group friend Aaron declines alcohol because the good lord doesn't approve. Tony points out that Jesus drank wine but Janice has an answer to this: 'He was Jesus, Tone – we can't make comparisons.'

The owner of La Pizza is appalled that one of his pizza pies was found at a crime scene. 'My pizza never hurt nobody.'

The owner's son says the pizza is a custom-made special order. The police want more information about who made the order. 'This pie fit a pattern?'

Paulie prefaces Tony's trip to the reptile house by saying snakes have both male and female reproductive organs. 'That's why we call someone a snake – how can us trust a guy who can literally go fuck themselves?'

Tony mishears when Carmela says Jackie Jr has taken Meadow to see *Aida*, Elton John's Broadway musical. 'I eat her?'

Soundtrack: 'State of Main' by the Miami Relatives (see Surveillance Report for this episode). 'Con Te Partiro' by Andrea Bocelli. Tony and the family sing 'Happy Birthday' to Carmela. 'Girl' by Vue. 'Make No Mistake' by Keith Richards. 'I Who Have Nothing' by Ben E King.

Surveillance Report: The real-life rock band Scout appear as the Miami Relatives in this episode and receive acting credits as Ashen Keilyn (Lead Singer), Nigel Rawles (Drummer), Rimas Remeza (Bassist) and David Weintraub (Guitarist). Janice may have become a born-again God-botherer, but she still snorts cocaine when the mood takes her.

The Verdict: 'How do you vandalise a swimming pool?' AJ gets busted for a teenage prank gone wrong, but gets let off by his school. Jackie Jr is also playing with fire by dating Meadow while trying to establish himself as an associate of the Soprano Family.

The writer Michael Imperioli contributes another cracking script for this episode, although it is not quite the equal of his work on #22, 'From Where To Eternity', in Season Two. Male characters court danger in this zinger-packed episode. Tony is smitten with his new mistress Gloria, ignoring the warning signs. Jackie Jr manages to convince Carmela that he is a gentleman with her daughter, but Tony's good opinion about the wannabe mobster is rapidly diminishing.

AJ is also endangering his future with bad-boy antics. How long before that suspended sentence of expulsion becomes reality?

36
To Save Us All From Satan's Power
US Transmission Date: 29 April 2001

Written by: Robin Green and Mitchell Burgess
Director: Jack Bender

Cast: Jana Januskova (Dancer), Joe Pucillo (Beppy),
Matt Cerbone (Young Jackie Jr),
Dominick Charles Carbone (Kevin Bonpensiero),
Domenica Galati (Mother),
Tyler Gulizio (Little Boy),
Loulou Katz (Little Girl),
Rosie Chavolino (Second Dancer),
Larry Clark (Cop),
Capathia Jenkins (Store Employee),
Diego Lopez (EMT), Michael Rispoli (Jackie Aprile Sr).

Storyline: Tony goes to the seaside to have his boat
winterised. He arranges a meeting with Paulie on the
boardwalk, prompting memories of another meeting he
had there with Pussy and the late Jackie Aprile Sr in 1995.
There was conflict between the acting boss Jackie and
Junior over a truck hijacking and Pussy had been to Boca
to persuade Junior to have a sit-down with Jackie. Pussy
moans about money troubles. Jackie says Pussy can always
come to him for help and Tony warns Pussy not to deal
heroin – it's too risky.

Back in the present, Tony and Paulie discuss Pussy.
Paulie has no time for the friend who turned rat. Instead
he bitches about a strike organised by Ralphie which is
costing Paulie money. Tony promises to speak with
Ralphie.

Carmela hassles Tony about Christmas preparations,
prompting him to have a panic attack. Janice wants to
cook Christmas lunch for the family and she needs Tony
to fix the fuse box at Livia's house.

Tony admits to Dr Melfi that he has not been taking his
medication regularly. He talks obliquely about having to
deal with Pussy.

At Livia's house Janice is composing a Christian rock
song with Aaron. Tony and Carmela arrive to help with
preparations for Christmas Day. Janice can't clean because
of nerve damage to her wrist. She tells Tony the injury
dates back to being beaten by the Russians. He adds
dealing with them to his Christmas list of things to do.

Janice is backsliding on her born-again beliefs but is enthused about the Christian contemporary-music scene – it's the fastest-growing market in the business.

At Satriale's Pork Store Tony's crew get out the Christmas decorations. Every year the store hosts a party for local children with presents and a Santa. The tradition was started by Tony's father, Johnny Boy Soprano. Pussy always played Santa, which prompts more discussion about the dead rat. Raymond Curto is among those present. He says he wishes he could have been along for the ride when Pussy was dealt with. Tony refuses to play Santa.

Tony visits a Russian friend, Slava, who launders his money. He gives him $250,000 to be cleaned and transferred to a bank account in the Isle of Man. Slava has a drunk friend, Valery, propping up a bar. Tony asks Slava to locate the Russian who beat Janice.

Silvio tells Tony he has been dreaming about Pussy ever since they dug out the Santa suit. Silvio realises Pussy was probably being flipped when he missed the sit-down between Junior and Jackie Sr in 1995.

Silvio, Tony and Paulie have a meal at Vesuvio. They discuss what Christmas gifts they are giving their respective mistresses. Tony says Gloria has gone to Morocco for the festive season and she bought the ticket herself. He thinks she's too good to be true. Paulie is impressed with the ass of a new waitress at Vesuvio. All three men are shocked when the waitress turns around – it's Artie Bucco's estranged wife, Charmaine. She jokes with them that the FBI are in the restaurant. She and Artie are still at each other's throats. Tony gets a phone call telling him where to find the Russian who beat Janice. The culprit is Igor Parnasky, a minicab driver.

Tony and Furio take a trip with Igor as their driver.

Tony gets home and discusses the new-look Charmaine with Carmela.

At Satriale's, preparations for the party continue. Baccala arrives with presents from Junior and is nominated to be Santa. He doesn't want to, because he is shy. But Paulie orders him to be Santa.

Janice sees a news report on TV which shows a badly beaten Igor, who was found under the sleigh in a sporting-goods window display. She cries with gratitude at the violence Tony has done for her.

Meadow comes home for Christmas. She believes Jackie Jr is visiting a friend in hospital.

Tony joins Christopher and Silvio at Vesuvio for a drink. Tony gets into an argument with Charmaine and decides to leave. Silvio suggests they try a rival strip club that has opened near the Bada Bing!. At the club Tony sees Jackie Jr getting a lap dance from a stripper. Tony drags Jackie into a bathroom and beats him. He also finds and confiscates Jackie's handgun.

Next morning Carmela and Tony argue about where he was last night. Carmela accuses him of being interested in Charmaine and brings up the fling Tony had with Charmaine during high school.

At a therapy session Dr Melfi tries to turn the conversation back to Pussy. Tony gets up and walks out.

The Christmas party is about to begin. When Baccala puts on the Santa suit, Tony realises Pussy was wearing a wire at the 1995 party. Baccala proves to be a very grumpy Santa. One of the children swears at him. Afterwards, Silvio says Baccala will have to go to Santa school before next year's party. Silvio, Tony and Paulie discuss Pussy. They all agree he made a good Santa.

On Christmas Day the Sopranos are opening their presents when Jackie Jr arrives. He apologises to Tony and admits to flunking out of university. He wants to design men's fashion. Jackie says he got the gun from Ralphie. Tony hasn't made his mind up what to do about Jackie Jr.

Meadow gives Tony a singing Billy Bass as a present. The rest of the family laugh as it sings at Tony. He tries not to pass out again . . .

Deep and Meaningful: Silvio, Tony and Paulie discuss Pussy after the Christmas party. Silvio is being haunted by the friend he helped murder, and Tony still finds himself thinking about Pussy. Paulie claims he isn't bothered with such thoughts, but Tony is unconvinced. He remembers how Paulie went to see a psychic after Christopher's near-death experience (in #22, 'From Where To Eternity'). Paulie says that was different because Christopher was shot: 'That was a paranormal event.' Despite their hatred of Pussy for becoming a rat, all three still miss him.

Bright Lights, Baked Ziti: In a flashback to 1995, Jackie Sr is eating pasta at a boardwalk café when Pussy returns from Boca.

Tony is keeping a Christmas list on things to do. It includes the words 'Transfer Cannolis' – this proves to be a reference to money laundering.

Carmela says Janice is insisting on cooking a goose for Christmas Day. The Sopranos always have shellfish on Christmas Eve. Janice has roped Carmela into making lasagne and gravy for Christmas Day.

Tony, Paulie and Silvio eat pasta at Vesuvio. Artie brings them plates of ravioli. Charmaine says Artie's cooking has been shit lately.

Janice is preparing the goose when she sees the news report about Igor.

Tony and Carmela argue about Charmaine while Carmela is preparing the lasagne for Christmas Day.

Mobbed Up: Tony turns on the TV and is dismayed to see Frank Capra's Christmas perennial *It's A Wonderful Life* being broadcast. 'Enough already!'

Next day Tony's crew discuss the origins of the Santa myth. Tony suggests *The Grinch Who Stole Christmas* borrowed elements from the myth. Silvio is appalled at the idea that Dr Seuss ripped off the concept. Christopher expresses his admiration for the film *The Grinch*, starring Jim Carrey, as it grossed $200 million.

During a flashback to 1995, Tony notices that Pussy has arrived already wearing his Santa costume. He suggests Pussy is trying to get into character, like the method actor Al Pacino. This prompts Silvio into an impersonation from *The Godfather Part II*: 'It was you, Fredo!'

How Do You Feel?: After the panic attack Tony says he had been feeling good but all of a sudden he's back to square one. Failing to take his medication regularly is just another thing to feel bad about. He admits part of the feelings may be driven by what happened to Pussy.

I Dream of Jeannie Cusamano: There are several flashbacks to 1995, when Jackie was acting boss, OJ Simpson was in court and Tony still had most of his own hair. Pussy talks about wanting a house by the ocean and says perhaps it will be in another life. This seems ironic, as Pussy was later murdered and his body dumped at sea by Tony, Silvio and Paulie.

Silvio dreams that the Bada Bing! is being troubled by petty thefts. He goes into the stripper's dressing room to investigate and finds Pussy's bloody body behind a rack of costumes.

Quote/Unquote: Dr Melfi says everyone is under a lot of pressure in the festive season. 'I call it Stress-mas.'

Janice ponders the lyrical content of a Christian song she is writing with Aaron called 'His Blood Cleans Stains'. 'What are we selling here – Ajax?'

When Hesh and Christopher unpack the Christmas decorations at Satriale's, Hesh says there's a branch but he doesn't see the rest of the tree. Christopher misunderstands his meaning. 'Fuck that philosophical shit!'

Paulie thinks Tony is banging a stripper and is stunned when told she has gone to Morocco for Christmas. 'Who is she, Bada Bing! Crosby?'

A small boy criticises Bacala's festive efforts: 'Fuck you, Santa!'

Soundtrack: 'Santa Baby' by Eartha Kitt. 'White Christmas' by the Drifters. 'Christmas Don't Be Late' by the Chipmunks. 'The Cycle' by Virgos Merlot. 'I've Got a Feeling' by the Campbell Brothers with Katie Jackson.

Surveillance Report: This Christmas tale broke American television tradition by being broadcast in late spring – either four months late or eight months early, depending on your perspective!

This episode was unusually short with a running time of just over forty minutes. Episode lengths often vary on *The Sopranos* because commercial-free HBO does not demand dramas meet a very specific timing. But this episode was nearly ten minutes shorter than any of the previous instalments, causing mystification among fans on the Internet. They speculated that scenes had been cut from the broadcast version for reasons unknown.

The official HBO website for *The Sopranos* names seven characters for this episode who are not listed in the credits of the show that was broadcast. These include FBI Agents Harris and Cubitoso, Dino Zerilli and four others. The HBO website does have minor inaccuracies, but never to such an extent. Were the FBI agents featured in a scene cut from the final version? Only the production team on *The Sopranos* knows the answers to that question . . .

Michael Rispoli reprises his role as Jackie Aprile Sr, appearing in the flashbacks to Christmas 1995. Also back from the dead for this show are Vincent Pastore as Pussy Bonpensiero and Joe Badalucco as Jimmy Altieri.

Tony realises Pussy was a rat by Christmas 1995. This seemingly contradicts what FBI Agent Skip Lipari said in Season Two, when he indicated that Pussy had been nurtured by the feds for two years.

The Verdict: 'It's the miracle of Christmas.' Tony and his crew are haunted by the ghosts of Christmas past but this is no Dickensian morality tale. Nobody becomes a re-formed character and all men do not receive peace and goodwill.

In terms of plot, very little happens in this episode to advance the underlying stories of this season. Instead it concentrates on what *The Sopranos* does best – character moments and interplay. The script is packed with great lines and neatly captures the highly stressful nature of the festive season.

One character ends this episode in a worse position than he started it. Jackie Jr can count himself unlucky to be caught by Tony enjoying a lap dance. The level of coincidence required for this does jar a little, but not as much as Jackie Jr's balls after Tony has finished with them . . .

37
Pine Barrens

US Transmission Date: 6 May 2001

Teleplay by: Terence Winter
Story by: Tim Van Patten and Terence Winter
Director: Steve Buscemi
Cast: Crystal Fox (Nurse), Dayna Gizzo (Rita),
Deepa Purohit (Ambujam), Anya Shetler (Llana).

Storyline: Gloria returns from her Christmas holiday in Morocco. She goes to visit Tony on his boat with a present. He is not around when she arrives but the phone is ringing, so Gloria answers it. Tony's former mistress Irina is calling. She pretends to be from AJ's school. Tony walks in and gets rid of the call from Irina. Initially he lies to Gloria, then tells her the truth. She gets angry at his deception, throws his present into the harbour and stalks off.

Paulie is having his nails done when Tony calls. He asks Paulie to collect $5,000 from Valery, Slava's drunken friend. The collection is on behalf of a flu-ridden Silvio, whom Tony is sending home to bed. Paulie protests that he has to take his mother to the social security office the next day but Tony is adamant.

Tony and Carmela attend a joint therapy session with Dr Melfi. She notes that the couple seem to be less argumentative with each other.

Meadow is also down with the flu. She plays Scrabble with Jackie Jr in her dorm room, but his vocabulary proves very limited. Once he realises he is not going to get sex from Meadow, he makes an excuse to leave.

Next day Paulie and Christopher visit Valery, who is drinking first thing in the morning. Paulie is rude to the Russian and breaks his universal remote control. The pair get into a fight. Christopher tries to intervene and Paulie throttles Valery with a lamp stand. The two mobsters think the Russian is dying. They wrap him in a rug and throw him into the boot of Paulie's car.

Gloria and Tony meet in a hotel room at lunchtime. Gloria apologises for her behaviour. She gives Tony a Moroccan robe as a present. They start fucking but are interrupted by a phone call from Paulie about the Valery problem. Tony tells Paulie to use his own judgement. Gloria has to go back to work but invites Tony to dinner at her place that night.

Paulie puts petrol in his car while Christopher whines about being hungry – he had no breakfast. Paulie decides the best thing to do is dump Valery's body in the Pine Barrens of South Jersey – a deserted area. Christopher reluctantly agrees.

Tony tells Melfi he is having an affair with Gloria.

Paulie and Christopher arrive at a deserted part of the Pine Barrens. When they open the boot Valery is still alive. They march him into the woods at gunpoint and order him to dig his own grave. Valery hits Christopher with the shovel, pushes Paulie over and runs off into the snowy forest. They chase him, shooting wildly. Paulie manages to shoot Valery in the head. But, when Paulie and Christopher reach the spot where Valery was shot, he has disappeared.

Paulie phones Tony with news of what's happened, but the mobile-phone connection keeps breaking up. Tony is furious – he has a meeting with Slava and he could be walking into a deathtrap. Paulie and Christopher try to retrace their steps to Paulie's car.

Tony goes to see Slava to launder $200,000. The Russian says he and Valery were soldiers in Chechnya. Valery saved his life but is now a drunk, tragic figure. Slava says he would do anything for Valery. Afterwards, Tony calls Paulie with more news about Valery. The drunk is an ex-commando from the Russian Interior Ministry who killed sixteen Chechen rebels single-handedly. But the message gets gabbled on the bad phone connection.

Christopher thinks he sees Valery and gives chase. Paulie follows but loses his right shoe. Christopher succeeds in shooting his quarry, which turns out to be a deer.

Jackie Jr calls Meadow, who is still sick. Jackie invents a lame excuse for not seeing Meadow. Afterwards she is suspicious.

Paulie and Christopher find an abandoned truck and shelter inside for the night. Paulie's shoeless foot is frozen, while Christopher thinks he may have concussion from the shovel blow to his head.

Tony has dinner with Carmela and AJ. Carmela's parents, Hugh and Mary, arrive unexpectedly. Hugh has been diagnosed with glaucoma and may need an operation. Tony had planned to go and see Gloria but now has to stay at home for several more hours. Paulie calls and admits to Tony they are lost. He tries to put the blame for what happened on to Christopher.

Meadow gets a college friend to drive her around to the apartment where Jackie Jr is staying while a friend is in Israel. They wait outside.

Tony finally gets to Gloria's place – three hours late. He apologises.

Paulie and Christopher bicker about what happened and what they should do next. Paulie calls Tony for help. He agrees to come find them. When Tony prepares to leave, Gloria goes ballistic. She calls him names and throws a hefty piece of cooked meat at him, hitting him in the back. He walks out and she starts smashing her own possessions.

Tony goes to Junior's place, where he is meeting Bacala. Tony borrows a shirt from Junior to replace the one Gloria hit with meat. Bacala arrives, dressed like an oversized Elmer Fudd hunter. Tony can't help laughing.

Meadow sees Jackie Jr come outside with another woman. A heartbroken Meadow confronts and dumps Jackie.

Tony and Bacala drive to the Pine Barrens. Tony apologises for laughing earlier. Bacala used to go hunting with his hit man father every year. Bacala envies Tony for having Junior as an uncle. Tony and Bacala reach the place where Paulie left his car – it's gone. Tony phones Paulie but reception is poor.

Christopher and Paulie are at each other's throats. Christopher threatens to shoot Paulie and says he overheard Paulie trying to shift the blame. Finally, Christopher can't help laughing at their predicament. He promises not to leave Paulie behind in the woods.

Meadow is admitted to the college medical centre. She is dehydrated and running a temperature. She is distraught about Jackie Jr.

Next morning Tony and Bacala begin searching for the lost mobsters. Paulie and Christopher start walking. Paulie has fashioned a makeshift shoe from carpet in the van but it soon comes loose. He snaps and starts firing his gun, which alerts Tony and Bacala to their presence. The lost pair are soon located and taken back to Tony's car, where he has food for them.

Tony gives Paulie the choice – to stay and search for Valery, or to go back to North Jersey. Paulie opts for the latter and Christopher backs up Paulie's version of events. Tony says if Valery survives, the consequences will all fall on Paulie. He drives everyone home. Paulie is very unhappy and looks at Tony with genuine hatred.

Tony discusses Gloria's erratic behaviour with Dr Melfi. She asks what attracted him to Gloria in the first place, or to Irina before? Both were depressive personalities, unstable and impossible to please – does that remind Tony of any other woman? He knows Melfi means his mother, but he says nothing . . .

Deep and Meaningful: After nearly 24 hours in the Pine Barrens, Paulie and Christopher snap. Christopher accuses Paulie of planning to murder him and Paulie lunges at him. They grapple and Christopher pulls a gun on Paulie, screaming, 'I'll leave you here, you one-shoe cocksucker!' All their conflicts throughout the season have been building to this moment.

Finally, Christopher starts laughing – he can't help himself. After a day of constant bitching, he can only find their ludicrous situation funny. The moment passes and afterwards Christopher supports Paulie's version of events when questioned by Tony. The two have bonded in the unlikeliest of circumstances.

Bright Lights, Baked Ziti: Gloria invites Tony to her place for dinner. She asks if he likes London broil.

Christopher moans through the whole episode about being hungry. He doesn't have breakfast before coming out with Paulie and lives to regret it. He tries to persuade Paulie to stop at a Roy Rogers restaurant, but Paulie wants to dump Valery's body first.

When they are lost in the woods, Christopher wants to eat some local berries but Paulie says they are probably dangerous. Christopher finds half-frozen sachets of ketchup when they shelter in the abandoned truck. Paulie suggests mixing ketchup and relish for maximum flavour. Paulie has a packet of Tic Tacs which he keeps to himself. Christopher decides to eat the berries, poisonous or not. 'At least I won't die hungry.'

At dinner Tony, Carmela and AJ eat pasta. Tony only picks at his food because he is saving space for dinner with Gloria, but claims he had a late lunch when questioned by Carmela about his lack of appetite. Carmela offers her parents food when they arrive but Mary turns it down.

Gloria throws the London broil of meat at Tony, splattering him with aromatic beef juices.

When Paulie and Christopher try to walk out of the woods next morning, they decide Denny's Restaurant should be their first stop. Christopher wants to have five Grand Slam breakfasts. When they finally get to Tony's car, the pair scoff a box of burgers he has brought for them. Paulie gets mayonnaise down his chin, which Tony points out.

Mobbed Up: Paulie says Russians can't be trusted, citing the Cuban missile crisis as an example. Christopher thought the crisis was just a bullshit movie.

Tony tells Dr Melfi he likes Gloria because she's smart, sexy and Italian. He believes you should stick to your own kind. Melfi compares his attitudes to a hit musical and movie of the past: 'What is this, *West Side Story* now?

Christopher worries about Valery, who is trained for hanging around in the woods. He likens their situation to the *Die Hard* movies.

How Do You Feel?: At a joint session with Dr Melfi, Tony attributes the lack of arguments between himself and Carmela to therapy paying off. But he comes clean at a later solo session, admitting he is seeing a fellow patient, Gloria. Dr Melfi says this means Tony's improved relationship with Carmela is predicated on a lie. 'Predicated on my ass, what's the difference?' He says he feels content and relaxed. He feels he is a better husband and a better father. Being with Gloria makes him happier than all the therapy and Prozac combined.

Tony changes his tune after Gloria throws the beef at him. He calls her a fucking lunatic and wonders why everything has to be so hard.

Quote/Unquote: Valery rants in Russian at Christopher and Paulie when they joke that he must be cold in the snowy woods: 'You think the cold bothers me? I wash my balls with ice water!'

Paulie uses oblique language on his mobile phone while telling Tony what happened with Valery: 'The package hit Chrissie with an implement and ran off.'

Christopher suggests they are lost. 'Stop getting cunty!' Paulie replies.

Paulie mishears when Tony says Valery was an assassin for the Russian Interior Ministry who murdered sixteen Chechens single-handedly. ' He killed sixteen Czechoslovakians – guy was an interior decorator.' Christopher is surprised: 'His house looked like shit.'

Soundtrack: 'Gloria' by Van Morrison. 'Coffee and TV' by Blur. 'Sposa Son Dispressata' by Cecilia Bartoli.

Surveillance Report: This episode is directed by the film actor and director Steve Buscemi, best known for starring in movies such as *Fargo* and *Reservoir Dogs*. His character spent much of *Fargo* stumbling around in the snow, making the setting for this episode very reminiscent.

There is an overhead shot when the camera looks down on Paulie and Christopher, just after Valery has disappeared. It cleverly prompts the viewer into thinking the Russian is hiding in the tree branches and he will jump down on the mobsters at any second – he never does.

New Jersey fans of *The Sopranos* complained about factual errors in this episode. The scenes set in the Pine Barrens were actually shot in New York state and the landscape shown apparently bears little resemblance to the real Pine Barrens. Also, one of the characters is shown pumping petrol into his own car. But the state of New Jersey does not allow self-service at petrol stations.

Jackie Jr's vocabulary is limited, judging by his best efforts at Scrabble – 'the', 'ass' and 'poo'. By comparison, Meadow scores highly with 'oblique', which Jackie thinks is Spanish.

The Verdict: 'How can we be lost like this? We're in Jersey.' Paulie and Christopher have an unhappy adventure in the Pine Barrens while the honeymoon is definitely over for two budding relationships.

The writer Terence Winter comes up trumps with one of the best episodes of Season Three. Tony discovers Gloria is prone to erratic behaviour while Meadow learns that Jackie Jr is an immature, self-centred shit. The warning signs have been obvious to viewers for weeks, now the characters are catching on. For Tony the tide is just turning, while Meadow gets wise and dumps Jackie.

But the centrepiece of this gem is the farcical efforts of Paulie and Christopher to deal with a drunken Russian ex-commando. Will Valery come back? And how much has this incident soured Paulie's relationship with Tony?

38
Amour Fou

US Transmission Date: 13 May 2001

Teleplay by: Frank Renzulli
Story by: David Chase
Director: Tim Van Patten
Cast: Isaach De Bankole (Father Obosi),
Paul Mazursky (Sunshine), Victor Truro (Dr Rotelli),
Joanie Ellen (PA), Anna Mastrionni (Woman In Car),
Michael Lee Patterson (Martin),
Stephen Peabody (Service Manager),
Anthony Zayas (Cholo #1),
Freddy Martinez (Cholo #2),
Cesar Deleon (Cholo #3).

Storyline: Carmela and Meadow visit an art gallery. Carmela is having problems with bleeding outside her usual period. She chides her daughter about poor grades at college. Meadow says her relationship with Jackie Jr is over, but will not elaborate. Carmela starts crying in front of a painting.

Gloria approaches Tony in a car park. She apologises for her behaviour. Tony agrees to see her later. He goes to therapy with Dr Melfi, who says Tony and Gloria have what the French called '*amour fou*' – crazy love. The therapist suggests Gloria is drawn to Tony like a moth to a flame.

Jackie Jr and Dino Zerilli meet with Ralphie. They give him $350, a cut from the proceeds of their activities. Jackie Jr whines that Tony did not intervene to stop him being kicked out of college.

Tony and Gloria meet in a hotel room for sex. Gloria complains about her strained family relations.

Jackie Jr and Dino chase three customers – who insist on smoking – out of the Ooh-Fa Pizza parlour. Christopher comes in and offers them part of a truck heist. The pair say they have aligned themselves with Ralphie.

Carmela is getting her Mercedes serviced but no courtesy cars are available. Gloria overhears the name Soprano and gives Carmela a lift home. Gloria politely grills Carmela for information about the Soprano family while driving her home way too fast.

Jackie Jr and Dino are having a midnight snack at the Aprile household when Ralphie comes in. He tells them an anecdote about how Tony and Jackie Sr broke into the big time by robbing a card game run by a made guy.

Carmela watches TV. She finds herself crying at dog food commercials.

Tony visits Gloria at home. Her car's tyres have been slashed. Tony wonders if Irina could have been responsible but dismisses the idea. He says he slapped the piss out of her last time something like this happened. Gloria is intrigued but goes mad when Tony offers to get her new tyres.

Jackie Jr and Dino decide to hit a card game run by Eugene Pontecorvo, a made guy under Ralphie's protection. Jackie wants to include Carlo Renzi, who has a shotgun. The pair go inside to call Carlo but are distracted by TV.

Carmela goes to confession with Father Obosi, a priest studying for his doctorate in psychology. She worries she may have ovarian cancer, which killed her cousin. She is too scared to go to a doctor. The priest says she could be pregnant. Carmela says her life is a lie, financed by Tony's crimes. Father Obosi suggests she learn to live off the good part of her husband. She should also go and see a specialist for her medical concerns.

Carmela tells Tony that Meadow and Jackie Jr have split up. Gloria phones Carmela while Tony is there, under the pretence of selling her a car. Tony hears about Gloria's recent contact with Carmela. He goes to the car dealership and tells Gloria the relationship is over – in no uncertain terms.

Carmela gets her ovaries scanned by a doctor.

Jackie Jr goads Dino into calling Carlo about hitting the card game.

Carmela, Rosalie Aprile, Angie Bonpensiero and Gabriella Dante have lunch. Carmela says the doctor diagnosed a small thyroid problem, nothing serious. The four women discuss the break-up of Jackie Jr and Meadow. Young women of today seem to get over heartache much more quickly. They discuss how much the First Lady, Hillary Clinton, had to put up with from her husband.

Gloria phones Tony at the Bada Bing!. She's sobbing and hysterical. He goes to see her at home. She just wants things back the way they were. He says that's impossible. Gloria uses the same phrases and tactics as Livia to attack Tony. He recognises what is going on and warns Gloria to stay away from his family. He chases her around the room, picks her up by the throat and throws her to the floor. She spits in his face and begs Tony to kill her. He starts throttling her but regains control of himself. Tony gets up and walks out.

Jackie Jr, Dino, Carlo and Matush pull up outside the card game. Carlo is eager to get on with it but Jackie Jr is having second thoughts. He offers them a way out. They collectively decide to rob the game before the drugs they took earlier wear off. Matush stays with the van as getaway driver while the other three go inside, armed with pistols and Carlo's shotgun.

The trio burst in to find a game laden with made men, including Furio, Christopher, Bacala and Eugene Pontecorvo. Dino freezes up and can't talk, so Jackie Jr shouts orders. The dealer, Sunshine, infuriates Jackie by spouting old adages. Another card player emerges from the toilet and Carlo blasts at him with the shotgun. Outside Matush hears the shot and drives off. Inside, Sunshine starts another saying and Jackie shoots the dealer repeatedly in the chest, murdering him. The small room turns into a shooting gallery. Christopher shoots Carlo through the head, while Jackie shoots Furio in the thigh. Jackie and Dino run out of the door but the getaway van is gone. Jackie hijacks a passing car and drives off, leaving Dino by himself. Christopher and another card player catch Dino. He pleads for his life, saying he is with Ralphie. They shoot him anyway. The card players leave the crime scene at speed, taking Furio.

Dr Fried is making a commercial for his penile-implant business when he gets a phone call from Tony asking for help. Furio can't be taken to a hospital for treatment because he's an illegal immigrant. Dr Fried operates on Furio, who swears profusely in Italian throughout the procedure.

Christopher tells Tony the other robber was definitely Jackie Jr. He wants to kill Jackie himself but Tony forbids it. Christopher is infuriated and calls Tony a hypocrite for protecting Jackie Aprile Sr's kid. Tony lays down the law to Christopher, who runs off.

Tony meets with Ralphie in the back office at Satriale's. He leaves the final decision about Jackie Jr to Ralphie, who is torn about what to do.

Tony discusses Gloria with Dr Melfi. She says the relationship with Gloria was about Tony reliving his relationship with his mother. The therapist doesn't know if Gloria poses a threat to Tony in the future.

Patsy takes a test drive with Gloria. He pulls a gun and warns her to stay away from Tony – or else. She gets the message.

Ralphie goes home to Rosalie and tells her Jackie Jr has a serious drug problem. He says he will do his best to save her son.

Carmela is reading about how to get into selling real estate when Tony comes home. He notices she is no longer wearing the ring he gave her. Carmela lies, saying it is being resized.

Deep and Meaningful: There are several great, character-defining moments in this episode. The confrontation between Tony and Christopher about Jackie Jr is prime stuff, with all Tony's rage revealed in its terrifying ferocity. But the best is perhaps when Tony puts the final decision about Jackie Jr's fate into Ralphie's hands. Ralphie realises it was his anecdote about Tony and Jackie's father robbing the card game that led to this crisis. Tony asked whether

Ralphie schooled Jackie Jr the best he could. Ralphie says he spoiled the young man. Ralphie walks out of the meeting and stands on the street, alone. He has to decide whether or not to obey the mob code and have Jackie Jr slain . . .

Mama Mia: Gloria all but morphs into Livia during her final confrontation with Tony. He protests that his life is no picnic. 'Poor you,' says Gloria, reviving one of Livia's catchphrases. She also wonders aloud if she should be like a mute and says nobody cares if she's alive or dead. All this jolts Tony to a crucial realisation: 'I didn't just meet you. I've known you my whole fucking like.' He says Gloria is just like his mother, a bottomless black hole.

Bright Lights, Baked Ziti: This action-packed episode has little time for food. Jackie Jr pulls a gun on the smokers in the Ooh-Fa Pizza parlour, telling them to go find a Taco Bell – a chain of Mexican fast-food restaurants.

Jackie Jr and Dino are eating spaghetti when Ralphie tells them anecdotes. Ralphie looks for marshmallows to put into his hot chocolate.

Tony has cereal when he and Carmela discuss Meadow and Jackie Jr.

Dino scoffs pizza as Jackie Jr goads him into calling Carlo.

Carmela, Angie, Rosalie and Gabriella have pasta for lunch at Vesuvio. Rosalie complains about Artie's cooking.

Carmela is cooking lemon snaps for the bake sale at church when Tony comes home as the episode draws to a close. He says they smell good.

Mobbed Up: Jackie Jr and Dino are transfixed by the film *Basic Instinct* when it is screened on TV. Jackie says the sequence where Sharon Stone crosses her legs to reveal she is wearing no panties is his favourite part.

Patsy warns Gloria not to attempt any *Fatal Attraction*-style antics with Tony or his family, or he will kill her. 'It will not be cinematic.'

How Do You Feel?: Tony says he and Gloria are like leather and lace or a burning ring of fire. They push each

other's buttons. He likes the fact that she's a very
independent woman, unlike Irina, who was a helpless
baby.

After he nearly kills Gloria, Tony wonders to Dr Melfi
if the relationship was a set-up from the beginning. He now
sees Gloria as just another Irina with a college degree. The
therapist asks why Tony is drawn to dangerous relationships. He suggests he's looking for a way out of his
marriage. Dr Melfi says he will never leave his wife – it's
the one good decision he has made about women in his life.
However, Carmela might leave him. Tony starts getting
angry at this and doesn't enjoy being told he's a very
conventional man, in spite of everything else.

How Do You Feel, Carmela?: Carmela thinks her whole life
is a lie. She worries she will die outside God's mercy
because of her complicity in Tony's crimes. Carmela tells
Father Obosi that it seemed so right when a psychiatrist
told her to leave Tony. She loves her husband and she
loves God, but her life is financed by crime. The priest
looks at the massive sapphire finger on her hand and
Carmela covers it up, ashamed. She decides to take his
advice and try to live only on the good part of her life.

Sleeping with the Fishes: This episode has a body count of
three – easily the highest of the season and all confined to
a few minutes of the show. The card dealer, Sunshine, is
first to die, shot repeatedly in the chest by Jackie Jr for
spouting old adages. Carlo Renzi gets it next, shot in the
head by Christopher. Last, but not least, Dino Zerilli is
executed by Christopher and another player from the card
game.

Quote/Unquote: Ralphie dismisses Jackie Jr's complaint
that Tony should have tried to save Jackie's college status.
'He should break the dean's legs 'cos you're too lazy to
read a fucking book?'

Carmela thinks it's terrible the English government
didn't tell people sooner about mad-cow disease. 'Probably
didn't want to create a stampede,' Tony quips.

Gabriella Dante sums up the life and career of Hillary Clinton: 'She took all that negative shit he gave her and spun it into gold.'

Tony lays down the law to Christopher: 'You don't gotta love me – you will respect me.'

Patsy Parisi gives Gloria her final warning about Tony while they test-drive a new Mercedes. 'You call or go anywhere near him or his family, you'll be scraping your nipples off these fine leather seats.'

Soundtrack: 'Sposa Son Dispressata' by Cecilia Bartoli. 'Return To Me' by Dean Martin. 'Walk Like An Egyptian' by the Bangles. 'Return To Me' by Bob Dylan. 'Affection' by the Lost Boys. 'No Hay Problema' by Pink Martini.

Surveillance Report: Dr Melfi says she is not charging Tony for his sessions because he overpaid last month. She will not accept gifts from Tony. This resolves a minor dangling plot thread from #35, 'The Telltale Moozadell'.

Carmela says Noah is moving to India for the United Nations.

During a phone call Tony conveniently recaps what's happening with his legal status. The authorities could prosecute him on simple fraud charges over the airline tickets but they want to roll that into a major RICO predicate case.

Lewis Stadlen reprises his role as the penile-implants specialist Dr Fried, last seen in #19, 'The Happy Wanderer'. Also returning from the same episode is the card dealer Sunshine, played by Paul Mazursky. Mazursky is an actor, writer and director, best known for the films *Bob and Carol and Ted and Alice*, *An Unmarried Woman* and *Down and Out In Beverly Hills*.

The Verdict: 'Kill me, you fuck!' Jackie Jr's attempt to jump-start his mob career goes horribly wrong, while Tony finally recognises Gloria for what she really is. Carmela perhaps finds a new way forward from her moral quandary.

After the outstanding #37, 'Pine Barrens', this is another cracking episode. At first glance, 'Amour Fou' seems like a rerun of elements from the second season. Jackie Jr and Dino replace Matt and Sean as the wannabe mobsters whose plans go wrong. Tony dumps his mistress in the penultimate episode. Carmela has a crisis over her relationship with Tony.

Yet the result is more exciting because so much more is at stake this time. Gloria represents much more of a threat than vodka-sodden Irina. Jackie Jr's actions threaten to destabilise the entire Family. Carmela comes closer than she has ever done to walking out on her marriage and Dr Melfi tells Tony it is a real possibility for the future.

The scene is set for the final episode of Season Three. But how many ongoing plotlines will it resolve, and how many will it leave for the fourth – and potentially final – season of *The Sopranos*?

39
Army Of One

US Transmission Date: 20 May 2001

Written by: David Chase and Lawrence Konner
Director: John Patterson
Cast: Fairuza Balk (Agent Deborah Ciccerone),
Normal Maxwell (FBI Agent),
Marc Damon Johnson (Detective Filemon Francis),
Danielle Cautella (Mackenzie Trucillo),
Melissa Marsala (Kelli Aprile), Patricia Mauceri (Marie),
Francis Esemplare (Nucci),
Ryan Homchick (Cadet Delaunay),
Candy Trabucco (Miss Giaculo),
Dick Latessa (Father L'Oiseau),
Michael Kenneth Williams (Ray Ray), Monique Lola
Berkley (Saleswoman), Lekel Russell (Leena),
Geoff Wigdor (Little Bruce), Phil Larocco (Wiseguy),
Dino Palermo (Junior's Friend),
Tobin Bell (Major Zwingli).

Storyline: AJ and his friend Egon Kosma hide in the school basement, waiting for the janitor to leave. Egon has to piss, prompting AJ into having a slash too. Afterwards they sneak into an office in search of something.

Jackie Jr hides out with a black family on a housing project.

Paulie takes his mother on a tour of Green Grove retirement community. She loves it. Paulie needs to raise $40,000 as a deposit. Later he meets with Silvio and Ralphie at a dinner. Paulie wants half the proceeds from the robbery of a safe for which he provided the details and codes to Ralphie. Ralphie netted nearly $100,000 from the job. He pretends to get a phone call on his mobile from Tony and uses it as an excuse to leave the meeting without giving Paulie anything. The message was actually a prearranged call from Vito Spatafore, who is part of Ralphie's crew.

Tony gets a phone call at home from a desperate Jackie Jr, who wants help. Tony refers him to Ralphie and hangs up.

Ralphie meets with Tony and says there's another $300,000 coming soon from the esplanade project. Tony says Jackie Jr called, and wants to know what Ralphie is doing about the problem. He delegates the final decision to Ralphie but indicates it should be resolved soon.

The principal at AJ's school invites AJ and Egon to his office. He compliments them on each getting 96 per cent for geometry, a subject they both usually fail. The principal claims to have got a DNA match to them from the urine the janitor found in the basement. Egon cracks and starts crying. AJ blames Egon for peeing first.

FBI agents meet to discuss the status of their investigation into the Soprano Family. Junior seems to have beaten cancer. The feds decide to try another tactic, using a female agent to get close to Adriana in the hope she'll divulge Family secrets. A young agent who has previously only done background checks is given the job.

Jackie Jr goes out for a walk. He is slain by Vito.

Tony goes to the office at the Bada Bing!. Christopher walks out, still in a huff with Tony. Paulie whines about the money dispute. He demands a sit-down with Ralphie and Tony. Tony gets a tearful phone call from Carmela.

AJ has been permanently expelled from Verbum Dei. Tony decides his son should go to a military academy. He has brochures for such schools, given to him by Janice. Carmela gets news that Jackie Jr is dead, murdered in a drugs deal gone awry. She goes to comfort Rosalie Aprile. AJ calls Meadow, who tells him the DNA test was a bluff – such results take six weeks. He tells her about the murder of Jackie Jr. Meadow is distraught.

Tony discusses Jackie's death with Dr Melfi. She says he foresaw this day would come. Tony says AJ would never survive if he tried to join the mob.

Tony and Carmela take AJ for an interview at Hudson Military Institute. AJ is appalled to learn the school day runs from 5.30 a.m. to 10 p.m. with no television. Major Zwingli tells Tony and Carmela about the school philosophy, which encourages students to become an army of one. That night Tony and Carmela have a screaming match about whether or not AJ should go to Hudson.

Attendance at the funeral home for Jackie Jr is poor. Rosalie bitterly attributes this to its being just two days to Superbowl – the climax of the sports betting season. Janice gives the funeral director Cozzarelli a demo CD of her Christian contemporary music to play. She says the boss of Sony Records is interested. Cozzarelli buries the CD under a pile of paperwork.

Christopher takes Tony to one side and apologises for doubting him about how to handle the Jackie Jr situation. Tony just walks away from him.

After seeing Jackie Jr's body, Carmela relents and decides to try Tony's suggestion of sending AJ to military school.

The sit-down goes badly for Paulie. Tony rules that Ralphie has to pay Paulie only $12,000 of the profits. Paulie is left bitter and stunned – he needed more money to pay for his mother to go to Green Grove.

Adriana makes a new friend while shopping for funeral clothes. FBI Agent Ciccerone succeeds in her assignment, adopting the name Danielle.

AJ puts on the military school's dress uniform at home for his parents. He starts crying because he doesn't want to go. Finally, it all becomes too much – he has a panic attack and passes out. Like father, like son.

Tony tells Dr Melfi that AJ can't go to military school because of the panic attacks. His son has the same problem as he has. Verbum Dei has belatedly admitted AJ had a previous panic attack during football practice, which was diagnosed as dehydration at the time by the school nurse. Tony is on the verge of tears – how are they going to save AJ?

Cut to Jackie Jr's coffin being unloaded from a hearse for burial. The police swoop and arrest Christopher and Silvio on gambling-related charges at the graveyard. Paulie runs off to escape arrest. Junior and Bacala turn up. When Junior sees the cops, he departs so fast he almost leaves Bacala behind.

Afterwards at the Aprile house Meadow argues with Jackie Jr's sister Kelli. Kelli believes Jackie was killed by one of the local mobsters. Meadow hits the vodka and defends her father, saying Tony is not a boss. She is stunned that Kelli shows no loyalty to the Family and talks about it in front of an outsider.

Nearly everyone gathers at Vesuvio for Jackie Jr's wake. Paulie leaves when Tony arrives, saying he has to look after his mother. Tony chats with Junior, who has been released from house arrest. Junior's trial on RICO (Racketeer-Influenced and Corrupt Organisation) charges is starting soon. Having survived cancer, Junior decides to enjoy life more.

Johnny Sack approaches Paulie outside. Paulie complains about Tony's ruling and Ralphie's attitude. Johnny Sack says the New York boss Carmine asks after Paulie. Paulie offers his services to Carmine, any time, for anything.

Junior sings an Italian song, 'Core 'ngrato' – ungrateful heart. It brings tears to the eyes of many in the restaurant. Artie stands by his wife Charmaine, but he looks lovingly at Adriana, who is with Christopher. Janice is all over

Ralphie like a cheap suit. Meadow throws bits of bread at Junior before running out, pursued by Tony. She runs away from him, just managing to cross the road safely in heavy traffic. Tony returns to Vesuvio, where he hugs AJ and Carmela. Junior continues singing . . .

Deep and Meaningful: Tony has a moment of intense self-loathing and fear when discussing AJ's fate with Dr Melfi. He says his son has got the same putrid, rotten, fucking Soprano gene as himself. Tony is on the verge of tears. He has already said AJ could not survive in the Family business, especially after what happened to Jackie Jr. Tony knows Meadow will be all right – but what future is there for his son?

Bright Lights, Baked Ziti: Paulie's mother worries when she hears Green Grove has a Parisian night – she doesn't want to eat snails. The staff assure her that the food will be dishes like coq au vin and blanket of veal.

Tony kicks the door off the mini-fridge at the Bada Bing! when he finds someone has eaten the lo mein (Chinese noodles served in a clinging sauce) he left there for later consumption.

Tony, Carmela and AJ have pasta for dinner while Tony looks at brochures on military schools for AJ.

Vesuvio serves dinner for Jackie's wake. Junior compliments the gravy. Meadow lobs lumps of bread at Junior when he starts singing.

Mobbed Up: Tony compares AJ in dress uniform to Sergeant Bilko, eponymous hero of the classic US sitcom starring Phil Silvers as a scheming soldier in the army.

How Do You Feel?: Tony feels that he failed Jackie Jr. He tells Dr Melfi that he is not going to make the same mistake with AJ, hence the military-school plan. Tony says the most important thing for Meadow is she get as far away as possible from the Family business.

Sleeping with the Fishes: Jackie Aprile Jr, executed by Vito Spatafore with a single bullet to the back of the head. The funeral home does a great job of reconstructing his face so Jackie can have an open coffin.

Quote/Unquote: Tony offers no sympathy when Jackie Jr asks for help, yet again using his dead father as a reason for special treatment. 'He's been dead for two years. As a matter of fact, the expiration date was last week on all your bullshit with that.'

FBI Agent Cubitoso asks Agent Ciccerone how she would like to make a new best friend for the next nine months. 'Let me put it this way – how big can you make your hair?'

Kelli Aprile correctly guesses the true circumstances of her brother's murder: 'He was killed by some fat fuck in see-through socks.'

Junior remembers Jackie Jr as a dumb fuck who nearly drowned in three inches of water. 'The penguin exhibition,' Tony says, nodding sadly.

Junior celebrates his freedom after getting released from house arrest. 'I've been farting into the same sofa cushion for eighteen months.'

Soundtrack: The residents at Green Grove sing Sammy Cahn's 'Call Me Irresponsible'. 'Wonderful Love' by Creeper Lagoon. Junior sings 'Core 'ngrato' at Vesuvio restaurant. During the song the music mutates into a medley of three other tracks, two of which are 'Parlez-moi d'amour' by Lucienne Boyer and 'La Enramada' by Los Tres Ases. The third song and performer remained unidentified by online fans as this book went to press. Meadow sings a line from 'Oops, I Did It again' by Britney Spears at the wake. 'Ambient music track 7 (blur)' by the Aphex Twin plays over the closing credits.

Surveillance Report: When they first meet to discuss the proceeds of the safe job, Paulie calls Ralphie Richie – but nobody seems to notice. Was this a slip of the tongue by the actor that went unnoticed or an attempt to wind Ralphie up?

It has to be asked – what is the significance of Junior's seemingly singing in tongues at the end of this episode? His own voice is replaced with three other voices singing in other languages, yet the music is cleverly timed so it appears Junior is lip-synching the words. Is this meant to represent the universal nature of the themes in his song? The global problems of family and the heart? Who knows? The viewers are left scratching their heads as the season closes with the most oblique moment yet in *The Sopranos* . . .

This episode drew 9.5 million viewers when it was first broadcast on US television. This is higher than the ratings for Season Two's finale, but down on the 11 million viewers who tuned into the double-length premiere for Season Three. By way of comparison, *The X Files'* finale screened at the same time on the Fox network got 14 million viewers. But only a third of US homes have HBO access, so *The Sopranos'* ratings are still very impressive.

FBI Agent Ciccerone is played by Fairuza Balk, an actress best known for playing the lead witch in the supernatural thriller *The Craft* and other Gothic films.

The Verdict: 'We're starting a new regime around here!' Jackie Jr meets his inevitable end. AJ gets expelled and only just escapes being banished to military school. Tony's man-management techniques leave something to be desired as he alienates Christopher and Paulie, storing up trouble for the future.

Viewers who tune in to this episode expecting a traditional season finale that neatly ties up long-running plot threads have come to the wrong place. The only things resolved are Jackie Jr's fate and Junior's beating cancer and house arrest. Aside from that, everything else is still up in the air. In fact, this episode sets up several new plot elements. Fairuza Balk debuts as an FBI agent assigned to making friends with Adriana, while Johnny Sack starts working on Paulie to have him betray Tony.

When the creator David Chase began planning Season Three, he asked for the first episode's broadcast date to be pushed back from the usual January slot to March 2001. This extra two months was spent plotting out both Seasons Three and Four. So this episode is really just the halfway point in a 26-episode run, rather than the expected apocalyptic season finale. On that basis it's another strong effort, if not the equal of the two preceding episodes.

Of course, this begs the questions – what will happen in Season Four? David Chase and the actor James Gandolfini are contracted to *The Sopranos* only up to the end of the fourth season and there has been much speculation about whether the show will be extended. For more on this, see the essay about Season Four at the end of the book.

Matriarchy Rules

In mob stories, the power structure is almost invariably patriarchal. Men rule the Family and also their own family. In the *Godfather* trilogy, women are confined to the roles of whores or madonnas. Either they are sex objects for men to use and abuse, or else they are long-suffering mothers who must cook, clean and look after the children, the heirs to the throne. Vito Corleone's wife fulfils the madonna role. Her only power is unintentional – Michael refuses to have his brother Fredo killed until their mother is dead.

Michael's wife does not come from the usual Italian stock and does not adhere strictly to the role expected of her by the Family. She divorces Michael, but still returns to him by the final part of the trilogy. Of all the women in the *Godfather* films, only Connie flexes any real muscle of will. By the third film she is influencing Michael's decisions and pressing for retribution against the Family's enemies. Her brother comments on her attitude, suggesting their foes should be more afraid of her than of him.

In *Goodfellas*, the madonna/whore equation is in full effect. The character played by Lorraine Bracco (who now plays Dr Jennifer Melfi in *The Sopranos*) comes from outside the Italian tradition and shows some initial spirit. But, once she marries Ray Liotta's character, she is quickly subsumed into the role of mob wife and mother. Mafia stories on film, television and in other media have almost without exception replicated this patriarchal power structure.

On the surface, *The Sopranos* follows this same structure. At the beginning of Season One, Jackie Aprile is acting boss and all his captains are men. When Jackie dies, Junior becomes the new acting boss – although it is actually Tony who is in control. Tony finally takes the mantle of acting boss after Junior is indicted on federal charges at the end of Season One.

But a small scratch to below the surface reveals women as the power behind the throne. Time and again characters comment on the hold mothers have over their children in *The Sopranos*. The scariest mother of them all has to be Livia Soprano. In flashback she is seen threatening to poke young Tony's eyes out with a fork. She also threatens to smother her own children rather than move to Nevada. She constantly talks about infanticide, such as news reports about mothers throwing their babies out of skyscraper windows.

Ostensibly, Livia fulfilled the role of mob wife, bearing Johnny Boy Soprano's children and raising them. In reality, she controlled her husband by passive/aggressive manipulation. Tony says Livia wore his father down until he was a squeaking little gerbil. She drove away her two daughters, Janice and Barbara. She estranged Carmela from her mother, as Carmela's mother revealed at Livia's wake in Season Three.

Only Tony remained to look after his mother in her elder years, tied to her by guilt. He cannot admit to hating his own mother, even though he undoubtedly does. He cannot recall a single warm, loving experience involving her. Such is Tony's need for a mother substitute that he becomes infatuated with his therapist. Later, he has an elaborate fantasy about Isabella, a loving, caring mother. He even imagines himself as a baby being nursed by Isabella.

Livia's power is not just over her own children. Junior goes to her for guidance when he becomes acting boss. He defers to her in making decisions and is led into arranging the attempted hit on his nephew. Livia carefully tells

Junior exactly the information necessary to gull him into action on her behalf. She manipulates him while simultaneously maintaining plausible deniability – even to herself. When the hit on Tony goes wrong, she fakes senility and then a stroke to escape his wrath. She constantly belittles everyone around her and badmouths those who are not present.

Her daughter Janice is cut from the same cloth. She is a frustrated mother, whose son Hal now lives in Canada. Janice ran away from New Jersey to escape her mother's power. She embraced hippie New Age ideals and feminism, but still uses the same ploys as Livia to manipulate and control the men in her life. Janice goads and bullies Tony until she gets her way about Livia's house. She gets engaged to Richie Aprile and controls him like a puppet. Janice nags him about his lack of power. She allows him to hold a loaded pistol to her head while they have sex, but renders Richie impotent by saying he should be boss instead of Tony.

Just like her mother, she carefully feeds Richie information about Tony that is designed to nudge him into whacking her brother. Janice holds all the power, with Richie reduced to the role of worker bee collecting money and goods for the queen bee. Finally, when Richie loses his temper and punches her in the face, Janice gets a gun and shoots him in the chest. Had she stopped there, you might believe it was an act of self-defence by an abused woman. Instead, she pauses, takes careful aim and then shoots Richie in the head – even though he had already suffered fatal injuries. This was murder, the ultimate act of control.

By comparison, Carmela is more content playing out the role of mob wife. She keeps herself at arm's length from Tony's criminal activities. Instead, she uses her power in more subtle ways to get what she wants. Carmela bullies Tony into agreeing to have a vasectomy, then changes her mind. She nags Tony about his mistress until he finally dumps Irina. Carmela controls what happens inside the family home. She even acknowledges the power of motherhood in a conversation with Livia, admitting that she uses it to get what she wants.

Carmela's daughter Meadow is a matriarch in the making. She knows what she wants and manipulates her parents and others to get it. Facing severe punishment after a teenage party at her grandmother's house gets out of hand, Meadow suggests her own penance – the loss of her credit card for a fortnight! Upset when she learns a friend is being used for sex by their soccer coach, Meadow lets slip about the relationship to her parents. When your father is Tony Soprano, such a revelation can only lead to one thing. Meadow immediately berates herself for telling them what's going on – exactly as her grandmother does after carefully planting information. Even in the pilot episode, Meadow is flexing her power. Carmela cancels a skiing trip after catching her daughter trying to sneak out at night. Meadow responds by refusing to take part in a mother-and-daughter trip to New York.

The ultimate example of matriarchal power is Annalisa, who appears in Season Two when Tony visits Italy on business. He finds himself negotiating with a woman boss – a totally alien concept to Tony. She explains that all her brothers have been murdered in gang wars and all the other men who could take charge are in prison, thanks to a government campaign against organised crime.

Annalisa says Italian men are in love with their mothers, so they are used to taking orders from women. This realisation enables her to run the Family, as well as her own family. Annalisa uses both sides of the madonna/whore equation to her own advantage. She runs her Family like a mother, but comes on to Tony sexually when they are negotiating business terms. Despite this, she is a loving, caring mother who looks after her children and her senile father.

The Sopranos' use of powerful matriarchal characters reflects its setting in a post-feminist society. It also goes some way to explaining why the series is so popular with women. The two greatest antecedents to *The Sopranos* are the *Godfather* trilogy and *Goodfellas*. Both of these are nostalgia pieces, set decades before they were made, and both are movies by men, for men, about men. *The*

Sopranos is of its own time, set at the dawn of the new millennium. The role of women in society has changed and this is reflected in the crucial roles played by women in the show. The programme would be so much less believable if all the women were still content to play the role of submissive wife, mother or whore. Despite what Tony Soprano may want to believe, it's not 1954 anywhere any more. Matriarchy rules, OK?

Generation XXX

The Sopranos began life as a movie idea for its creator David Chase. A veteran writer and executive producer for television series such as *The Rockford Files* and *Northern Exposure*, Chase always wanted to write and direct feature films. Television was something he fell into while trying to break into movies.

The original story revolved around a mobster's troubled relationship with his mother, a relationship so irritating that it drives him into therapy. It had been inspired by Chase's fractious relationship with his own mother. Chase proposed the story as a pilot and America's Fox Network paid for a script to be developed. But Fox passed on the project when Chase finished his screenplay. The script was pitched to every major network in America and every one of them turned it down. This was undoubtedly frustrating at the time, but proved to be a godsend for the show. Enter Home Box Office, better known as HBO.

HBO is a cable network in the USA that commissions and broadcasts original films and television series. Viewers have to pay for their cable connections, which restricts the potential audience. However, it enables HBO to screen programmes with extremely adult content – nudity and sexual scenes, graphic violence and profanity – and without breaks for commercials. Both these factors would enable *The Sopranos* to break new ground.

HBO paid for the pilot episode to be shot, which Chase himself directed. Six months later HBO Commissioned a further twelve episodes to create a three-month-long season of thirteen weekly episodes. *The Sopranos* made its TV debut on 10 January 1999. The impact was immediate and unprecedented for a series on HBO. Critics raved about the show and audience numbers began climbing rapidly. By the time the final episode of Season One screened on 4 April, *The Sopranos* was a smash hit – a cult had been born.

That cult soon became a phenomenon as the show was nominated for 16 Emmys – America's most prestigious television industry award. The cast and crew attended the ceremony in a New Jersey bus but took away only two major awards. Edie Falco beat her co-star Lorraine Bracco and three other nominees to win Best Actress in a Dramatic Series. The 'College' episode won for Best Writing in a Dramatic Series, but that was hardly a surprise. Four of the five scripts nominated were from Season One episodes, so the law of averages dictated that *The Sopranos* virtually had to win that category.

The Sopranos went on to win almost every other award it was eligible for, picking up trophies from the Screen Actors' Guild, the Writers' Guild and the Golden Globes. But its poor showing at the Emmys rankled with the cast and crew. *The Sopranos* was the first cable show ever nominated for Best Dramatic Series and everyone thought it the clear favourite to win. Instead, the award went to *The Practice*, a series about a law firm from the creator of *Ally McBeal*.

Despite the Emmy snub, the impact of *The Sopranos* was enormous. Within weeks of its broadcast, real-life gangsters were recorded by law-enforcement authorities talking about the show and comparing themselves to its characters. One of the major networks approached the programme makers to see if a sanitised version could be created for mainstream broadcast – they politely refused. For HBO, the show was a massive boost. By the time the second season began in January 2000, people were having cable television connected to their homes just to watch *The Sopranos*. The show dominated magazine covers on newsstands. The final episode of Season Two attracted more than 9 million viewers, the largest ever audience for a drama broadcast on cable television. The premiere of Season Three in March 2001 broke that record, with an audience of more than 11 million people. It got a larger audience than shows screening at the same time on some of the major networks, despite the fact they reach four times at many homes in America.

In Canada, the CTV network aired uncut returns of Season One against a rival channel's coverage of the 2000 Sydney Olympics and won the ratings battle every night. It also bested other popular US TV series such as *Ally McBeal* and *The West Wing*. The screenings sparked a national debate about sex, violence and swearing on Canadian television.

When *The Sopranos* held an open casting call for extras in Harrison, New Jersey, the organisers expected between 500 and 1,000 people. In fact, the event attracted more than 14,000 hopefuls – effectively doubling the small town's population for one day. More than 150 police had to be called in from neighbouring towns and cities to sort out the chaos.

But what makes the series so significant and its followers so fervent? A major factor must be the level of reality it brings to its subject. In a society stricken with angst over the collapse of the family unit and the loss of traditional values, *The Sopranos* addresses those same problems in the context of compelling drama. People's lives are fracturing into two halves – their family life and their life at work. Most people find themselves spending more time with their work colleagues than they do with their families. For Tony Soprano, this conflict is heightened by the conflict of his family versus his Family. As the show's publicity material suggests, if one doesn't kill him, the other will. That's why a murderer has to go into therapy. It's a sad commentary on life in America where a mobster needs the help of psychiatry to cope with the stresses and strains of modern society.

The Sopranos seems real because it is able to break the rules that bind other television dramas. The characters swear and have sex like real people. No major network show could ever contemplate having a strip club like the Bada Bing! as a central locale. America is a violent society where gun ownership is a right enshrined in the Constitution – yet this is rarely reflected on television screens. *The Sopranos* pulls no punches in holding a mirror up to the bloody face of a culture where a million children take guns to school with them.

Thanks to HBO's respect for the programme makers' wishes, *The Sopranos* does not suffer from the supermodel syndrome visible in most television shows. Unlike them, *The Sopranos* is not populated by a cast of beautiful people with perfect teeth, narrow waists and pouting breasts. Instead, characters are played by men with paunches, women with wrinkles and children who don't conform to some impossible stereotype.

The lack of commercials in *The Sopranos* gave its creators the chance to pace the show entirely at their own discretion. A one-hour drama on the major networks has to be written and produced in four acts, to accommodate breaks for adverts. This creates an artificial structure requiring the creation of several cliffhangers within each episode to keep the audience watching. *The Sopranos* has the luxury of ignoring that stricture. Viewers outside the USA do have the episodes interrupted by commercial breaks, but it is a sign of *The Sopranos*' quality that this does not lessen the show's impact.

Episodes can be given whatever pace the makers want. In interviews, Chase says his creation is actually much slower than network series, but this has the effect of making what happens all the more absorbing. The show also doesn't feel obliged to explain itself for some imaginary viewer with lowest-common-denominator intelligence. Most TV shows tell you something is going to happen, show it to you and then tell you what just happened afterwards. *The Sopranos* doesn't bother. Even its dream sequences are oblique slices of surrealism which mostly go unexplained, rather than trite devices used by lazy writers to throw crucial plot information at the audience.

The use of music in *The Sopranos* is another area where its embrace of reality will have a major impact in the way television dramas are made. Conventional dramas have a specially composed score that swells and surges at appropriate moments to prompt the audience into an emotional response. *The Sopranos* uses real songs, carefully chosen to complement or comment on its action. Securing the rights to broadcast these songs is far more expensive than having incidental music written to order, but Chase insisted this money be factored into the budgets for the show and HBO agreed.

Clashes between Chase and HBO are rare, but two examples of the cable channel behaving like a normal network have been reported. When the series was in development, HBO objected to its name. The executives thought viewers would be turned off by the title, perhaps thinking it was a drama about high-voiced classical singers. HBO suggested *Family Man* instead. Chase and company objected right back and dozens of potential names flew around. The matter was finally settled when Fox, the network that first got the show rolling, launched a series called *Family Guy*. That killed HBO's suggestion and *The Sopranos* became the permanent title.

The other clash was over the award-winning 'College' episode. During that instalment Tony sees a mobster who turned rat for the FBI. He tracks the informant down and murders him – the first time in the series Tony is seen killing someone. HBO objected because the series had spent five episodes establishing an audience empathy with the mobster. If he murdered someone, that empathy could be fatally eroded. Chase stood his ground, saying that if Tony did not kill the rat it would alienate the viewers. Chase won the argument and the result won an Emmy award for outstanding writing. Since that incident, HBO seems to have kept its opinions to itself.

A Hit is a Hit

In this Internet age, any television show that generates as much interest as *The Sopranos* is also going to generate a vibrant and highly dedicated following on the Web. Sure enough, websites began springing up within a few weeks of the show's debut. These have evolved rapidly over the past two years and now *The Sopranos* has dozens of sites, e-groups, bulletin boards and newsgroups. Any attempt to catalogue these in a programme guide is pretty futile, since the details are liable to be long out of date by the time this tome goes on sale. However, a handful of significant URLs are worth mentioning here, as they have the look of permanence – if such a thing exists on the Web. Try any of them and navigate around from these using the usual links pages most sites include.

http://www.hbo.com/sopranos/
This is the official HBO site for *The Sopranos* and is loaded with episode guides, video clips and background information. There's an extensive list of bulletin boards, including the eternal quest to identify each and every song used in the show. Start your web explorations into *The Sopranos* here.

http://www.jeffreywernick.com/
This site was established by HBO in March 2001 to coincide with the debut of Season Three. It features vast amounts of background information to the Soprano Family, as gathered by the fictional investigative journalist

Jeffrey Wernick. Some material is repeated from the excellent book that takes a similar approach, *The Sopranos: A Family History*. But there are also many screens of fresh material from Season Three to update entries in the book.

http://www.nj.com/sopranos/

New Jersey's *Star-Ledger* daily newspaper found that its website contained so much coverage of *The Sopranos* that it gave the TV its own subsection. There's a great archive of old articles about the series, many interviews with the cast and crew, and authoritative critics of the show and its themes.

http://sopranoland.com/

This fan site is carving out a niche for its coverage of the show's location filming around New Jersey. There are complete transcripts of the dialogue from most episodes and lots of fan photography of the actors. From this site you can find links to almost any other fan website worth visiting. Two such sites are *http://clubs.gist.com/tvclubs/fanclub.jsp?fanclub=sopranos/* and *http://the-sopranos.com/*

http://www.sopranosfanclub.net/

This fan site has developed strong links with HBO and its official site. As home of the web-based *Sopranos* Fan Club, it also hosts online chats with key cast members from the show, and provides access to The *Sopranos* e-group.

http://www.dvd.com/stories/play/sopranos/

Last, but not least, this short-lived site gave visitors the chance to discover their mob nickname simply by typing in their own name. Hopefully it will still be online when this book is published, as it is a lot of fun!

Any show that can generate and sustain dozens upon dozens of websites can also sell merchandise, and *The Sopranos* is no exception. Books, soundtrack albums, videos, DVDs, t-shirts, glasses, mugs, posters, calendars – you name it, somebody is probably contemplating sticking *The Sopranos'* logo on right now. Expect the Bada Bing!

range of Zippo lighters and crotchless panties any day. While you're waiting, here's a selection of the spin-off merchandising available as this edition went to press ...

BOOKS

The Sopranos: A Family History, by Allen Rucker
This authorised volume purports to be an investigation into the history and structure of the Soprano crime Family. This fictionalised exposé includes material from FBI surveillance documents, extracts from private journals and interviews with characters from the show. It presents the world of *The Sopranos* as reality and draws heavily on the files of the investigative journalist and author Jeffrey Wernick. This lush hardcover is copiously illustrated with photographs and provides a fascinating insight into the show. The book closes with cast profiles, plot synopses for the first two seasons and an interview with its creator David Chase. An invaluable purchase for any fan wanting to know more about the fictional backstory of the Soprano Family and family.

The *New York Times* on *The Sopranos*
This unofficial volume was rush-released in early 2000 to fill a void in the market for books about the show as Season Two was broadcast. It collects essays and articles from the pages of the *New York Times* about the show and is illustrated with grainy photos of cast members at show-business parties and functions. The low production values and newsprint paper all scream cheap and shoddy, although some of the writing inside is quite perceptive. A new version was released in early 2001 to coincide with the debut of Season Three on HBO. The new version adds very little fresh material and smacks even more of a quickie cut-and-paste job. Not highly recommended.

The Sopranos Scriptbook
This official TV tie-in is due to be published in October 2001. According to advance listings on e-commerce web-

sites, the book will be a 256-page hardcover featuring five scripts selected from all three seasons. Among the scripts included are the very first episode, 'Pilot/The Sopranos', and the Season Three opener, 'Mr Ruggerio's Neighorhood'.

VIDEO

The first place in the world to get *The Sopranos* on video was actually the United Kingdom. Warner Vision International released Season One over six VHS PAL tapes, just after the show finished its first run on Britain's Channel 4 in October, 1999. Volume 1 featured the first three episodes, while the remaining five tapes had two episodes each. The episodes were presented as full-screen versions, even though the shows were created in widescreen. All six volumes were subsequently collected as a boxed set. American fans had to wait until December 2000 before Season One was made available on five VHS tapes in the NTSC format used by US television.

Britain was also the first country in the world to get Season Two on video. The first six episodes were released over three tapes in May 2001, with the remaining seven episodes split over another three tapes in June 2001. These releases coincided with the debut of Season Two on DVD in the UK, but the videos did not include any of the bonus material available on DVD. Fans in the US were still awaiting news of a local video release for Season Two when this book went to press.

DVD

America was the first country to have *The Sopranos* available on Digital Versatile Disc, or DVD as it's more commonly known. The Complete Season One was a four-disc Region 1 set released in December 2000. All thirteen episodes are presented in widescreen format with a total running time of 680 minutes. The boxed set also contained a number of bonus features. The pilot episode has a commentary track by the show's creator David Chase and the film director Peter Bogdanovich, who appears as Dr Elliot Kupferberg in Season Two. Disc 4 includes an in-depth interview with Chase by Bogdanovich, providing plenty of interesting background material about the show's genesis and production. There are also two behind-the-scenes featurettes which don't add much to the package, and weblinks to the official HBO website for *The Sopranos*.

British fans had to wait until April 2001 for the release of *The Sopranos* on DVD in a Region 2 format. The first thirteen episodes were split over six discs. These could be bought individually, or as a boxed set. Alas, the Region 2 discs did not feature many extras from the Region 1 version, such as the interview or director's commentary. Instead, British fans were fobbed off with a cheap and cheerful 30-minute behind-the-scenes documentary, split over the first five discs. Volume 6 had the music video for Alabama 3's 'Woke Up This Morning' as its added extra. Most galling, the UK release was in conventional television proportions of 1.33:1, instead of the widescreen version in the US.

By way of compensation, Britain was first to get Season Two on DVD. The first six episodes were released on three discs in May 2001, available separately or as a boxed set. The remaining seven episodes were split over another three DVDs released in June 2001. These releases coincided with the debut of Season Two on video in the UK. After the poor effort on Season One, the discs for Season Two were a distinct improvement. The episodes were released in widescreen and each disc included brief promotional trailers and cast interviews originally prepared by HBO to promote Season Two in America. Plans for the US Region 1 release of Season Two on DVD were still being finalised as this book went to press.

MUSIC

The Sopranos: Music From The HBO Original Series was released in December 1999 by Playtone/Columbia. Its fourteen tracks are an eclectic selection culled from the dozens of songs featured in the show's first two seasons. The soundtrack album has sold about half a million copies. Here is the full track listing, with the source episode noted.

ALABAMA 3: Woke Up This Morning (Chosen One Mix) – this is the theme music for *The Sopranos*. An instrumental version also appears in some episodes. The shows creator, David Chase, had originally planned to use a different song over the titles of each episode but abandoned the idea after seeing how well this track fitted the opening sequence.

RL BURNSIDE: It's Bad You Know (from 'I Dream of Jeannie Cusamano')

FRANK SINATRA: It Was a Very Good Year ('Guy Walks Into a Psychiatrist's Office . . .')

BOB DYLAN: Gotta Serve Somebody ('House Arrest')

LITTLE STEVEN & THE DISCIPLES OF SOUL: Inside Of Me ('I Dream of Jeannie Cusamano') – Little Steven is Steven Van Zandt, who plays Silvio Dante in the show

CREAM: I Feel Free ('Isabella')

THEM FEATURING VAN MORRISON: Mystic Eyes ('Down Neck')

BRUCE SPRINGSTEEN: State Trooper ('I Dream of Jeannie Cusamano')

BO DIDDLEY: I'm A Man ('Pilot/The Sopranos')

ELVIS COSTELLO & THE ATTRACTIONS: Complicated Shadows ('Denial, Anger, Acceptance')

NICK LOWE: The Beast In Me ('Pilot/The Sopranos')

LOS LOBOS: Viking ('Toodle-Fucking-oo')

WYCLEF JEAN FEATURING G&B (THE PRODUCT): Blood Is Thicker Than Water ('Commendatori')

EURYTHMICS: I've Tried Everything ('Guys Walks Into a Psychiatrist's Office . . .')

The Sopranos – Peppers and Eggs: Music From The HBO Original Series was released in May 2001 by Playtone/ Columbia. This double-CD compilation collects tracks from all three seasons, but the emphasis is on songs featured in Season Three. Here is the full track listing, with the source episode noted.

THE POLICE & HENRY MANCINI: Every Breath You Take/Theme From Peter Gunn (Mr Ruggerio's Remix) (from 'Mr Ruggerio's Neighborhood')

BATTLEFLAG: Pigeonhead (from '46 Long')

THE CAMPBELL BROTHERS WITH KATIE JACKSON: I've Got A Feeling (from 'To Save Us All From Satan's Power')

KASEY CHAMBERS: The Captain (from 'He Is Risen')

RL BURNSIDE: Shuck Dub (from 'Another Toothpick')

THE LOST BOYS: Affection (from 'Amour Fou')

OTIS REDDING: My Lover's Prayer (from 'From Where To Eternity')

MADREBLU: Certamente (from 'Commendatori')

NILS LOFGREN: Black Books (from 'Second Opinion')

CAKE: Frank Sinatra (from 'The Legend of Tennessee Moltisanti')

FRANK SINATRA: Baubles, Bangles And Beads (from 'Funhouse')

THE ROLLING STONES: Thru And Thru (from 'Funhouse')

ELVIS COSTELLO & THE ATTRACTIONS: High Fidelity (from 'Mr Ruggerio's Neighborhood')

THE KINKS: Livin' On A Thin Line (from 'University')

VUE: Girl (from 'The Telltale Moozadell')

CECILIA BARTOLI: Sposa Son Dispressata (from 'Pine Barrens' and 'Amour Fou')

BEN E. KING: I Who Have Nothing (from 'The Telltale Moozadell')

BOB DYLAN: Return To Me (from 'Amour Fou')

KEITH RICHARDS: Make No Mistake (from 'The Telltale Moozadell')

JOVANOTTI: Piove (from 'Commendatori')

THE PRETENDERS: Space Invader (from 'House Arrest')

TINDERSTICKS: Tiny Tears (from 'Isabella')

VAN MORRISON: Gloria (from 'Pine Barrens')

DOMINIC CHIANESE: Core 'ngrata (from 'Army of One')

BONUS TRACK: Dialogue from *The Sopranos*

Bob Dylan recorded his cover version of the Dean Martin hit 'Return To Me' especially for *The Sopranos*. The Lost Boys was a band formed by Steven Van Zandt due to his love of 1960s garage bands. The group recorded an album which was never released. The song 'Affection' was rescued from that album and used in Season Three. This is the first time the track has been available to the public.

Advance listings for the double CD included the track 'Time Is On My Side' by Irma Thomas, which was featured in #14 – 'Guy Walks Into A Psychiatrist's Office . . .'. But this was replaced with Van Morrison's 'Gloria' on the release edition, for reason unknown. The bonus track of dialogue features dozens of memorable quotes culled from all three seasons, following by a reprise of Alabama 3's 'Woke Up This Morning.'

MEMORABILIA

The Sopranos has spawned a range of official memorabilia, as well as the usual, illegal bootleg merchandise. Officially licensed and sanctioned items include T-shirts, coffee mugs, beer mugs, shot glasses, posters, calendars, glass tumblers, an ashtray and a cappuccino mug. These feature the show's logo, the logo of the Bada Bing! strip club or publicity images from the programme. The name Bada Bing! has been trademarked to protect it from those looking to trade off the show's popularity.

Unseen Sopranos

Like any television series the script for each episode of *The Sopranos* goes through many drafts and revisions before it is filmed. Even when an episode has been shot, scenes may still be shortened or cut completely in the editing process, for reasons of pacing or length. Normally this material remains on the cutting room floor, unseen and unknown. However, scripts from films and television shows are becoming increasingly available to a curious public.

During research for this book the author found and purchased a script for *The Sopranos* #02, '46 Long', from a London store which specialises in entertainment media merchandise. The David Chase script is labelled as the fourth revision, dated June 19th, 1998. It notes that the production draft was completed on May 28th, 1999, with further revisions on June 11th, 15th and 17th. The cast list matches that of the broadcast episode, but it notes that Giacomo 'Jackie' Aprile was formerly called Pat Aprile. The name Pat also survives in one of the scene descriptions.

Structurally, the script is very similar to the final version screened by HBO in January, 1999. The running order of scenes only differs in a few places. The dialogue is almost a word-for-word transcription of what was broadcast. However, most scenes were trimmed either at their beginnings or ends in the final show – a process known as topping and tailing. Two scenes were dropped and several were severely truncated.

'46 Long' begins with Tony and his crew watching TV in the back room at the Bada Bing!. In the script it specifies that they watch the popular US talk show, *Larry King*. In the broadcast version, Larry and his show were substituted for a generic talk show and host. Perhaps Larry was unavailable or too expensive. In the script, Silvio's Al Pacino imitation misquotes *The Godfather*.

Some intriguing dialogue appears in the scripted scene where Tony comes down to breakfast and hears about the teacher's car being stolen. Tony is unconcerned – he says the insurance company will pay out because the teacher is white. Carmela says Mr Miller's wife just had twins. She asks Tony to intervene and says the teacher was nice to AJ when the boy missed a lot of school because of sickness.

The next unseen material appears in the script when Tony calls his mother as she is cooking mushrooms. 'Always with the mushrooms,' Tony says to himself. While he waits for her to come back to the phone, Tony berates Christopher for bitching about not being made yet. He says Christopher will not rise up in the world by hanging around with people like Brendan Filone.

When Carmela invites her mother-in-law to live with the rest of the family, the draft version foreshadows a development for much later in Season One. Livia says it's a very nice offer, but she isn't an Alzheimer's case yet. By the end of this season, Livia will be showing Alzheimer's-like signs of senility.

During Tony's first session with Dr Melfi, the script has him revealing more about his siblings. He says he has one sister living at an ashram in California, while the other is called Annette and lives in upstate New York with her husband and four kids. Annette would be renamed Barbara in future episodes. Tony asks for Dr Melfi's diagnosis of his mother's condition. The therapist reluctantly suggests Livia is dystymic – incapable of experiencing joy. In the draft script, Tony cites two examples of loving, warm experiences from his childhood, rather than just the one broadcasts. He remembers at age twelve buying his mother the album 'Smoke On The Water' when it was obviously a gift for himself. Tony says Livia didn't get that pissed at all. Melfi presses him for examples of emotional nourishment or support by his mother. Tony replies that 'old guineas' like his mother are not demonstrative.

In the scene where Tony and Junior have a sit-down with Jackie about the raid on Comley Trucking, Tony suggests in the draft script that Junior watch *Gone With The Wind* on DVD. In the broadcast episode his suggestion is much funnier – *Grumpy Old Men*. The script has the meeting being watched by two Feds in a surveillance van parked opposite the pork store. When Tony leaves the meeting he raps on the side of the unmarked vehicle and suggests the Feds are having a mutual masturbation session inside. 'I saw the van rocking, guys. You having a taffy-pull in there?' All of this was either never filmed or was cut from the final version. The Feds don't appear on screen until the funeral scene at the end of #04, 'Meadowlands'.

When Tony is chastising Christopher and Brendan for not paying their tribute to Junior, the draft script has some heavy-handed dialogue recapping what happened in the first episode. Tony says he has not talked to Jackie about Christopher getting made, because Jackie still remembers the wannabe mobster clipped a guy without permission. 'The proof is in the pudding' Christopher replies. Brendan pisses Tony off by joking about Jackie's illness. In the script Brendan talks about Jackie adopting 'the waif look'. In the broadcast episode, he talks about Jackie becoming the chemo-sabe – a much subtler reference to the effects of cancer treatment.

An entire scene between Livia and her temporary carer Perrilyn appears in the draft script but never made it to broadcast. The pair are finishing lunch and carrying their dishes to the kitchen. Perrilyn tells an anecdote about her grandson, which actually brings a small smile to Livia's lips. Perrilyn washes dishes and Livia dries. The carer suggests they could go for a walk around three o'clock and accidentally calls her Olivia. That was the name of Perrilyn's sister, who died as a baby. Livia agrees that some fresh air would be nice. The old woman stops and chooses exactly what she wants to say to Perrilyn. The dialogue does not appear in the script, but the reader infers it must be something very offensive. The draft script cuts to the next scene, when Carmela arrives just as Perrilyn storms out of the house. This is where the broadcast version resumes.

Tony has another session with Dr Melfi after Livia runs down Fanny in her car. In the draft script he says the doctors are going to test Livia for infarc dementia, but no mention of this was made in the final version. Instead, Livia would not be tested for dementia until after the attempted hit on Tony. Dr Melfi talks with Tony about depression. In the script, she describes it as anger not acted out, and says depression is very common in the elderly. On screen, the scene ends with Melfi talking about seniors who are inspired and inspiring. In the draft script, the scene continues as the session comes to an end. Tony says he received Dr Melfi's bill in the mail. He pulls out a wad of cash that could choke a horse and starts dropping hundred dollar bills on her desk, which makes the therapist uneasy. She asks if Tony is on a health plan where he could post the money. The mobster replies he is covered by the plumbers' union, but he doesn't want to submit psychiatrist's bills. He says cash is better for her, anyway, and leaves. Dr Melfi gives a false smile and closes the door after him.

The scene where Christopher, Adriana, Brendan and his girlfriend stand outside the nightclub runs much longer in the draft script. After Martin Scorcese has gone into the club, Christopher and Brendan get into an argument with the bouncer. Brendan tries to frighten the bouncer by invoking the name of the Sopranos, without success. Brendan starts getting a weapon out of his pocket to attack the bouncer, but is interrupted by his beeper going off.

Once they get inside the club, Christopher and Brendan talk about Junior's tribute. Brendan shows a poor grasp of the English language in a line which didn't make it on screen: 'He's throwing down the gimlet.' Brendan probably means gauntlet, since a gimlet is a small boring tool for penetrating wood. Christopher wonders whether the old greats like Charlie Lucky and Neil Dellacrocce felt like this when they were just starting out. Brendan gets almost philosophical in another line cut from this scene. He has heard they are the first generation of Americans who are not going to do as well as their parents.

A classic line of Livia dialogue was lost from the scene where she tries to give her son a vibrating chair. Tony tries to reassure his mother, saying she's not ready to die. Livia is unimpressed: 'Listen to him. God speaks right to him.'

There's a funny sequence involving AJ which didn't make it into the final episode. Tony and Carmela have returned from installing Livia at Green Grove. Tony is making lunch when AJ enters from the back of the house carrying a large can of charcoal lighter, some highway flares and a box of matches. Carmela demands to know what he is doing with this highly combustible combination. AJ explains that it is his science project, a volcano. Carmela bans the boy from lighting any fires in the house. Tony offers to cut up some shotgun shells so he and AJ can use the gunpowder from inside. Carmela hands Tony a greeting card from the post. It shows a sad basset hound with the words 'Missing You' printed above it. The card is signed from 'Your friends in the 3rd Federal Judicial District'. Tony smirks.

Last but not least, the draft script has an extended sequence which gives the episode its name. After Tony orders Christopher and Brendan to take the Italian suits back to Comley Trucking, he selects a beautiful blue pinstripe for himself. It's 46 long – his size. Paulie points out that Tony already has a suit exactly like it. Tony notices Pussy admiring it so he finds a pair of metal shears and cut the arms off the suit so it is ruined. Only Tony gets to wear a beautiful blue pinstripe Brioni suit.

Speculations on Season Four

What will happen in Season Four of *The Sopranos*? God knows creator David Chase and his team are not short of plotlines to explore in the forthcoming 13 episodes. Production of the fourth season is not due to begin until October 2001, so what follows can only be idle speculation, but trying to second-guess what will happen next is part of the fun of *The Sopranos*.

The first question to contemplate is whether Season Four will be the grand finale of *The Sopranos*. David Chase and lead actor James Gandolfini are contracted only up to the end of the fourth season and there has been much speculation about whether the show will be extended. HBO will no doubt be happy to pay handsomely for further episodes. *The Sopranos* is the subscription channel's greatest asset and directly responsible for a surge in viewers signing up.

David Chase has said many times in interviews that he does not want his creation to become just another TV zombie, dragging on season after season simply to keep everyone making money. He wants *The Sopranos* to finish at its peak – an understandable goal. When Season Three began with the best ratings yet for the show, Chase seemed to relent slightly on his edict that there would only be four seasons. So, there's a glimmer of hope for viewers.

Best guess? Chase will pull the plug after Season Four, deciding that 52 episodes are enough – one for every week of the year. His life-long ambition is to write movies. The success of *The Sopranos* has brought him much closer to that dream, but that same success is now stopping him making the leap to film. There is no show without David Chase, so Season Four could well be the last hurrah for Tony and family (and Family). Whatever happens, there are a number of lingering plot threads from Season Three that may reappear . . .

Tony's tempestuous affair with Mercedes sales rep, Gloria Trillo, was wrapped up in #38, 'Amour Fou' – or was it? Will Gloria return like aggrieved mistress Glenn Close in the film *Fatal Attraction*? David Chase has professed to a dislike of doing the predicable, so such a development seems unlikely. **SPECULATION**: Tony has seen the last of Gloria Trillo.

During Season Three, Tony's life and business became increasingly intertwined with members of the Russian Mafia. Slava Malevsky is laundering the vast sums of money Tony is netting from the New Jersey esplanade project. But a shadow has been cast over the relationship by Paulie and Christopher's bungled efforts to execute Russian hardman, Valery. He disappeared after being headshot in the Pine Barrens, seemingly taking Paulie's car. Valery is a man with a grudge and Tony puts the blame for the cock-up on Paulie. **SPECULATION**: Valery returns for revenge and the resulting violence sours relations between Tony and the Russian Mafia.

Johnny 'I don't stick my beak in' Sack seems intent on sticking his beak into Soprano Family business. He was acting as mentor to Ralphie before Tony got smart and made Ralphie a captain. In the Season Three finale Johnny starts making nice with Paulie, trying to woo the disaffected captain over to the New York Families. There are millions of dollars at stake in the esplanade project and Johnny is intent on getting the biggest slice for NY. **SPECULATION**: This will be a major plot thread for Season Four. Johnny Sack's underboss status should protect him from Tony's wrath, but others will be hurt in the crossfire.

Two characters started making recurring appearances during the third season. State Assemblyman, Ronald

Zellman, is a politician in Tony's pocket, delivering the esplanade project. Another crony of Tony, Reverend James Jr, popped up twice during Season Three. It seems unlikely he's just there to add local colour. **SPECULATION**: Expect more appearances by these characters.

Made man Raymond Curto only showed up in a handful of episodes during Season Three, but he was revealed as a rat for the feds. Can he gather crucial evidence against Tony and the Family? And how many others have been flipped by the Government? **SPECULATION**: Curto is revealed as a rat and gets a bad case of lead poisoning from a bullet to the back of the head.

Carmela's parents, Hugh and Mary DeAngelis, emerged from the shadows after the death of Livia, becoming regular visitors to the Soprano household. Hugh has been diagnosed with the eye disease glaucoma, while Mary seems intent on taking Livia's place as nagging mother. **SPECULATION**: More medical problems and an untimely death for Hugh, giving Carmela a dilemma about where her mother should live.

The FBI did not have a very successful campaign during Season Three. Elaborate efforts to get a bug into Tony's house were unwittingly thwarted by Meadow, while the deaths of Pussy, Livia and Richie Aprile rescued Tony from several potential prosecutions. Rat Raymond Curto doesn't seem to be doing the business and Tony is too smart to fall victim to routine surveillance. A new ploy was introduced during #39 – a female agent has been assigned to becoming Adriana's new best friend. Will this produce results? **SPECULATION**: Adriana gets Christopher into big trouble with her big mouth, but the FBI still can't lay a finger on Teflon-coated Tony.

Artie and Charmaine Bucco split up during Season Three, thanks to Artie's infatuation with Adriana and his plans to go into business with Tony. Charmaine responded by getting a makeover and declaring her independence. **SPECULATION**: The closer Artie gets to Tony, the worse his life will get. Charmaine will prosper while her estranged husband suffers.

Eugene Pontecorvo was introduced during Season Three – he was the other guy being made when Christopher got his button. Eugene is part of Ralphie's crew and hosted the card game that Jackie Jr tried to rob. He is being established as part of the next generation of gangsters in the Family. **SPECULATION**: An increased role for Eugene under Ralphie's tutelage.

Like Paulie, Christopher was becoming disenchanted with Tony's leadership as the third season ended. Christopher does not know he is in danger from the FBI targeting his fiancée Adriana for close surveillance. The newly-made man survived an attempted assassination during Season Two – how will he fare in Season Four? **SPECULATION**: The wedding of Christopher and Adriana is the mob marriage of the year. But the proud husband spends his honeymoon in jail after being arrested by the FBI for information gleaned from his loose-lipped wife.

Junior spent Season Three under house arrest and fighting cancer. By the end of #39 things were looking up – cancer apparently beaten and the terms of his house arrest relaxed. But his trial on twelve RICO predicates is drawing ever closer. Can he beat the rap? **SPECULATION**: David Chase has said he doesn't want to turn the show into a legal drama, so don't expect to see much courtroom action in Season Four. Junior has buried his differences with Tony – expect him to act as elder statesman and advisor to his nephew.

AJ was the kid going off the rails in Season Three. He lurched from one disaster to the next, got expelled from Verbum Dei and only escaped being banished to military school because of his panic attacks. AJ is not the sharpest tool in the box, so academic excellence looks beyond him and he doesn't seem tough enough to make it in the Family. So what will happen to Tony's only son? **SPECULATION**: The fate of AJ will be a major plotline for Season Four. It's hard to see a future for the boy beyond entering the Family business. Perhaps he can emulate the loveable Bacala, the nicest mobster in the world.

Meadow had a tumultuous year – going to college, losing her virginity with Noah, falling in love with Jackie Jr and then having the brutal reality of mob life shoved in her face. After three years of criticising the mob lifestyle, she tore into Jackie Jr's sister for lacking loyalty to the Family and discussing business in front of an outsider. Does Meadow now consider herself part of the Family? **SPECULATION**: Meadow will continue her studies at Columbia during Season Four but find herself drawn ever closer to the Family business.

Dr Melfi began Season Three still questioning whether she should be treating Tony. The rape and its consequences were a turning point for the character. She could have used Tony as a weapon to gain revenge against her rapist but, instead, she reaffirmed her own belief system. **SPECULATION**: Dr Melfi will continue to treat Tony, sometimes in joint sessions with Carmela. There may even be family therapy sessions involving AJ. Do not expect to see the rapist plotline revived or any romance between Melfi and Tony!

Carmela continued to question the gap between her beliefs and her actions. After being shaken to the core by Dr Krakower's urgings that she leave Tony, Carmela found another way forward when Father Obosi suggested she live off only the good part of Tony's nature. As Season Three ended, Carmela was contemplating a career in real estate sales. **SPECULATION**: Twice Carmela has flirted with the idea of an affair – Season Four may finally see her taking the plunge. Certainly she will be trying to extend the boundaries of her independence and reduce her financial dependence on Tony's blood money.

Last, but not least, what will happen to Tony Soprano? Traditionally mob sagas like *The Godfather* trilogy and *Goodfellas* have charted the rise and fall of Mafia men. The leading characters often survive to die of old age, but they always end up living unhappy lives – as if some price has to be paid for their actions. To date *The Sopranos* has taken a firmly amoral stance, refusing to pass judgement upon the actions of its characters. This doesn't seem likely to change during Season Four.

SPECULATION: If Tony Soprano dies, the show dies with him. He is the centre of it all, the sun about which the other characters orbit. So don't expect to see Tony die in a bloody gunfight before the final episode of Season Four, #52. The legal actions against him seem to be on hold, so he will probably be a free man for most of the fourth season. But the threats against him are building up: dissension within his own Family, interference from the New York Families, danger from the Russian Mafia, and constant surveillance by the FBI.

But, as always, the greatest threat to Tony is Tony himself. If he continues to involve himself in dangerous relationships like the affair with Gloria, he risks losing the thing most precious to him: his family. Carmela leaving Tony and taking the children with her would be far more devastating than any bullet or imprisonment. That is also the most fertile ground for a compelling drama show like *The Sopranos*. In interviews, David Chase says he wants to make mini-movies about the conflict between a family and a Family. Expect that to be the major focus of Season Four.

Bright Lights, Baked Ziti Online!

This book aims to be the definitive unofficial guide to *The Sopranos*. But no such volume is ever perfect. Think you've spotted mistake? Tell the author about it online. Go to the URL listed below and you can join the *Bright Lights, Baked Ziti* online discussion group.

This e-group has been established as a forum to discuss *The Sopranos*, this book and related matters. It's the perfect place to debate the ideas, opinions and speculations presented in these pages. Has this book left out your favourite moment from the first three seasons? Set the record straight! Have you identified that Kate Bush-like song from #38? Share the news with everyone. Want to contact the author? Do it at the brightlights-bakedziti e-group! Just go to:

http://groups.yahoo.com/group/brightlights-bakedziti